Cultural Tourism
The Partnership Between Tourism and Cultural Heritage Management

Cultural Tourism
The Partnership Between Tourism and Cultural Heritage Management

Bob McKercher, PhD
Hilary du Cros, PhD

Routledge
Taylor & Francis Group
New York   London

First published by
The Haworth Press, Inc
10 Alice Street
Binghamton, NY 13904-1580

Reprinted 2010 by Routledge

Routledge
Taylor & Francis Group
270 Madison Avenue
New York, NY 10016

Routledge
Taylor & Francis Group
2 Park Square
Milton Park, Abingdon
Oxon OX14 4RN

Cover design by Anastasia Litwak.

Library of Congress Cataloging-in-Publication Data

McKercher, Bob.
  Cultural tourism : the partnership between tourism and cultural heritage management / Bob McKercher, Hilary du Cros.
      p. cm.
  Includes bibliographical references (p.).
  ISBN-13: 978-0-7890-1105-3 (hc. : alk. paper)
  ISBN-10: 0-7890-1105-0 (hc. : alk. paper)
  ISBN-13: 978-0-7890-1106-0 (pbk. : alk. paper)
  ISBN-10: 0-7890-1106-9 (pbk. : alk. paper)
  1. Heritage tourism. I. Du Cros, Hilary. II. Title.

G156.5.H47 M35 2002
338.4'791—dc21

                                                    2001039564

To Eve-Louise

ABOUT THE AUTHORS

Bob McKercher, PhD, is an Associate Professor in Tourism in the Department of Hotel and Tourism Management at the Hong Kong Polytechnic University. He has been a tourism academic since 1990, working in both Australia and Hong Kong. Previously, he worked in the Canadian tourism industry. His industry experience includes policy and advocacy work as the executive director of Canada's largest regional nature-based tourism association, as well as operational experience in the nature-based tourism sector.

Dr. McKercher has published more than 100 scholarly papers and research reports on a variety of topics, including nature-based tourism, regional tourism development, tourism marketing, and tourism education. He received his PhD from the University of Melbourne in Australia, a master's degree from Carleton University in Ottawa, Canada, and his undergraduate degree from York University in Toronto, Canada.

Hilary du Cros, PhD, is a cultural heritage analyst and academic living in Hong Kong. She worked for nearly 15 years as a heritage consultant in Australia and owned one of the largest heritage consulting firms in that country.

Dr. du Cros is a member of the International Council on Monuments and Sites (ICOMOS) International Scientific Committee on Cultural Tourism. Between 1997 and 1999, she was an executive committee member of the ICOMOS Australian chapter. In 2000, Dr. du Cros was engaged as a sociocultural analyst for a World Tourism Organization tourism master plan in Yunnan, China. She is currently assisting UNESCO as one of its cultural heritage experts advising on tourism projects in the Asia region.

Dr. du Cros received her PhD from Monash University in Melbourne, Australia, and her undergraduate degree from the University of Sydney. Her nearly 40 publications include *Much More than Stone and Bones: Australian Archaeology in the Late 20th Century* and *Women in Archaeology: A Feminist Critique*.

CONTENTS

Preface   xi

Acknowledgments   xiii

Chapter 1. Introduction   1

Defining Cultural Tourism   3
Conceptualizing Cultural Tourism—A Thematic Approach   6
The Key Issue: Linking Cultural Heritage Management
    and Tourism Management   9

**Chapter 2. Challenges in Achieving Sustainable Cultural
Tourism**   11

Introduction   11
Culture and Tourism—Collaborators or Competitors?   11
The Independent Evolution of Tourism and Cultural Heritage   13
Seven Possible Relationships Between Tourism and Cultural
    Heritage Management   15
The Consequences   21
The Solution?   23

Chapter 3. How Tourism Works   25

Introduction   25
The Nature of Tourism   26
Attractions Drive Tourism   31
Factors Influencing Visitation Levels   33
Tourist Behavior   36
Cultural Tourism   39
Conclusion   42

Chapter 4. Cultural Heritage Management   43

Introduction   43
Core Concepts   44
Cultural Heritage Management and Tourism   58

Negative and Positive Impacts of Tourism   60
Conclusion   63

Chapter 5. Tangible Heritage   **65**

Introduction   65
Process-Driven Conservation of Tangible Cultural Heritage   66
The Scope of Tangible Heritage Assets   67
Cultural Significance of Heritage Assets   71
Authenticity   73
Tourism, Authenticity, and Commodification   76
Visitor Accessibility to Tangible Heritage Assets   79
Consultation As an Important Element of the Management
    Process   81

Chapter 6. Intangible Heritage and Its Management   **83**

Introduction   83
Recognition of Intangible Cultural Heritage Management   84
Intangible Heritage Assets—Management and Tourism
    Issues   88
Authenticity and Cultural Space   94
Tourism and Changes to Intangible Heritage   96
Culturally Appropriate and Sustainable Use of Assets   97
Stakeholder Consultation in Setting Management Priorities   98

**Chapter 7. Cultural Tourism Products—A Regional
    Perspective**   **101**

Introduction   101
Products   102
Benefits of Adopting a Marketing Approach to Product
    Development   107
Hierarchy of Attractions   109
Developing Cultural Tourism Attractions   110
Conclusions   114

**Chapter 8. Commodification, Environmental Bubbles,
    and Cultural Tourism Products**   **115**

Introduction   115
Consumption—Strangeness versus Familiarity
    and the Environmental Bubble   116

Creating Cultural Tourism Products or Attractions   122
Tactics   127
Conclusions   134

**Chapter 9. The Cultural Tourism Market: A Cultural
Tourism Typology**   **135**

Introduction   135
Who Are Cultural Tourists?   135
A Typology of Cultural Tourists: Recognizing Different
    Shades of Cultural Tourists   139
Five Types of Cultural Tourists   144
Testing the Model: Hong Kong As a Case Study   147
Implications for Cultural Tourism   150

Chapter 10. Gatekeepers   **153**

Introduction   153
Using Cultural and Heritage Assets to Brand a Destination 155
The Role of Gatekeepers in Conveying Messages   162
Effect of Many Gatekeepers on the Message Passed
    to the Tourist   169

Chapter 11. Assessment   **171**

Introduction   171
Assessing the Tourism Potential of Assets   172
Considering the Wider Context   173
Understanding the Asset in Its Setting   176
Asset Specific Issues: "Place" and Cultural Spaces   177
Stakeholder and Consultation Issues   180
People, Skills, and Financial Resources   183
Conclusions   184

Chapter 12. Asset Auditing and Planning   **185**

Introduction   185
An Audit Model   185
An Audit Procedure   189
Testing the Procedure—Hong Kong   192
Planning   195

Chapter 13. Marketing   **201**

Introduction   201
Marketing As a Management Tool   201
Unique Features of Marketing in Cultural Tourism   204
Thinking Strategically   205
Sustainable Competitive Advantages   208
Role of Research   209
Putting It Together—The Marketing Plan   211
The Four Ps—The Marketing Mix   212
Conclusions   214

**Chapter 14. Presentation and Management of Heritage
Assets**   **215**

Introduction   215
Reinvestment of Revenue in Conservation As One Benefit
    of Tourism   220
Fees and Levies Raised at the Source   223

Epilogue   **231**

References   **233**

Index   **255**

Preface

In our journeys around the world over the past number of years, we have been continually amazed that cultural tourism and cultural heritage management (CHM) operate as parallel activities in most places, with remarkably little dialogue between the two. This fact remains even though CHM professionals and the tourism industry have mutual interests in the management, conservation, and presentation of cultural and heritage assets. Instead of working together to produce truly outstanding products, this historic isolation results in cultural tourism that is poorly provided for and executed.

The result is many lost opportunities to provide quality visitor experiences while managing rare and fragile resources in a socially, environmentally, and ethically responsible and sustainable manner. Sometimes, this loss results in some (and we stress *some*) unscrupulous tourism operators exploiting local cultures and heritage assets for their own personal gain, while providing little in return for the host or the continuing care of the assets. Likewise, *some* cultural heritage managers have a deep hatred of tourism and do whatever they can to thwart it. In these situations, tourists also lose, as visitor experiences are often well below their expectations. Finally, if the assets and host are no longer able to support a quality tourism experience and meet visitors' expectations, those visitors go elsewhere.

In most cases, though, the underperformance of many cultural tourism activities can be attributed to a lack of awareness and naiveté about each sector. We have seen far too many cases in which well-meaning cultural heritage managers have struggled with the roles of manager and promoter of cultural tourism attractions when they have assumed or have had those roles thrust upon them. On the other hand, we have seen far too many tour operators and tourism marketers show incredible cultural insensitivity about local cultural and heritage assets—again, mostly out of naiveté. We have also witnessed far too many tourists acting in appropriate ways, again not out of malevolence, but largely because either they are responding to signals given to them by the tourism industry about accepted behavior or they have not been informed about how to act otherwise.

We have written this book in an attempt to bridge the gap between cultural heritage management and tourism. The book has been conceived so that professionals and students from each field of study can read it and gain better understandings of the roles of their own discipline in cultural tourism management and of the needs, interests, and values that drive the other discipline. Most important, it outlines how tourism and cultural heritage management can work in partnership to achieve mutual benefits.

In a very real sense, the book represents a marriage of tourism and cultural heritage management. The book adopts both tourism marketing and cultural heritage management perspectives and includes our observations of what actually happens at many cultural sites as well as theory. Bob McKercher has devoted much of his professional life to tourism, first in an operational role and more recently as an academic. Hilary du Cros has devoted most of her professional life to cultural heritage management, as the owner of one of Australia's leading consulting archaeology and heritage management firms and more recently as an academic. Together, over the past decade, we have also devoted much of our lives to understanding each others' unique perspectives in these fields. For each of us, this book represents both vocation and our avocation.

Acknowledgments

Many organizations and individuals have contributed to this book, either directly or indirectly. For a start, we must thank the Hong Kong Special Administrative Region of China government, and especially the University Grants Committee, for funding a large ongoing study of cultural tourism in Hong Kong. In addition, thanks goes to the Lord Wilson Heritage Trust for its foresightedness in funding research into planning for sustainable cultural tourism in Hong Kong. We would also like to thank Chris Johnston of Context Proprietary Ltd. Cultural Heritage Planners in Melbourne, Australia, and Billie Chow So Ming and Pamela Ho Sau Ying from Hong Kong for their comments on earlier drafts of this manuscript. We would also like to thank the many hundreds of cultural heritage managers, owners, and operators of tourism attractions and academics with whom we have spoken formally or informally over the years. Finally, we would like to thank Oscar, Lily, Poppy, Ben, and Mimi for their love and support. Although many people must share in any success this book has, we alone must be responsible for any of its weaknesses.

Chapter 1

Introduction

Cultural tourism is arguably the oldest of the "new" tourism phenomena. People have been traveling for what we now call cultural tourism reasons since the days of the Romans; it is just that they were never recognized as being a discrete group of travelers before. Visiting historic sites, cultural landmarks, attending special events and festivals, or visiting museums have always been a part of the total tourism experience. Indeed, all travel involves a cultural element. By its very nature, the art of traveling removes tourists from their home culture and places them temporarily in a different cultural milieu, whether in an adjacent city or in a village halfway around the world. But cultural tourism is seen as offering something more or different both to the tourist and the community that hosts the tourist.

Cultural tourism began to be recognized as a distinct product category in the late 1970s when tourism marketers and tourism researchers realized that some people traveled specifically to gain a deeper understanding of the culture or heritage of a destination (Tighe 1986). Initially, it was regarded as a specialized, niche activity that was thought to be pursued by a small number of better educated, more affluent tourists who were looking for something other than the standard sand, sun, and sea holiday. It is only since the fragmentation of the mass market in the 1990s that cultural tourism has been recognized for what it is: a high-profile, mass-market activity. Depending on the source and the destination, between 35 and 70 percent of international travelers are now considered cultural tourists (Richards 1996c; Antolovic 1999). Based on these figures, as many as 240 million international journeys annually involve some element of cultural tourism. Today, arguably, cultural tourism has superseded ecotourism as the trendy tourism buzzword. It is not surprising, then, that destinations are clamoring to get on the proverbial cultural tourism bandwagon by promoting their cultural or heritage assets for tourist consumption, often without due consideration of the impact that tourism may have on them.

Cultural tourism did not go unnoticed by the cultural heritage management sector either. In fact, the growth of cultural tourism coincided with the emergence of a broader societywide appreciation of the need to protect and conserve our dwindling cultural and heritage assets. However, cultural tourism was seen as a double-edged sword by the cultural heritage management community. On the one hand, increased demand by tourists provided a powerful political and economic justification to expand conservation activities. On the other hand, increased visitation, overuse, inappropriate use, and the commodification of the same assets without regard for their cultural values posed a real threat to the integrity—and in extreme cases, to the very survival—of these assets. At about the same time, then, cultural heritage management advocates began to promulgate policies to protect cultural values from inappropriate tourism uses (International Council on Monuments and Sites [ICOMOS] 1976).

Thus began the parallel yet largely independent evolution of cultural tourism as both a product and cultural heritage management issue. To a large extent, both sectors still operate in parallel, with little real evidence being shown of true partnerships forming between them. But cultural tourism can, could, and should achieve both cultural heritage management (learning about conservation of cultural heritage assets) and tourism management (market appeal, commercial viability of products) objectives. In theory, this aim is supported widely by both sectors. In practice, though, the achievement of this dual objective has proven elusive, as the pursuit of one objective has often been regarded as being inimical with the attainment of the other (Berry 1994; Boniface 1998; Jacobs and Gale 1994; Jansen-Verbeke 1998). Instead, in many instances one element has been sacrificed or traded off. Tourism values are compromised to ensure that the cultural integrity of assets is maintained or that cultural values are not compromised for tourism gain. The resulting cultural tourism sector operates at a suboptimal level, failing to achieve either its tourism or cultural heritage management potential fully.

Sustainability can occur only when the practice of trading off one set of values for another ceases and, instead, tourism and cultural heritage management interests work toward the achievement of common goals. This task is complicated by the historic lack of understanding of the role each plays and is reflected in the sentiment that both sectors work toward different and mutually incompatible goals. Other than sharing the same assets, they often feel they have little else in common. Each sector has a different disciplinary focus and mandate, serves a different role in society, has different political overlords, and is accountable to different stakeholder groups. The end product is ignorance, often leading to suspicion of the other's motives. This book seeks to dispel some of that ignorance and foster greater understanding of the mutual interests that tourism and cultural heritage management have in cultural tourism.

DEFINING CULTURAL TOURISM

What is cultural tourism? This seemingly simple question is actually very difficult to answer because there are almost as many definitions or variations of definitions of cultural tourism as there are cultural tourists. The American chapter of ICOMOS, the International Council on Monuments and Sites, observed that "cultural tourism as a name means many things to many people and herein lies its strength and its weakness" (USICOMOS 1996: 17). A number of definitions of cultural tourism were reviewed when preparing this text that support this assertion. They fell into four broad categories: *tourism derived, motivational, experiential,* and *operational.*

Perhaps this diversity is to be expected given the emerging nature of the sector and the diversity of products and/or experiences that constitute cultural tourism. Moreover, people will shape their definition of an amorphous concept to suit their own needs. Some of the definitions are comprehensive while others are clearly narrow and self-serving. Politically oriented definitions of cultural tourism tend to be as inclusive as possible to show the level of consumer interest and thus provide further justification for investment in cultural heritage management activities. Likewise, the undercurrent of many marketing-oriented definitions is to strive for greater allocation of marketing resources to the sector. On the other hand, definitions that tend to focus on one or a narrow set of activities seek to position those activities as the core elements of cultural tourism and, by extension, position others as being peripheral to true cultural tourism.

Tourism-Derived Definitions

Tourism definitions place cultural tourism within a broader framework of tourism and tourism management theory. Cultural tourism, for example, is recognized as a form of special interest tourism, where culture forms the basis of either attracting tourists or motivating people to travel (McIntosh and Goeldner 1990; Zeppel 1992; Ap 1999). Others place it in a tourism systems context, recognizing that it involves interrelationships between people, places, and cultural heritage (Zeppel and Hall, 1991), or define it in the context of the temporary movement of people (Richards 1996c). Cultural tourism has also been conceptualized from a business perspective as involving the development and marketing of various sites or attractions for foreign as well as domestic tourists (Goodrich 1997).

Motivational Definitions

A number of authors and nongovernmental organizations (NGOs) feel that cultural tourists are motivated to travel for different reasons than other tourists and, therefore, feel that motivation must be considered an important element when defining cultural tourism (Richards 1996b). The World Tourism Organization (WTO) defines cultural tourism as "movements of persons essentially for cultural motivations such as study tours, performing arts and cultural tours, travel to festivals and other events, visit to sites and monuments, travel to study nature, folklore or art, and pilgrimages" (WTO 1985:6). Likewise, the province of Ontario in Canada uses the definition of "visits by persons from outside the host community motivated wholly or in part by interest in the historical, artistic, scientific, or lifestyle/heritage offerings of the community, region, group, or institution" (Silberberg 1995: 361).

Experiential or Aspirational Definitions

Motivation alone, though, does not seem to encapsulate the full magnitude of cultural tourism. Cultural tourism is also an experiential activity, with many people feeling it also includes an aspirational element. As a minimum, cultural tourism involves experiencing or having contact of differing intensity with the unique social fabric, heritage, and special character of places (TC 1991; Blackwell 1997;

Schweitzer 1999). It is also hoped that by experiencing culture the tourist will become educated as well as entertained (VICNET 1996), will have a chance to learn about the community (IDCCA 1997), or will have an opportunity to learn something about the significance of a place and its associations with the local community, its heritage, and a cultural or natural landscape (AHC and TCA 1999). Some people even liken cultural tourism to a quest or search for greater understanding (Bachleitner and Zins 1999; Hannabus 1999). These people suggest that by leading the observer into the cultural past, cultural tourism can help them see the present from a different viewpoint.

Operational Definitions

An operational definition is the most common definitional approach used. Most of the tourism derived, motivational, and experiential definitions also include an operational component, often to illustrate the point being made. Cultural tourism is defined by participation in any one of an almost limitless array of activities or experiences. Indeed, it is common to avoid defining cultural tourism, instead stating that "cultural tourism includes visits to . . . " By inference, if someone visits one of these attractions, that person must be a cultural tourist; thus the activity must be a cultural tourism activity. Motivation, purpose, or depth of experience count less than participation.

The tourism literature identifies the range of cultural tourism activities as including the use of such cultural heritage assets as archaeological sites, museums, castles, palaces, historical buildings, famous buildings, ruins, art, sculpture, crafts, galleries, festivals, events, music and dance, folk arts, theatre, "primitive cultures [sic]," subcultures, ethnic communities, churches, cathedrals and other things that represents people and their cultures (Richards 1996a; Goodrich 1997; Miller 1997; Jamieson 1994). Likewise, the array of cultural tourism products can include existing structures, modified facilities, and purpose-built attractions. The scale can vary from one building, to a cluster of buildings, a streetscape, a precinct within a community, an entire city or town, a region, or arguably to entire countries.

The operational definition highlights the potential scope of this activity, while at the same time illustrating the very real problems that exist in setting meaningful parameters about what is and what is not cultural tourism. By its very nature, cultural tourism has fuzzy boundaries, for it is almost impossible to ascribe absolute parameters either to the resources used or to the tourist using them. In fact, cultural tourism has become an umbrella term for a wide range of related activities, including historical tourism, ethnic tourism, arts tourism, museum tourism, and others. They all share common sets of resources, management issues, and desired aspirational outcomes.

CONCEPTUALIZING CULTURAL TOURISM— A THEMATIC APPROACH

The definitions examined are not without their weaknesses, not because they are poor definitions, but because it is almost impossible to capture the full essence of cultural tourism in one or two sentences. Rather than adding to the growing list of incomplete definitions, we wish instead to place cultural tourism within the context of a number of common themes apparent in these and other definitions that shape our understanding of this phenomenon. The book will focus on an examination of the interrelationships between these themes.

Cultural tourism involves four elements:

1. Tourism
2. Use of cultural heritage assets
3. Consumption of experiences and products
4. The tourist

Tourism

To state that cultural tourism is a form of tourism may seem self-evident and rather tautological. But, as discussed in Chapter 3, it is important to appreciate that "tourism" is a noun and "cultural" is an adjective used to modify it. Above all else, cultural tourism is a form of tourism. It is not a form of cultural heritage management. As a form of tourism, the decision to embark on cultural tourism must be based on sound, commercial tourism reasons first and cultural heritage management reasons second. This point is sometimes not appreciated by some members of the cultural heritage management community who may see tourism as a means of achieving other agendas or who fail to appreciate just what is needed to make an asset work as a tourism attraction. As a tourism activity, it will attract nonlocal visitors (or tourists) who are traveling primarily for pleasure on limited time budgets and who may know little about the significance of the assets being visited. Successful cultural tourism products must be shaped with this type of visitor in mind.

The Use of Cultural Heritage Assets

Having stated the above, however, cultural tourism's principal building blocks are a community or a nation's cultural heritage assets. The International Council on Monuments and Sites (ICOMOS), defines *heritage* as a broad concept that includes tangible assets, such as natural and cultural environments, encompassing landscapes, historic places, sites, and built environments, as well as intangible assets, such as collections, past and continuing cultural practices, knowledge, and living experiences (ICOMOS 1999). These assets are identified and conserved for their intrinsic values or significance to a community rather than for their extrinsic values as tourism attractions. In fact, the tourism potential of assets is rarely considered when they are first identified. At this time, most documentation of an asset's significance concentrates on its aesthetic, architectural, historical, social, spiritual, or educational values, with tourism sitting hazily within the educational or social values sections.

One of the paradoxes of cultural tourism is that although the decision to enter this sector must be driven by tourism considerations, assets are managed by the principles of cultural heritage management. In addition, cultural or heritage assets may serve a multitude of user groups, including tourists, but also including local schoolchildren, "traditional owners" (indigeonous or ethnic community groups that own the intellectual cultural property or land righs associated with a cultural asset), and other local residents. These groups may value the asset for different reasons and seek different benefits from its use, making the task of presenting the asset appropriately more difficult. These competing approaches can be a source of friction between tourism and cultural heritage management interests. Chapters 4 through 6 introduce the key principles of cultural heritage management and how they are applied to tangible and intangible assets.

Consumption of Experiences and Products

All tourism involves the consumption of experiences and products (Urry 1990; Richards 1996c), and cultural tourism is no different. Cultural tourists want to consume a variety of cultural experiences. To facilitate this consumption, cultural heritage assets must be transformed into cultural tourism products. The transformation process actualizes the potential of the asset by converting it into something that the tourist can utilize. This transformation process, though abhorrent to some, is integral to the successful development and sustainable management of the cultural tourism product. This issue is discussed in more detail in Chapters 7 and 8.

Throughout the book, a distinction is made between a cultural or heritage asset and a cultural tourism product. A cultural or heritage asset represents the uncommodified or raw asset that is identified for its intrinsic values. A cultural tourism product, on the other hand, represents an asset that has been transformed or commodified specifically for tourism consumption (see Photo 1.1).

The Tourist

Finally, cultural tourism must consider the tourist. A number of the definitions suggest or imply strongly that all cultural tourists are motivated to travel for deep learning, experiential, or self-exploration reasons. Others recognize that the motivations for cultural tourism participation fall along a continuum, from those who travel exclusively or primarily for cultural tourism reasons to those for whom cultural tourism participation is an accidental element of the trip. Chapter 9 identifies five different types of cultural tourists who exhibit markedly different behaviors. The typology is based on the importance of cultural tourism in the decision to visit a destination and the depth of the experience for the tourist.

In addition, the type, quality, and veracity of information tourists consume prior to arrival will shape their expectations of the asset and their expected behavior while visiting. Ideally, the asset managers can communicate directly to the tourist and accurately impart the desired information in a desirable manner. In reality, as discussed in Chapter 10, many information gatekeepers have more direct access to the consumer prior to the visit and, therefore, may play a more important role in shaping expectations of the experience than the asset itself.

PHOTO 1.1. Middle Kingdom, Ocean Park Theme Park in Hong Kong, China

Cultural tourism is first and foremost a tourism activity in which a destination's cultural or heritage assets are presented for the consumption of tourists. In some cases, consumption can be highly commodified, as in this example of traditional dancers at the Middle Kingdom precinct of the Ocean Park theme park in Hong Kong, China. This precinct's selective and stylized presentation of Chinese traditional culture was specially designed to appeal to the European and North American tourists. It was reasonably popular when it first opened. However, since the opening up of China to foreign tourists and the return of Hong Kong to China in 1997, this attraction saw a decline in popularity. It has since closed and is being redeveloped for other activities. Highly commodified attractions such as this often have a shorter life cycle than less commodified attractions. They must be revised constantly to remain attractive to their target markets.

THE KEY ISSUE:
LINKING CULTURAL HERITAGE MANAGEMENT AND TOURISM MANAGEMENT

The challenge facing the cultural tourism sector is to find a balance between tourism and cultural heritage management—between the consumption of extrinsic values by tourists and conservation of the intrinsic values by cultural heritage managers. This challenge was noted first by the cultural heritage community as long as twenty-five years ago (ICOMOS 1978) and is only recently being recognized as an important issue by the tourism community. The advent of tourism as an interested and legitimate user group has made the heritage resource management process even more demanding. At times, conflicts have emerged between the two sectors as they vie to use the same resource base (Bowes 1994; Jamieson 1994).

Greater urgency than ever exists as demand increases and as pressure is being placed on many assets to perform in a more businesslike manner in order to secure funding (Sugaya 1999). The main stumbling blocks seem to be the continued operations of tourism and cultural heritage management in parallel rather than in partnership, combined with ignorance of the other's needs and suspicion of the other's motives. Integration and partnerships can be achieved only if each side develops a stronger understanding of how the other views the assets, values them, and seeks to use them.

The conservation sector seems to appreciate that use, be it by local residents or tourists, is an important element in creating public awareness of and support for conservation of tangible and intangible assets that will translate into greater political and finding support for further conservation activities (Sugaya 1999). Many others in the conservation sector—sometimes begrudgingly, sometimes with open arms—accept that a partnership between heritage management and tourism is both necessary and beneficial. As a general rule, the tourism industry, historically, has been much slower to recognize the need for partnership. Chapters 11 through 14 present a number of management approaches that both tourism and cultural heritage can use to identify a mutually agreeable set of goals and to manage assets to achieve those goals.

Chapter 2

Challenges in Achieving Sustainable Cultural Tourism

INTRODUCTION

The emergence of cultural tourism as a fashionable tourism activity presents both opportunities and threats to its sustainable management. We defined sustainable cultural tourism in Chapter 1 as a partnership that satisfies both tourism and cultural heritage management objectives. But is this ideal realistic, and can it be achieved across the broad spectrum of cultural tourism products and experiences? Ideologically, most tourism and cultural heritage management stakeholders acknowledge the mutual benefits that can accrue from such a partnership (Robinson 1999). For example, ICOMOS, in its second tourism charter, states "Tourism can capture the economic characteristics of heritage and harness these for conservation by generating funding, educating the community and influencing policy" (ICOMOS 1999: paragraph 5). In practice, though, the partnership seems to be an uneasy one, for tourism and cultural heritage management seem often incompatible (Berry 1994; Bowes 1994; Boniface 1998; Jacobs and Gale 1994; Jansen-Verbeke 1998; Garrod and Fyall 2000).

CULTURE AND TOURISM— COLLABORATORS OR COMPETITORS?

Partnerships work best when a limited number of stakeholders are involved and each holds similar values. On the other hand, conflict, or the potential for conflict, is more likely to emerge when many stakeholders are involved who hold diverse values or when the actions of one set of stakeholders interfere with the achievement of another group's goals (Jacob and Schreyer 1980). Goal interference can occur directly, such as when direct actions of others affect one's enjoyment, or indirectly, such as when a general and more pervasive feeling of dislike or an unwillingness to appreciate the other's views exists (Jackson and Wong 1982). Over time, if conflicts are not resolved, they tend to evolve from an essentially intellectual and therefore distant debate to one that becomes personal and emotive in nature (Burgess, Limb, and Harrison, 1988).

This situation occurs often, or at least has the potential to occur often, in cultural tourism. Kerr (1994: 2) observes that "what is good for conservation is not necessarily good for tourism and what is good for tourism is rarely good for conservation." In practice, cultural values have been compromised for commercial gain where culture assets are presented as commodified tourism products for easy consumption by visitors (Urry 1990; Daniel 1996; Stocks 1996; McKercher and du Cros 1998). Likewise, tourism values have been compromised for some assets when a management attitude exists that any *tourism-ification* is considered to be a corrupting influence (Hovinen 1995; Fyall and Garrod 1996).

Much of the recent history of cultural tourism has been typified by competition for use of the same resource, rather than cooperation to achieve mutually beneficial goals. Competition is often erroneously seen as a zero-sum game that produces winners and losers, when in reality most competitors display both complementary and conflicting interests (Pinkley 1990; Quirk 1989). In other words, although both tourism and cultural stakeholders may have some divergent goals, they also share much in common. Both can benefit from building on this common ground.

Competition may also be exacerbated when the power balance between stakeholders changes, as is happening in many cultural tourism places (McKercher 1996). A power shift, leading to the emergence of a new, dominant stakeholder, be it either tourism or cultural heritage management, and the concomitant relative disempowerment of the other stakeholder, will produce feelings of resentment and distrust toward the new player. Thus, it is not uncommon for heritage managers, for example, to question the benefits of heritage tourism and to argue that they are based on anecdotal information or hope rather than empirical evidence (Jamieson 1995).

The history of cultural tourism, especially during its nascent stages or during the rapid development stage of tourism in general, has been one of permitting tourism to become the dominant stakeholder and then trading off cultural values to maximize tourism benefits. The tourism industry in general and destination marketers in particular, who are primarily interested in maximizing visitation numbers, often have little knowledge of or regard for the impacts of tourism activities on the cultural assets they are promoting.

Likewise, the history of conservation management, especially in mature destinations or in the developed world, has been one of trying to reassert cultural heritage management as the dominant stakeholder and in doing so to reduce or limit visitor numbers. David Lowenthal (1998) raises this issue when he observes that cultural heritage managers can sometimes take their stewardship of assets so seriously that they become overly possessive or selfish in their treatment of such assets when challenged by other stakeholders whose requirements for using such assets may differ or ultimately overlap. Host communities may also have conservation requirements that initially clash and then overlap with that of tourism.

THE INDEPENDENT EVOLUTION OF TOURISM AND CULTURAL HERITAGE

It is not surprising that tourism and cultural heritage management view each other with suspicion, for they share little in common apart from their resource base. Each discipline evolved independently with different core ideologies and values, to serve different sets of stakeholders, different political masters, achieve different objectives, and perform significantly different roles in society. Tourism industry professionals value cultural assets as raw materials for their products to generate tourism activity and wealth. Cultural heritage management professionals value the same assets for their intrinsic merits.

The lack of cross communication is disappointing, if not surprising, in spite of the fact that cultural tourism has been as a distinct tourism product category for more twenty years. We have been amazed in our world travel at how few tourism people attend cultural tourism conferences organized by the heritage sector and how few heritage people attend similar conferences organized by the tourism sector. This lack of cross communication leads to a lack of cross-fertilization of ideas and lack of an understanding of the legitimate needs of each stakeholder. Ignorance breeds suspicion, which breeds mistrust.

Table 2.1 highlights just how different cultural heritage management is from tourism. Cultural heritage management evolved to conserve and protect a representative sample of our heritage for the future. Its goal is to serve the broader public good. Cultural heritage management is largely structured around public sector or not-for-profit organizations. Its stakeholders tend to be community groups or representatives of indigenous or ethnic groups, and it regards assets for their intrinsic worth. Cultural heritage management professionals tend to come from a social science or arts background.

TABLE 2.1. Comparing Cultural Heritage Management and Tourism

	Cultural Heritage Management	Tourism
Structure	Public-sector oriented Not for profit	Private-sector oriented Profit making
Goals	A broader social goal	Commercial goals
Key stakeholders	Community groups Heritage groups Minority/ethnic/indigenous groups Local residents Organizations for heritage professionals/local historical groups/religious leaders	Business groups Nonlocal residents National tourism trade associations, other industry bodies
Economic attitude to assets	Existence value Conserve for their intrinsic values	Use value Consume for their intrinsic or extrinsic appeal
Key user groups	Local residents	Nonlocal residents
Employment background	Social science/arts degrees	Business/marketing degrees
Use of asset	Value to community as a representation of tangible and intangible heritage	Value to tourist as product or activity that can help brand a destination
International political bodies/NGOs	ICOMOS/ICOM/UNESCO (promote conservation of culture)	WTO/WTTC (promote development of tourism)
National/regional political/bureaucratic bodies	National, state, and local agencies and some museums concerned with heritage management, archives	National, state, regional tourism bodies

Conversely, tourism is essentially a commercial activity that is dominated by the private sector and is driven by profit or the desire of governments to achieve economic objectives. Its stakeholders tend to represent the commercial sector and to be driven by commercial objectives. Because of this focus, tourism is much more interested in the use value of assets rather than in their existence value. Tourism industry professionals tend to come from the commercial world and increasingly are receiving business educations focusing either on the business of tourism or marketing.

SEVEN POSSIBLE RELATIONSHIPS BETWEEN TOURISM AND CULTURAL HERITAGE MANAGEMENT

This historic isolation leads to a number of possible relationships between tourism and cultural heritage management. Insights about possible relationships can be gained from an examination of the relationship between tourism and the environment, which has been the subject of academic inquiry for more than twenty-five years. Budowksi (1976, 1977) argued that three possible relationships could exist between tourism and those people advocating the conservation of nature. Coexistence tended to occur in the nascent stage of tourism development when small numbers of operators took relatively few clients into natural areas. Because their activities were widely dispersed, few contacts occurred between tourists and conservationists. Tourism was seen as a nonthreatening activity. However, as tourism numbers increased, a state of conflict was more likely to emerge, especially in the vacuum of effective conservation management plans. Conflict is most likely to emerge when tourism is perceived to be detrimental to nature and its resources. A symbiotic relationship can exist whereby tourism is seen to be complementary to overall management objectives, but symbiosis is rare and occurs only as a result of direct management intervention.

Much the same situation applies when considering the relationship between tourism and those people who advocate the conservation of tangible and intangible cultural and heritage assets. This issue was canvassed in a special edition of the *Journal of Sustainable Tourism* (JOST 1999). Table 2.2 outlines seven possible relationships on a

TABLE 2.2. Possible Relationships Between Tourism and Cultural Heritage Assets

Cooperation/partnership ◄──────────────────────► Conflict

Full Cooperation	Working Relationships	Peaceful Co-existence	Parallel Existence/Blissful Ignorance	Mild Annoyance	Nascent Conflict	Full Conflict
True partnership for the mutual benefit of both sectors	Realization of common needs and interests	Sharing of the same resource	Separate and independent	Goal interference attributable to one stakeholder	Problems defying easy solutions emerge	Open conflict between stakeholders
Likely imposed or heavily managed	Begin dialogue Work to ensure that both interests are satisfied	Derive mutual Benefits from its use, but still largely separate and independent. Some dialogue, but little cooperation or recognition of need to cooperate	Little or no contact Out of sight, out of mind	Lessened satisfaction One stakeholder exerts adverse effects, but little real conflict Lack of understanding between stakeholders	Changing power relationships with emergence of one dominant stakeholder whose needs are detrimental to the other established stakeholder	

cooperation/conflict continuum from full partnerships to open conflict. Partnerships are unlikely to evolve spontaneously; instead, they usually require intervention from a dominant management agency, while conflict is most likely to occur in a management vacuum.

At one end of the spectrum, true partnerships between stakeholders may occur. This situation is easiest to achieve in purpose-built facilities, such as museums, art galleries, or heritage theme parks, or in purpose-designed cultural tourism experiences, such as dance shows and minority/indigenous cultural shows. Here, the desired experiences can be crafted for the tourist around a desired set of cultural or heritage management objectives (see Photo 2.1). Mass tourism attractions, such as historic theme parks, may seek to provide an entertainment- or *edutainment*-oriented tourism experience that purposefully provides a more shallow but still meaningful experience for visitors. On the other hand, museums, art galleries, and cultural tours may shape their products to provide visitors with the opportunity to engage the attraction or experience at a much deeper and more intellectually challenging level.

Full cooperation is easier to achieve in such facilities because the number of competing stakeholders is limited, a clearly defined set of management objectives has been identified and agreed to by all parties, the economic necessities of tourism are appreciated along with cultural heritage management ideals, and a clear power/management hierarchy exists to ensure that both objectives can be achieved in a balanced manner. Top-down leadership, coupled with a shared vision that such facilities serve both tourism and cultural goals, ensures that necessary compromises are made to satisfy both parties' needs.

True partnerships are much harder, but not impossible, to achieve in non–purpose-built facilities. In such cases, there must be a mutual agreement among all stakeholders that either tourism or cultural heritage management interests will dominate the management process and that the other's needs will be modified to serve the needs of the overall management goals. Thus, different management approaches and attitudes to the delivery of experiences will be applied to historic buildings developed for tourism use than for one conserved primarily for its intrinsic values. In the former case, the facility will be managed in such a way as to facilitate its consumption; in the latter case, consumption will be permitted but only to the point that it does not interfere with the cultural values being conserved.

PHOTO 2.1. Jorvik Viking Centre, York, England

Tourism and cultural heritage management can be powerful allies. Tourism revenue generated by visitation to the Jorvik Viking Centre in York, England, provides
most of the income for the York Archeological Trust's research activities. Tourists
are also encouraged to join a live dig to learn more about the past. The Jorvik
Viking Centre is a historical attraction based on the archeological examination of
a 1,000-year-old Viking village. It serves domestic tourism as well as the international market, while also being attractive to schools as a trigger to interest children
in history. The Viking Centre was considered quite controversial among heritage
managers and archaeologists when it first opened due to its popularization of
archaeology. Although controversial, its success has influenced the thinking
behind the design of many other on-site visitor centers.

Working relationships, rather than full partnerships, are more likely to occur in extant assets that are shared by tourism and cultural heritage management. Both sets of stakeholders appreciate that the other has legitimate interests in the asset in question, and both also appreciate that while they may have their differences, they also share much in common. Over time, a working relationship develops between stakeholders with each willing to make some accommodations to satisfy the needs of the other. Management structures are put in place to retain the relationship that has evolved.

This situation works well providing that power relationships remain relatively stable and that no new stakeholders claim an interest in the asset. The empowerment of one stakeholder or the introduction of others, such as the "discovery" of a cultural asset by a new tour operator who decides to bring large numbers of tourists to the place, can throw this relationship out of balance. Productive working relationships can exist at both high-visitation or low-visitation cultural tourism products, provided that they are managed for such use levels.

Peaceful coexistence is likely to exist when both sets of stakeholders share the resource but feel little need to cooperate. This type of situation is most likely to occur when visitation levels are low or when large numbers of tourists consume the product in an unobtrusive manner. Likewise, they are most likely to occur when cultural heritage management activity is low or when management occurs in a manner that does not interfere with tourism use. Examples of peaceful coexistence are the preservation of historic streetscapes or heritage buildings that tourists may visit. Here, large numbers of tourists may consume the streetscape but otherwise exert little adverse impact on how the conserved buildings are managed. Indeed, tourism may be cited as a justification for the continued conservation of such places, even though most tourist use is passive. Likewise, management structures exert few restrictions on tourists.

Parallel existence occurs when tourism and cultural heritage management operate independently and tourists have little interest in a destination area's cultural assets. This situation is akin to *blissful ignorance,* or an "out of sight, out of mind" attitude toward each other. These situations are most likely to occur where little tourism activity exists (see Photo 2.2) or when that activity is focused around a destination's other attributes, such as the beach, resorts, outdoor recreation,

PHOTO 2.2. Midden, West Coast, Republic of South Africa

Tourism and cultural heritage management can coexist when tourism pressures are low. However, this is often a veneer, for an increase in tourism activity without proper management can create conflicts. In this example, taken from the west coast of the Republic of South Africa, the small numbers of tourists that visit an ancient midden have minimal impact. If this site were to become more popular, management activities to restrict disturbance would have to be introduced. Appropriate measures might include a raised viewing platform or walkway around the edge of the midden to prevent the erosion of vegetation holding the midden in place and the trampling and fragmentation of the shells by visitors. Signage would also be needed to explain the significance of the site to visitors unfamiliar with shell middens and their role in past lifestyles.

or gaming. Cultural tourism is not seen as part of the region's product attributes, is not promoted, and assets are little used.

Mild annoyance, possibly leading to a later state of conflict, occurs when the actions of one set of stakeholders interfere with the desired goals of another set. It does not stop the individual from participating in an activity but lessens the level of enjoyment. Mild annoyance is likely to occur when the stakeholders feel that the current situation is beginning to evolve in an unfavorable direction. It may be that greater numbers of tourists are beginning to visit an asset, reducing the pleasure felt by the existing users. It may be that changing management plans is affecting the ability of the tourism stakeholders to achieve its goals.

Nascent conflict is the step between mild annoyance and full conflict. The actions of one stakeholder have an adverse effect on the other. Moreover, the problems that arise defy easy resolution. Nascent conflict will emerge when a stable system is pushed out of stasis due to external factors. It is also likely to emerge when the power relationship between stakeholders changes fundamentally. Thus, the decision to include a cultural heritage asset in a tour itinerary without consulting the asset managers may lead to a state of nascent conflict. Likewise, alterations to a management plan that are seen to benefit one stakeholder at the direct cost of another could trigger a nascent conflict.

At the far end of the spectrum, *full-scale, open conflict* can emerge between heritage and tourism stakeholders. Conflict is most likely to occur when real or perceived differences exist between stakeholders and how they view assets (McKercher 1992, 1993), threats to access or exclusivity (Pigram 1984; McKercher 1992), differences in activity styles (Jacob and Schreyer 1980; Jackson and Wong 1982), or differences in participants' desires and motivations for pursuing a specific activity (Manning 1985). This type of conflict was noted when the Walt Disney Company sought to build an American history theme park near the Gettysburg battlefield site (Gallagher 1995). A powerful new stakeholder sought to fundamentally change how a cultural asset had been used and in doing so would seem to pose a threat to the ongoing integrity of that asset. Open conflict is most likely to occur in a management vacuum that cannot stop or slow change.

Likewise, a change in power relationships between stakeholders can trigger conflict. The emergence of tourism as the dominant user coupled with the perception that assets are being managed for tourism use at the cost of their intrinsic values can produce a state of conflict among cultural heritage management advocates (see Photo 2.3). Alternatively, the imposition of stringent management plans that restrict a number of tourism uses that previously had been permitted may engender a sense of loss of power and conflict among tourism stakeholders.

THE CONSEQUENCES

Unfortunately, it has been our experience that, in many cases, the type of relationship between cultural heritage management and tour-

PHOTO 2.3. Boudhanath Stupa, Kathmandu, Nepal

The influx of large numbers of tourists can shift an asset out of equilibrium, changing the nature of the relationship between tourism and cultural heritage management. At Boudhanath Stupa, outside of Kathmandu, Nepal, tourist facilities have been built right up to the edge of the shrine. The holy area is surrounded by small hotels and souvenir shops which crowd so close that on busy days tourists jostle worshippers spinning the Buddhist prayer wheels around its base. This situation is particularly curious given that the site has been inscribed on the World Heritage List since 1979 and that most development occurred after its inclusion. The development of unplanned tourism infrastructure close to heritage assets is often a problem for heritage managers in developing countries where town planning mechanisms are lacking. The UNESCO World Heritage Center now encourages those nominating places for inclusion on the World Heritage List to provide evidence that such mechanisms are already active before inclusion will be considered (UNESCO World Heritage Centre 2000).

ism tends to be weighted toward the conflict end of the spectrum, with blissful ignorance and mild annoyance being the most common attitudes expressed. Destination marketers either ignore cultural heritage managers when devising strategies promoting the consumption of their region's cultural assets or express frustration that these people do not understand the benefits that tourism can bring. Tour operators continue to bring people to cultural attractions and continue to foster inaccurate or inappropriate attitudes toward places. Cultural heritage managers, on the other hand, choose to ignore the reality of tourism and, in doing so, lament the perceived adverse impacts that tourism imposes on heritage assets.

As discussed throughout this book, the failure to appreciate the nexus between cultural heritage management and tourism results in the suboptimal delivery of cultural tourism products and the continued unsustainable development of this sector. The failure to accept that tourism is a legitimate user results in the failure to develop and present cultural assets in a manner that is amenable to the needs of the tourist. The consequence may mean lowered visitation levels and decreased satisfaction, threatening the commercial viability of the asset. Worse still, the consequence may mean continued high levels of visitation without signaling how the asset is to be used, resulting in tourists defining the experience themselves, at the peril of the asset.

The failure by tourism interests to accept that cultural and heritage assets have legitimate intrinsic values of their own, above and beyond their use values as products, and that these values are meaningful to other users beyond tourists, means that tourism may overwhelm that asset and damage the very essence of what makes it appealing in the first place. Further, the failure of some elements of the tourism industry to explain the intrinsic values detracts from the quality of the experience provided. Moreover, the unethical actions of some tourism operators that not only permit but encourage inappropriate uses of cultural assets can lead directly to the destruction of the asset or open conflict with local custodians or tradition bearers.

Fortunately an increasing number of asset managers realize that tourism plays an important role in the overall management and presentation of their facility. They are working to incorporate tourism needs into their activities and are striving to develop products that meet the interests of the tourism industry. In addition, a number of tourism professionals are now appreciating that cultural tourism products must be treated in a somewhat different manner than other tourism products and that they exist to satisfy more than the narrow interests of tourism.

THE SOLUTION?

Partnerships are most likely to emerge when stakeholders understand one anothers' needs and appreciate that both tourism and cultural heritage management stakeholders have a legitimate interest in the cultural heritage asset being used by tourism. Understanding can occur only by truly developing an appreciation of the other side's interests and values. This means that tourism interests must develop an awareness of cultural heritage management concepts, ideals, and practices. Likewise, cultural heritage management stakeholders must also develop an understanding of what tourism is and how it works. Through mutual understanding, both groups can then work to build on their shared interests in the asset and work to resolve differences. Throughout the rest of the book, we discuss cultural heritage management and tourism management and illustrate how they can be integrated into an overall, mutually beneficial management approach to cultural tourism.

Chapter 3

How Tourism Works

INTRODUCTION

People sometimes lose sight of the fact that cultural tourism is first and foremost a form of tourism. They forget that the word *cultural* is an adjective that modifies the noun *tourism*. Thus, while cultural tourism uses the cultural or heritage assets of a destination, its performance is guided by the same principles that drive any other form of tourism. Understanding cultural tourism, therefore, is predicated on developing an understanding of what tourism is, how it works, and what drives tourism decisions.

Few people really understand tourism, but that does not seem to stop them from commenting on it and telling willing audiences how tourism should work. Indeed, tourism is one of those activities that produces an inordinate number of instant experts who confuse emotions and feeling with fact. Because people have traveled or because they have witnessed change in places they have visited, they feel qualified to become tourism experts. The academic literature is replete with stories portraying tourism as destroyer of communities and cultures (O'Grady 1981; D'Sa 1999). These observations are usually personal in nature and are often emotional in context. Comments such as the one made by Dana (1999) are typical and reflect an attitude in much of the literature documenting alleged social impacts based more, we suspect, on personal disappointment in a vacation experience than on any hard evidence. He concludes his paper on the social costs of tourism by stating, "One could argue that the island residents are wealthier in monetary terms, but I question whether they and their island remain as rich as they were before tourists arrive" (Dana 1999:5), without ever having asked the local residents that very question.

For the most part, though, the large body of empirical research shows that residents affected by tourism feel its net benefits outweigh its costs (Liu, Sheldon, and Var 1987; Perdue, Long, and Allen 1987a,b; Milman and Pizam 1988; Getz 1993, 1994; Clements, Schultz, and Lime 1993; King, Pizam, and Milman 1993; Madrigal 1993; Parlett, Fletcher, and Cooper 1995; Derrett 1996; Fowler 1996). Likewise, a whole host of impacts has been identified that, on closer scrutiny, has more to do with the overall modernization or development process than with tourism per se (Singh, Thuens, and Go 1989; Pearce 1989). There is still a widespread belief that the tourism-ification of cultural assets will invariably lead to their destruction, when the evidence is at best ambivalent (Berry 1994; Boniface 1998; Jacobs and Gale 1994; Jansen-Verbeke 1998).

Indeed, if there are two lessons we have learned in our various journeys around the world, attendance at conferences, or in discussions with public sector nontourism officials, they are (1) how little some people really know about tourism, and (2) how little communication occurs between tourism and heritage management people. Resolution of real problems can occur only by seeking answers based on a deep understanding of the factors that have led to their emergence, not through emotional tirades. This is especially true for cultural tourism where, by its very nature, the potential for problems is heightened. This chapter identifies fifteen underlying principles or structural realities that drive tourism (as shown in Table 3.1). Some relate to tourism in general, while others relate to how cultural assets are used for tourism purposes. The list presented is a personal list based on our examination and observations of tourism and tourists. You may not agree with all the items but at least consider them before commenting on tourism in the future.

THE NATURE OF TOURISM

Tourism Is a Commercial Activity

Tourism is essentially a commercial activity. This axiomatic principle seems to be overlooked in much of the literature examining tourism from different academic or intellectual perspectives. Although tourism may be an interesting intellectual phenomenon, in practice it is a business—a big business. Indeed, it is arguably the world's larg-

TABLE 3.1. Underlying Principles of Cultural Tourism

Issue	Principle
The nature of tourism	• Tourism is a commercial activity. • Tourism involves the consumption of experiences. • Tourism is entertainment. • Tourism is a demand-driven activity that is difficult to control.
Attractions drive tourism	• Not all tourism attractions are equal. • Cultural heritage attractions are part of tourism. • Not all cultural assets are cultural tourist attractions.
Factors influencing visitation levels	• Access and proximity dictate the potential number of visitors. • Time availability influences the quality and depth of experience sought.
Tourist behavior	• The tourist experience must be controlled to control the actions of the tourist. • Tourists want controlled experiences. • The more mainstream the market, the greater the need for user-friendly tourism products.
Cultural tourism	• Not all cultural tourists are alike. • Cultural tourism products may be challenging and confronting but not intimidating or accusatory. • Tourists want "authenticity" but not necessarily reality.

est or second largest business. Businesses enter the tourism sector with hopes of profiting by providing goods and services for the hundreds of millions of people who travel every year. Destinations pursue tourism because of the economic benefits it provides and for the ensuing social benefits that accrue from its generation of wealth. States and provinces pursue tourism because it generates new money for their jurisdictions. Nations pursue tourism because it is such a valuable source of foreign exchange. Although we may travel to satisfy inner needs, such as escape, rest, recreation status, or learning (Hawkins 1994), destinations pursue tourism for the economic benefits it provides. But tourism is unique because the majority of revenue is generated by facilitators of experiences rather than by experience providers. The tourism industry enables tourists to consume experiences but does not necessarily provide the experiences themselves.

Indeed, only a small fraction of the cost of a tour is spent at what can be called attractions; the rest is spent on transport, accommodation, food, drink, tips, sightseeing, and commissions to the travel trade. Yet it is these attractions that draw tourists to region in the first place, enabling the rest of the benefits to accrue.

Tourism Involves the Consumption of Experiences

Tourists satisfy their personal needs by consuming enjoyable experiences (Urry 1990; Sharpley 2000). Some commentators decry tourism consumption as being nothing more than a search for photo opportunities (Urry 1990; Allcock 1995; Richards 1996c; Human 1999), while others argue that consumption of experiences is a worthy goal in itself (Sharpley 2000) (see Photo 3.1). Cultural tourism is no different from any other form of tourism in that cultural tourists are interested in consuming experiences. But, tourism represents an insidious form of consumption (McKercher 1993). Unlike most other economic activities that enjoy virtual exclusive rights over the use of their resource base, tourism resources are typically part of the public domain or are intrinsically linked to the social fabric of the host community.

Tourism activities can be invasive, especially when the perception exists that they have been imposed on the host community (Gorman 1988). Addressing the radically different needs of the tourist, who is traveling to seek experiences, and the community, which seeks some financial benefit from the traveler, poses the greatest challenge for tourism in general and for cultural tourism in particular. The tourism-ification of cultural heritage assets presents a number of issues for the management of these assets, not the least of which is the challenging task of accommodating both the needs of the tourism industry and the ideals of cultural heritage management (Bazin 1995; Cheung 1999; Peleggi 1996; Robb 1998; Sletvold 1996).

Tourism Is Entertainment

Tourism experiences, especially many cultural tourism experiences, have their basis in entertainment. To be successful and therefore commercially viable, the tourism product must be manipulated and packaged in such a way that it can be consumed easily by the public (Eden 1990; Cohen 1972). Tight tour schedules, limited time

PHOTO 3.1. Cook Islands

Tourists in the Cook Islands consuming a cultural show. Consumption can be overt, as in this case, or it can be more subtle, such as when the tourist absorbs local culture.

budgets, and the need to process large numbers of visitors mean that the product must often be modified to provide regular show times and a guaranteed experience. As one ex-president of the Hawaiian Visitors Bureau said many years ago, "Since real events do not always occur on schedule, we invent pseudo events for tour operators who must have a dance of the vestal virgins precisely at 10 am every Wednesday" (Stalker 1984). Although dated, this observation still applies to a large extent.

Clearly, learning opportunities can be created from the experiences, but their primary role is to entertain (Ritzer and Liska 1997). Even museums and art galleries that are developed to provide educational and cultural enlightenment have recognized that they are in the entertainment business and have arranged their displays accordingly (Zeppel and Hall 1991; Tighe 1986; McDonald and Alsford 1989; Prideaux and Kininmont 1999). The reason is that only a small number of tourists really seek a deep learning experience when they travel.

The rest are traveling for pleasure or escapist reasons and wish to participate in activities that will provide a sense of enjoyment. Some people explain this phenomenon by arguing that tourists accept entertainment or commodified experiences as being a manifestation of the modern consumerist lifestyle; tourism becomes an end in itself and not a means to some loftier goal.

Tourism Is a Demand-Driven Activity
That Is Difficult to Control

One of the great myths of tourism promoted by public sector tourism agencies and NGOs is that by controlling supply, adverse impacts of tourism can be controlled. Although this may be true at an operational level where undesirable elements can be refused entry or forcibly removed, the global history of rampant tourism development, even under a supply-driven approach, illustrates that this policy rarely works on a regional or national basis. The great challenge for any destination is to control the genie of tourism once it is let out of its bottle (McKercher 1993). The history of spontaneous development and the resultant social and environmental costs associated with it attest to the challenges faced by any destination that seeks to promote tourism (Foster 1985; Pearce 1989). The best that governments can do is hope to influence the direction tourism will take.

Tourism is fundamentally a demand-driven activity that is influenced more by market forces (tourists and the industry that seeks to satisfy tourists' needs), rather than by governments that try to control or manage it. The ability to control tourism must be predicated on the assumption of being able to control tourists. But proponents of a chaos theory (McKercher 1999; Faulkner and Russell 1997; Russell and Faulkner 1999; Diamond 1993) illustrate that tourism markets are dynamic, erratic, nonlinear, and are noted for their great volatility. If the driving force behind tourism functions in a chaotic manner, then the entire system will be driven by the principles of chaos. Tourism, tourists, and the tourism industry behave in a manner similar to a bottom-up, self-organizing, living ecosystem that cannot be controlled using traditional Newtonian supply systems.

Further, it has been our experience that many advocates of the belief that supply can control tourism are elitist in their attitudes. They assert that encouraging the "right" type of development will attract the "right" type of provider, which will appeal to the "right" travel distributor who will reach the "right" type of tourist. This person is usually an affluent experienced traveler who is aware of and sensitive to local cultures, will want to stay in local accommodations, eat locally produced food, and who will be satisfied with basic facilities, at the same time paying high tariffs. The problem is that this type of person represents a tiny portion of the traveling public. How do you satisfy the needs of the vast majority of people who travel, even if they do not fit this ideal description? They are not going to stop traveling; they will continue to place demand for services and facilities.

ATTRACTIONS DRIVE TOURISM

Not All Tourism Attractions Are Equal

Tourism is driven by attractions or, in marketing terms, demand generators. However, not all tourism attractions have equal demand-generation potential. A clear hierarchy of tourist attractions exists that can be defined according to the degree of compulsion felt by tourists to visit. The more dominant the attraction is, the greater the sense of obligation to visit (Bull 1991). On the other hand, the purchase decision becomes increasingly discretionary for lower-order attractions, until visits to the lowest-order ones are typified by low involvement decisions involving little effort required on behalf of the visitor.

It is important to appreciate where any attraction sits in this hierarchy, for it will dictate how much visitation it will receive and how it will be used. Primary attractions will draw people who specifically want to see the asset and who therefore will be somewhat knowledgeable of it. The quality of interpretation and presentation will differ from lower order attractions. They, on the other hand, will likely draw a different type of tourist seeking a different experience. As a more discretionary activity, these attractions will draw people seeking a lighter experience or who are looking for discretionary activities to round out their trip. They will be less familiar with the asset, less willing to spend large amounts of time consuming it, and less likely to invest substantial emotional resources for the experience.

Cultural Heritage Attractions Are Part of Tourism

Cultural tourism attractions are recognized widely as being an important element of the tourism mix of any destination (Richards 1996a). Many of them, though, fall into the category of being lower-order attractions. A wide array of publicly and privately owned cultural tourism products is available (Prentice 1993; Swarbrooke 1995), including cultural tours, art galleries, museums, heritage buildings, historical assets and/or complexes, and purpose-built theme parks. Many cultural heritage managers, however, seem to resist accepting that the assets they manage have touristic appeal. As a result, they resist introducing management structures that will optimize the quality of the experience provided while at the same time minimizing the impacts that tourism may have.

The first key to the successful management of any cultural heritage tourism attraction is to accept that the attraction is indeed a tourism attraction and must be managed as such, at least in part, for tourism use. The challenge for managers of cultural heritage assets with tourism potential is that some visitation will occur regardless of whether it is wanted or not and regardless of what management structures are imposed. Accepting this reality means that proactive managers must develop management plans that will ensure the needs, wants, and desires of tourists visiting the assets are satisfied, while at the same time ensuring that the cultural heritage values and integrity of the cultural heritage asset are maintained.

Not All Cultural Assets Are Cultural Tourist Attractions

Although cultural tourism attractions form part of the tourism mix, not all cultural assets have tourism potential. Cultural heritage places are usually designated by communities for reasons other than their tourism potential (Belland and Boss 1994, Jamieson 1994). They may be locally significant or locally unusual assets. But because an asset is listed does not mean that it will be attractive to tourists. It is sad to see the honest mistakes that well-meaning people have made by overinflating the perceived tourism value of an asset when, indeed, it has limited appeal. Valuable resources have been wasted developing infrastructure and services to cater for anticipated tourist use that has not eventuated.

Cultural heritage places with tourism potential share a number of common features. They are known beyond the local heritage community; they provide experiences that can be consumed; they are interesting and unique; they are robust; they can absorb visitation; and they are accessible. Most important, they provide the tourist with some compelling reason to visit, even if they are lower-order attractions (see Photo 3.2). A temple is a temple is a temple, unless it offers something unique or unusual for the tourist that entices a visit. Festivals provided for the benefits of local residents may be intriguing events but may have little appeal or relevance for tourists unless they satisfy the above criteria.

FACTORS INFLUENCING VISITATION LEVELS

Access and Proximity Dictate the Potential Number of Visitors

Demand for tourism products is influenced by a range of factors, including *distance decay* (Greer and Wall 1979; Truong and Hensher 1985; Bull 1991; Drezner and Drezner 1996; McKercher 1998a,b), *market access* (Pearce 1989; McKercher 1998a,b), and time availability (Chavas, Stoll, and Sellar 1989; Walsh, Sanders, and McKean 1990; McKean, Johnson, and Walsh 1995). Distance decay theory suggests that demand for tourism attractions varies inversely with distance traveled; that is, demand declines exponentially as distance increases. Similarly, market access states that demand is influenced by the number of similar, competing products or destinations available between the tourist's home and the prospective product or destination. Time availability has been shown to accentuate or minimize the effect of market access and distance decay (Johansson and Montagari 1996; Sjögren and Brännäs 1996).

The proximity of an attraction to a large population base, a major tourism destination, or a gateway will influence its potential visitation and consequently how the asset is to be used. Demand, in turn, influences the revenue generation potential for the asset, which should, therefore, influence the size, level of development, and level of investment. The basic rule of thumb is that attractions that are located close to large population or tourist centers will attract significantly larger numbers of visitors than more distant attractions.

PHOTO 3.2. Port Arthur, Tasmania, Australia

Not all cultural heritage assets are necessarily cultural tourism products. Cultural tourism products must have something that sets them apart from all other heritage assets. Port Arthur, the remains of a nineteenth-century prison in the Australian state of Tasmania, succeeds as a tourism product for a variety of reasons, including its sheer scale, unique history, status as one of the most notorious convict settlements in Australia, and the level of human suffering that is associated with the site. It is also one of the earliest cultural tourism attractions in Australia. Even in the 1890s, its appeal was evident. One visitor to the site noted "every visitor is anxious to see it, and if carefully looked after, it could have been made a permanent source of revenue" (Ballard in Davidson and Spearitt 2000: 26).

Prior to World War I, the remains fell into neglect. However, the awakening of interest in Australia's convict past in the 1920s spawned renewed interest in Port Arthur and other convict-housing sites. In the 1970s, the Tasmanian National Parks and Wildlife Service (TASNPWS) made numerous pleas to the state and federal governments for funding to maintain and conserve the site and its visitors' facilities from rapid decay and build a better tourism infrastructure, such as better access roads. Since then, it has been occasionally suggested that the site manager should reconstruct the ruins and add a more theme park–type atmosphere to the site to repay the money or make it financially self-sufficient. However, TASNPWS holds the view that Port Arthur is a cultural asset foremost, and any commodification should present the cultural values, not detract from them or overly commercialize them.

The same maxim holds true on a micro or destination-specific scale. Readily accessible attractions will enjoy greater visitation levels than out-of-the-way assets, unless the compulsion to visit them is so great that remoteness becomes a nonissue. Museums located in downtown areas or in tourist precincts, for example, will enjoy greater visitation than isolated museums located in outer suburbs. The physical location of the asset, vis-à-vis its major markets, must, therefore, be taken into consideration when assessing its tourism potential. Only truly superlative assets are capable of overcoming the realities of distance decay and market access. Their drawing power must be so strong that people are motivated to see them, regardless of the time, effort, cost, or distance involved.

Time Availability Influences the Quality and Depth of Experience Sought

Most tourists are traveling on finite time budgets, with many having their time strictly controlled by tour operators or children. They have only a limited amount of time available at any one destination and, being rational consumers, will choose to spend that time in the most cost-effective manner (see McKercher and du Cros 1998). As such, many tourists will seek to consume as many experiences as possible during their stay and will show a predilection for those activities that can be consumed quickly, easily, and where they feel certain they will get a guaranteed experience. Especially when cultural tourism participation is an incidental aspect of the trip, the amount of time a tourist is willing to allocate to a cultural tourism experience will depend on the amount of discretionary time available and the number of possible competing uses for that time. Those experiences that consume large blocks of time will tend to be avoided if an attractive alternative exists. Bear in mind that in tourism terms, large blocks of time can be counted in hours, and not days.

Unfortunately, the very nature of cultural tourism often demands that substantial amounts of time or emotional effort be expended to appreciate fully the experience. This creates two challenges for providers. On the one hand, providing experiences that require greater effort to consume may result in lower visitation, which could affect the commercial viability of a product. On the other hand, making the product simple to consume may result in higher visitation, but at what cost to the quality of the message being sent?

TOURIST BEHAVIOR

The Tourist Experience Must Be Controlled to Control the Actions of the Tourist

The best way to control tourists and, therefore, to limit the adverse impacts of tourism on cultural heritage, is to control the tourism experience. The best way to control the tourist experience is to standardize, modify, and commodify that experience. For many, this is heresy, especially given the significant volume of literature that condemns tourism for the commodification and trivialization of culture. Yet the standardization, modification, and commodification of the experience represents a pragmatic means of controlling the movement of people through an asset, while ensuring that the visitor gains as much from the experience as possible. It is for this reason that purpose-built heritage products often function better as tourism attractions than extant assets, especially if significant asset modification is required to cater to the needs of the tourist.

The problem has been and continues to be that the experience is being standardized and commodified by the tourism industry for the benefit of tourism operators and not by asset managers or asset owners as the best interpretation and protection of the asset's fabric (Vukonic 1996). The result has been the unfortunate type of cases still seen where the only interpretation many visitors receive is from the bus driver, whose main qualification is his ability to control a bus and not his knowledge of the area being visited. The challenge for the asset manager or museum board is to control the experience on site and to wrest control from the tour operator.

Tourists Want Controlled Experiences

It may be difficult for many to appreciate, but most tourists actually want to have their experience controlled and are amenable to having the asset presented in a manner that facilitates easy consumption. The reason is that most domestic tourists and virtually all international tourists may visit an asset only once in their lifetime and consequently wish to get the most out of the experience (see Photo 3.3). Standardizing the presentation of the product ensures that, as much as possible, the quality of the experience can be maintained at a consistently high level, guaranteeing a high-caliber experience for as many visitors as possible.

Controlling the experience also ensures that people on limited time budgets can experience the essence of the attraction while not wasting their time consuming elements that they feel are not essential to the core experience. Further, standardization, modification, and commoditization add value to the experience being consumed and can thus justify charging an admission or consumption fee.

PHOTO 3.3. Alcatraz Prison, San Francisco, California

Contrary to popular belief, most tourists wish to have their activities controlled somewhat to ensure that they get the highest experience. Many tourists will visit a place only once in their lifetime and, thus, wish to get the most out of a visit. Alcatraz Prison in San Francisco, as with many other heritage attractions, does this in an unobtrusive way by encouraging visitors to take an individualized guided tour following an audiotape.

The More Mainstream the Market, the Greater the Need for User-Friendly Tourism Products

The more mainstream the market being drawn to the attraction is, the easier the product must be to consume. Two factors are at play here. Mainstream or mass tourists are usually motivated by pleasure or escape reasons for their holidays. They are tourists who are seeking enjoyable experiences that do not tax them mentally or ideologically. They cannot be confused with anthropologists or archaeologists (de Kadt 1979). D'Sa (1999) adds to this when he reports on the opinions of some in the travel trade: "the major motive of tourism is recreation. . . . we are in no position to educate our clients" (1999:65).

As well, many of these people will be fundamentally ignorant of the assets they are visiting. The more culturally distant the asset is from the individual's own frame of reference, the greater the likelihood of ignorance about it (Sizer 1999), while, ironically, the greater the interest in experiencing cultural tourism (McKercher and Chow 2000). At best, many tourists not have studied history formally beyond the level of elementary or lower-level high school. At worst, they have not studied it at all in relation to the asset. As such, they often have the same real knowledge as a twelve- to fourteen-year-old. Whatever additional knowledge they will have acquired likely is from the mass media, documentary and lifestyle television shows, and the cinema. This information often presents a distorted history of the asset. This, of course, raises the ethical question of whether and how to present assets to tourists and further drives home the need to control the experience and the actions of the tourist.

Managers of heritage attractions must accept that the level of knowledge of most people visiting the asset will be limited. They are often likely to hold stereotypical images of the destination and seek experiences that confirm their stereotypes. For many, no real learning will accrue from their visits to these assets, apart from the type of indirect learning that comes from being in a different environment. Managers of cultural heritage attractions must accept that many of their visitors are fundamentally ignorant of their attractions and should adjust their presentations accordingly.

CULTURAL TOURISM

Not All Cultural Tourists Are Alike

The World Tourism Organization (WTO) estimates that 37 percent of international tourists are cultural tourists (Richards 1996a; Gratton and Richards 1996). This figure is derived from applying an operational definition of cultural tourists as those who visit a cultural or heritage attraction, a museum, or attend a performance *sometime* during their trip. As Hughes (1996) illustrates, confusion over the use of terminology and the indiscriminant application of the label serves only to confuse the understanding of cultural tourism.

But, as we discuss elsewhere, there are many kinds of cultural tourist. We identify five types in this book. They include (1) the *purposeful* cultural tourist, the person normally associated with cultural tourism who travels for cultural tourism motives and seeks a deep cultural tourism experience; (2) the *sightseeing* cultural tourist, who travels for cultural tourism motives but who seeks a shallow experience; (3) the *serendipitous* cultural tourist, for whom cultural tourism is not a stated reason for visiting a destination but who ends up getting a deep cultural tourism experience; (4) the *casual* cultural tourist, who identifies cultural tourism as a weak motive for visiting a destination and seeks a shallow experience; and (5) the *incidental* cultural tourist, for whom cultural tourism is not a stated motive for visiting a destination but who does visit cultural heritage attractions.

Cultural Tourism Products May Be Challenging and Confronting but Not Intimidating or Accusatory

Remember, most tourists are on vacation and are looking for a break from their normal stressful, hectic lives. Most do not want to be challenged while on vacation and, if confronted, most are not receptive to accept such a message. Cultural heritage products can be presented in an emotionally demanding manner but not in an intimidating or accusatory manner. Even here, the degree of challenge will depend on the type of tourist being attracted with mass, leisure tourists less willing to be challenged than those people specifically traveling for a more meaningful experience.

This is not to say that cultural heritage products cannot and should not be challenging. Indeed, this can be a useful strategy to differentiate one's product from the array of other cultural tourism products available in the marketplace. It may also be regarded as necessary if the asset is a heritage place that is associated with a particularly gruesome or reprehensible experience in the past. But the assets cannot be presented in an intimidating or accusatory manner that blames the visitor as being the cause of the problem. Remember that most tourists are pleasure travelers who are traveling for fun and escape. They are seeking experiences that may leave an impression on them but ultimately will contribute to an overall enjoyable vacation.

Many tourists visiting heritage attractions seem to be seeking affirmation of how modern they are and how much modern society has evolved from the past. As Craik (1997: 115) states so eloquently, "Tourism is a process of seeing and experiencing the other, but it is not about otherness, except as a means of coming to terms with one's own culture." Cultural tourism product designers think that tourists do not want to be reminded that many social ills (oppression, racism, etc.) outlined in site interpretation remain unresolved today. It is for this reason that many attractions present the past as being a vestige of a bygone era. For instance, Australian Aboriginal or Native American asset managers tend to present historical attempts at cultural or actual genocide in the past tense, but rarely show a direct link from past atrocities imposed on people to the current economic and social difficulties affecting indigenous communities.

Tourists Want "Authenticity" but Not Necessarily Reality

Building from the previous point, many tourists want "authenticity" but not necessarily reality. Authenticity is a social construct that is determined in part by the individual's own knowledge and frame of reference. Many tourists are interested in cultural heritage but most have minimal knowledge about the past. As such, they may be traveling to have their stereotypical or romantic images of a destination reinforced or possibly challenged, depending on their political leaning.

People going to cultural heritage attractions, be they historic parks, forts, prisons, or purpose-built historic theme parks, are seeking a stereotypical image of the past (Sizer 1999). It has been observed that travel is about reaffirmation, not change, and the resources that make up tourism are transformed into elements of a symbolic system (Craik 1999). The past is seen as very distant, and, as such, many historic assets are presented in an idyllic manner, with pristine gardens, clean streets, paved roads, and neat buildings (Lowenthal 1985). The reality of pollution, oppression, poor sewerage, and indifferent maintenance of some landscapes (particularly penal, industrial, and urban) is not an experience tourists can easily put in context. Without extensive historical and archaeological knowledge of the asset's era, much of this would be considered "overkill" by tourists. Many tourists wish, therefore, to experience what they are happy to believe to be authenticity at an attraction but not necessarily reality (see Photo 3.4). Reconstruc-

PHOTO 3.4. Sovereign Hill, Ballarat, Australia

Tourists want authenticity but not necessarily reality. Authenticity lies in the eyes of the consumer. This is one of the reasons why heritage theme parks, such as Sovereign Hill in Australia, are so popular. Visitors can get an authentic experience, in the sense that they can experience a number of distinct gold mining eras, while knowing fully that they are not visiting a real gold mining settlement. They often satisfy a nostalgic need for the past but are not necessarily true to it.

Heritage theme parks also offer an opportunity for greater customer entertainment as this does not have to be balanced against conservation of fabric. Another advantage of theme parks is that they can be built in high-traffic areas, enhancing their chances of commercial success. Further, as purpose-built entertainment and education centers, management can take greater liberties in providing themed experiences, including costumed actors and purpose-built, idealized artificial landscapes. In doing so, a desired type and quality of visitor experience can be assured.

tions such as the fortified town of Louisburg, Nova Scotia, in Canada or purpose-built heritage theme parks such as Sovereign Hill in Australia satisfy this need for an authentic experience for most visitors.

CONCLUSION

Successful tourism development does not occur by happenstance. Many people suffer from the misconception that if they post a sign claiming "tourists welcome" or "George Washington slept here," hordes of tourists will flood to their attraction. The reality is quite different. Developing successful tourism attractions involves first and foremost understanding what tourism is and how it works. The preceding discussion identified what we believe are fifteen key principles of tourism; others no doubt exist. These principles explain the rationale behind entering this sector, what attracts people to destinations, the factors that encourage or inhibit visitation, and why tourists behave the way they do. The next four chapters explore these issues in greater detail.

Chapter 4

Cultural Heritage Management

INTRODUCTION

Cultural heritage management (CHM) is the systematic care taken to maintain the cultural values of cultural heritage assets for the enjoyment of present and future generations. Cultural heritage management is now a global phenomenon. A series of internationally recognized codes and charters, such as the Venice Charter (ICOMOS 1994) and the UNESCO World Heritage Convention, dictate its core principles. These principles are embodied in most countries in formal heritage protection legislation or accepted heritage management policies. Since cultural tourism is reliant on the use of a destination's cultural or heritage assets, no discussion of this topic is complete without developing at least a basic understanding of cultural heritage management.

Finding ways to manage assets in a truly sustainable manner is clearly in the best interests of the asset, those who manage it, and the community. Tourism is increasingly being recognized as one of the potential uses for heritage, placing greater pressure on tourism and CHM stakeholders to collaborate for their mutual benefit (TCA 1998; Hall 1999; JOST 1999; Australian Heritage Commission and the Tourism Council of Australia 1999; UNESCO World Heritage Centre 2000; World Bank 2000; World Monuments Fund 2000; du Cros 2000). Ultimately, the better understanding each has of the other's philosophical framework and requirements, the better the partnership will be.

The following three chapters introduce the reader to some of the core concepts and applications of cultural heritage management. This chapter presents an overview of cultural heritage management by discussing a number of principles, grouped into four broad themes: core concepts, sustainability, stakeholders, and tourism; these are presented in Table 4.1. Chapters 5 and 6 look, respectively, at issues related to the management and presentation of tangible and intangible cultural heritage.

CORE CONCEPTS

In all jurisdictions, cultural heritage management is the more widely recognized term, except in the United States, where cultural resource management is in common usage (Pearson and Sullivan 1995; Macintosh 1999). The substitution of the word *heritage* for *resources* was made out of deference to the different connotations of each word. *Resources* implies that the asset being considered has an economic value and can be exploited. *Heritage,* on the other hand, recognizes the noneconomic values of the asset and further acknowledges its legacy, which implies certain obligations and responsibilities. Regardless, most cultural heritage managers still perceive that *cultural resources* as a term is neither readily understood nor current among the public to whom they are ultimately responsible (Pearson and Sullivan 1995).

Conservation of a Representative Sample of Cultural Heritage

The main goal of cultural heritage management is to conserve a representative sample of our tangible and intangible heritage for future generations. Recognition exists that the speed with which the world is changing is so fast that much of our heritage is at risk of being lost either through physical destruction or loss of knowledge. Cultural heritage management seeks to establish a formal system of identifying a sample of that heritage and conserving it for the future. As such, clearly it cannot include everything; only the best or most representative samples of things are preserved.

People have always produced and will continue to produce different kinds of physical remains and traditions, each of which is unique and nonrenewable. There will never be another genuine wreck of the *Titanic,* Egyptian pyramid, Angkor Watt, or peat bog Iron Age burial. These artifacts and remains were created under a special set of social, cultural, and economic circumstances, which are impossible to recre-

Table 4.1. Cultural Heritage Management Principles

Cultural Heritage Management	Sustainability	Stakeholders	Tourism
CHM aims to preserve and care for a representative sample of humanity's cultural heritage for future generations.	The identification, documentation, and conservation of heritage assets are essential parts of the development of sustainability.	Most heritage assets have multiple stakeholders.	Tourism needs are not the only ones considered in cultural heritage management.
Conservation of intrinsic values is important.	Each cultural heritage asset will have its own meaning and assessable cultural significance or values.	Consultation with stakeholders is important for defining their needs in the conservation process.	Tourism may be seen as an important use of a heritage asset, but not the only use.
Caring for both intangible and tangible heritage is becoming increasingly important.	Some cultures differ in their view about how much intervention or change can occur before an asset ceases to be authentic.	A stakeholder other than the cultural asset manager may have greater control over the asset.	Tourism can cause adverse impacts.
The scale among heritage assets conserved varies greatly, and the management process needed for each type also varies accordingly.	Cultural heritage assets should be used only in culturally appropriate and sustainable ways.		Tourism requirements may sometimes clash with those regarding conservation of an asset.
Cultural heritage management has an evolving framework.	Some heritage assets are too fragile or sacred to be fully accessible to the public, including tourists.		Tapping into the revenue generated by tourism for reinvestment in the conservation of heritage assets is an important goal for most cultural heritage managers.
CHM and conservation are ongoing activities that aim to provide some structure to the conservation of heritage.	Consultation of stakeholders is an important part of developing an asset sustainably.		
Conservation of heritage assets is rarely carried out without some requirement for their presention and interpretation to the public.			

ate truly. When a cultural heritage asset's significance is recognized, preserving it for future generations to observe and understand is imperative. Although we may not run out of heritage, we may lose certain types altogether or be overwhelmed by others in a way that gives a lopsided view of a culture or historical period.

The range of assets includes more than just icon attractions or highly visited places. It may also include more mundane examples that represent normal, everyday life, values, or traditions. Likewise, age is less important than the value of the asset being conserved. Contemporary assets that are evocative of late twentieth century or early twenty-first century life also need to be conserved, for they will become tomorrow's heritage (for instance, Berlin Wall fragments and the first Macintosh computers).

Conservation of Intrinsic Values

An underlying tenet of CHM is that there is "social good" to be derived from the conservation of heritage. The message that CHM needs to convey to the public is about the value of heritage to society. One of the hard things to appreciate for those in the tourism industry and elsewhere who tend to look at assets only from the perspective of their commercial value, is that they are identified for their intrinsic values rather than for their use values. The value of an asset comes from its meaning to a community or its existence value, not from its revenue-generating potential (see Photo 4.1). It is for this reason that relatively few cultural heritage assets have significant tourism appeal.

Most Assets Are to Be Presented and Interpreted to the Public

If the main goal of cultural heritage management is to conserve a representative sample of assets for future generations, it is also important that aspects of those heritage assets be made accessible to present generations. Good presentation of tangible assets requires that the cultural values of those assets are fully interpreted in a way that visitors of all kinds can understand. Information on intangible heritage can also be presented as part of the interpretation of tangible assets, particularly when a close association still exists between them (NTHP 1999).

PHOTO 4.1. The Presidio, San Francisco, California

Cultural heritage management values assets because of social good derived from conserving heritage rather than for their use value. Thus, assets on which it is hard to place an economic value, such as archaeological remains associated with Civil War–era houses at the Presidio in San Francisco, have value in their own right. Such remains are particularly important to research pertaining to the Civil War period and to complement what is known from historical records, diaries, gravestones, and other sources of information. Eventually data from the excavation will be interpreted and integrated with such information to expand on the Civil War–period visitor interpretation available at the Presidio. However, this is not its sole purpose, as it will also add to studies on the Civil War being carried out elsewhere.

Cultural heritage managers increasingly are being urged to plan for presentation to visitors of a heritage asset as an important part of its ongoing conservation and management (Pearson and Sullivan 1995; Shackley 1998; ICOMOS 1999). A balance between education and entertainment must be achieved when presenting assets. The main objective is, usually, general educational or awareness building. Museums, for example, whether associated with sites, objects, or cultural practices, are predicated on mainly educational objectives (Ghose 1992; Ambrose and Paine 1993; Lord and Lord 1999). However, entertainment-oriented presentation may serve to broaden the market base for an asset, presenting an opportunity for heritage managers to transmit the message about the value of heritage to more people, thus enlisting greater support for it (see Photo 4.2).

Tangible and Intangible Heritage Are Important

When most nonheritage management specialists think of conserving heritage, they tend to think of heritage places, routes, and objects such as old buildings, historic sites, archaeological sites, and other physical remains. However, cultural heritage management involves more than just the conservation of tangible assets. It also recognizes that intangible heritage, cultural landscapes, and traditions embodied in such things as folklore, storytelling, customs associated with worship, festivals, and other expressions of cultural traditions must also be protected. Both tangible and intangible heritage assets form the base for many cultural tourism products.

Concern is growing from international conservation organizations about how to integrate the management of both kinds of heritage management more closely (ICOMOS 1999; UNESCO 2000). Cultural heritage managers in places with strong indigenous cultural traditions have been doing this for awhile. Australia, New Zealand, and parts of North America are aware that it is important to allow the principles already held within some traditions to guide how tangible heritage assets are managed. For example, understanding the relationship between folklore and sacred heritage places is important for designing appropriate conservation measures.

Assets Differ in Scale, Complexity, and Management Challenges

Cultural and heritage assets can vary in scale and complexity from tangible remains as large as historic towns to assets as small as a snuff box collection. Likewise, intangible assets can be as complex as the folklore of twenty ethnic groups in a region or as simple as a favorite story told by a market storyteller. These different scales present different management challenges and opportunities, meaning that each asset must be treated as unique and must have its own unique management plan or policy.

PHOTO 4.2. Fort Chambly, Quebec, Canada

Interpreting and presenting material aids in creating interest in the past, educating the public, and generating support for further conservation activities. Information can be presented in an entertaining manner, such as this display of a "chest of archaeological drawers" that presents artifacts from different historical periods at Fort Chambly in Quebec, Canada. Archaeological concepts such as "super-imposition" are not always easy to explain to nonarchaeologists. Taking an imaginative approach such as this to show how different periods can be excavated in layers can make some esoteric issues of archaeological practice clearer to visitors. It also has a "dig-like" quality to it in the arrangement of the artifacts, which are usually more conventionally shown to visitors in display cases. Sometimes one of the curators acts as a museum guide and completes the picture by putting on gloves and waving a trowel around as part of the performance of interpreting the drawer's message to visitors.

It is important to remember that conferring a heritage designation status on an asset is a form of contemporary recognition of the intrinsic value of a tangible or intangible cultural feature that evolved for different reasons. In other words, the assets are not purpose built and as such often have qualities such as differences in scale, complexity, periodicity, and use, which inevitably complicate and shape the way that they are managed. The Silk Road through Asia, now an emerging important "heritage tourism route," is recognized because of its historic role as a travel-and-trade route. How transnational heritage assets are managed may depend on each country's heritage protection legislation, the understanding of the asset's cultural significance, political goodwill, and the way in which human resources can be organized to oversee the implementation of any conservation policy. Alternatively, small location-specific assets, such as a pottery scatter in Arizona, will have different legislation, fewer stakeholders, and possibly less cultural value outside that held for it locally. Its conservation policy will differ accordingly.

A similar situation applies with intangible heritage assets, although the study of the requirements for the conservation of intangible heritage is still in its infancy. It is likely that in most places, those associated with maintaining such practices do not work closely with government cultural heritage managers of tangible heritage. Historically, however, tradition bearers associated with intangible assets were more likely to collaborate with archivists, academics, or musicologists when requiring assistance in contextualizing cultural objects in their care or in documenting the "living" heritage of which such tradition bearers are the main custodians. As custodians, tradition bearers also seek to establish control of the management of particular cultural heritage places and objects, which are closely associated with their intangible heritage by establishing their own site registers, museums, and keeping places. Again, scale can play a role as resources often do not allow tradition bearers to manage such cultural heritage assets nor political or financial goodwill to allow management of these assets.

Cultural Heritage Management Has an Evolving Framework

Cultural heritage management is still a relatively new paradigm; as with any new model, it is still evolving. It is interesting to note, however, that regardless of the jurisdiction, it appears to evolve through a five-stage life cycle as the value of culture is first recognized, political interest grows, and the level of professionalism increases. No doubt more phases will be identified in the future as development continues. These five current phases include (1) the initial and continuing inventory phase, (2) the initial enacting of protective legislation, (3) the increase in professionalism phase, (4) the stakeholder consultation and participation phase, and (5) the review of the professional and state responsibility phase. The key features undertaken in each phase are identified in Table 4.2.

TABLE 4.2. Cultural Heritage Management's Evolving Framework

Phase	Key Features
Inventory	• Growing community interest • Documentation • Evolution from amateurs to professionals conducting work
Initial legislation	• First-generation legislation to guide identification and protection of heritage assets • Focus on tangible not intangible heritage • Creation of government heritage agencies • Little integration with other government agencies or laws
Increased professionalism	• Formation of heritage international governmental organizations (IGOs) and NGOs • Formalize codes of ethics, conservation principles in charters, etc. • Development of related heritage professions (public and private)
Stakeholder consultation	• Wide array of stakeholders emerge • Areas of conflict identified • More attention paid to community interests
Review	• New understanding of responsibilities • New or revised legislation • More integrated planning and practice • Greater awareness of intangible heritage • Recognition of other users • New paradigm in place • Maturity

The five-stage process begins with an initial recognition by academics, community leaders, and politicians of the value of heritage and the need to conserve it. The first stage, therefore, usually involves nascent attempts to document assets and is often driven by keen amateurs or a small group of heritage professionals. Once the scope of a jurisdiction's assets is recognized, the second stage involves invoking some form of legislation to recognize and conserve these assets. It may also involve systematically cataloguing the work of enthusiasts and engaging them further. The creation of formal heritage departments or the establishment of heritage units in other government departments often coincides with this action. Although this is important step, these actions often mean that the long-term conservation of the heritage is not addressed. Problems can occur when planning for or anticipating use conflicts is not done clearly. CHM must become a process that is both professional and systematic.

Hence, the third phase reflects increased professionalism in the sector and by its political overlords. Formal codes of practice and conservation charters are adopted, with countries typically becoming signatories to international charters. Formalizing the management process, rather than only enacting legislation to protect tangible assets, leads to greater professionalism in how assets are identified, their values assessed, and how they are managed in the long term. It is at this stage that a wide array of public- and private-sector heritage professionals, ranging from architects to consulting archaeologists, enter the sector. Similarly, it is often at this point that universities begin to offer specialist heritage-oriented degree programs. Much of the expertise in these areas currently exists in developed Western countries (Byrne 1991).

The fourth and fifth stages reflect even greater sophistication in cultural heritage management. Acknowledging the roles of stakeholders not only as interested parties but also as legitimate managers and comanagers of assets begins to occur. In doing so, more attention is paid to community concerns with the goal of achieving a consensus approach to management. This sophistication usually means that existing legislation must be modified and a more integrative approach to management must be adopted.

The evolutionary process starts with the initial recognition that conservation of cultural values will serve a broader societal good. It then progresses through initial and tentative steps toward conservation with growing professionalism and sophistication. The need to adopt an integrated, consensual management approach is recognized only in the latest stages of the process. The evolution of specific cultural heritage management actions, therefore, coincides with the more general societal and political evolution of the value of culture and ways to manage it. As a result, it is almost impossible to impose the final two evolutionary stages successfully in jurisdictions that have just begun to appreciate the need to conserve their heritage and in which CHM has few links with other stakeholders.

Museums—Special Cases

The International Council of Museums (ICOM) definition of a museum is "a non-profit making, permanent institution, in the service of society and its development, and open to the public, which acquires, conserves, researches, communicates and exhibits, for the purposes of study, education and enjoyment, material evidence of man and his environment" (Ambrose and Paine 1993: 296). There is a whole body of literature available in museum studies relating to professionalism, repatriation to indigenous groups, community involvement, and education. Such writing indicates that many museums and galleries are following a similar progression to that of heritage place management identified in this chapter (Leon and Rosenzweig 1989; Boylan 1992; Kavanagh 1994; Kaplan 1994; Arduin and Arinze 1995). Cataloguing and processing objects, and later updating these records by computerization, were important duties for museums initially; this process is still ongoing in many countries. In the past decade, many museums have also had their professionalism, community involvement, and curatorial responsibilities challenged by outside parties.

But museums also face special challenges not faced by other sectors of the cultural heritage management community. Most museum managers must deal with collections that often have a dubious or colorful history as well as deciding how much interest they should take in purchasing objects that were originally purchased by private collections. Accordingly, issues about claims of ownership in the dispute over cultural properties have been classified by heritage ethicist Karen Warren as "the 3Rs":

1. Claims concerning restitution of cultural properties to their country of origin (e.g., Greek government claims to the Elgin Marbles housed for many years in the British Museum)
2. The restriction on imports and exports of cultural properties as a debate over ownership of the past (e.g., between the private and public sector or local and international collectors)
3. The rights (of ownership, access, and/or inheritance) retained by relevant parties (e.g., claims by Native American and Australia Aboriginal groups to human remains and cultural material in museums) (Warren 1989)

However, these items are part of a nonrenewable resource that many heritage and museum managers believe should be enjoyed by the community at large, unlike certain private collectors (who indiscriminately purchase the resources and therefore create a demand). An increasing number of managers support the position of indigenous groups in this issue and provide assistance in establishing museums to be run by indigenous groups. Warren (1989) notes that any real discussion of the 3Rs and associated arguments needs to follow a step-by-step process which is nonhierarchical and nonadversarial for each proposed case.

Conservation and Cultural Heritage Management Are Ongoing Structured Activities

Cultural heritage management and conservation are structured activities that are part of a process that requires ongoing input about the condition of heritage assets and their use. The reason such a process has been developed lies in the way the international codes and conventions have developed that underlie much of its philosophy. Now many developing countries rely on such codes as a basis for conducting CHM and enacting or amending protective legislation.

The use of or adherence to international standards and principles is increasing. Such charters and associated documents emphasize the importance of making sure that conservation of heritage assets is an ongoing process, as is the pursuit of sustainability. One example of such a set of standards is the Venice Charter. The International Council on Monuments and Sites (ICOMOS), an NGO established in 1965 to act in an advisory role to UNESCO on issues concerning cultural heritage conservation, uses the Venice Charter (ICOMOS 1994) as a set of guiding principles for the conservation of tangible heritage assets with a strong emphasis on built heritage. It was adopted in 1964; by 1994, it had been translated into forty-two languages as a basis for developing guidelines for heritage conservation planning (ICOMOS 1994).

The scope of work allowed to conserve heritage assets has been extended over the years, but the Venice Charter still has a very strict view about how modification or damage to an asset should be handled (ICOMOS 1994). The key features of the Venice Charter are the five main principles or definitions of terms provided for

- historic buildings (extended now to groups of buildings),
- conservation (restrictions on modification),
- restoration with authenticity in mind (no reconstruction),
- archaeological investigation to be professionalized, and
- documentation (any action should be documented systematically and a public record kept).

A number of other international bodies have also developed charters or programs to recognize and manage heritage assets. These include the following:

- UNESCO—United Nations Educational, Scientific, and Cultural Organization (began the international focus on heritage with the Convention on the Protection of Cultural Property in the Event of Armed Conflict, 1954)
- IUCN—International Union for the Conservation of Nature (also known as the World Conservation Union)
- IATF—UN-based Inter-Agency Task Force (for improving risk-preparedness for world heritage places—a more recent development)
- ICCROM—International Centre for the Study of the Preservation and Restoration of Cultural Property (established in Italy by UNESCO in the early 1960s)
- ICOM—International Council of Museums (also an NGO that advises UNESCO)

Of these, UNESCO's World Heritage Sites and properties listed under the Convention Concerning the Protection of the World Cultural and Natural Heritage, 1972 (UNESCO and Nordic World Heritage Office 1999) is probably the best known. The objectives of UNESCO for the protection of world cultural and natural heritage are embodied in the convention. It seeks to encourage the identification, protection, and preservation of cultural and natural heritage around the world that is considered to be of outstanding value to humanity (UNESCO 1996). It is hailed by some as being one of UNESCO's success stories in terms of widespread influence with over 150 countries as signatories and over 690 sites placed on the World Heritage List, representing 122 countries as of August 2001 (Stovel 1998; Leask and Fyall 2000; UNESCO World Heritage Centre, 2001).

Certain site types, such as cultural landscapes, test the efficacy of current cultural heritage management processes. Cultural landscapes are environmental settings with cultural as well as natural values. They present unique management challenges because of their intangible nature and, more significant, because they often overlap state and national boundaries. Even so, some proposals have been debated for managing them. One strategy concerns the consistent implementation of international charters and conventions by using such instruments as the Endangered World Heritage List to ensure they receive adequate attention (Rössler 1994; UNESCO World Heritage Centre, 2000). Another strategy calls on governments to assist in the building of partnerships between countries and organizations to further their management and conservation (Dienne 1994). However, the efficacy of such proposals has been questioned as international agencies have little real influence when dealing with domestic political issues.

Sustainability

When cultural heritage managers are talking about long-term preservation or conservation planning, they are concerned about maintaining the resource at a sustainable level. The items listed under the sustainability section of Table 4.1 relate to the identification and value assessment of assets and how they should be used. These issues are discussed in more detail in the next two chapters with special reference to tangible and intangible heritage.

It must be recognized, however, that each cultural heritage asset will have its own meaning, cultural significance, and will also be placed in different social or cultural contexts. These conditions mean that each asset must be considered individually in relation to its physical and cultural robusticity. For example, some cultures differ in their views about how much intervention or change can occur before an asset ceases to be authentic. In some instances, the asset can be almost totally reconstructed and still maintain its values, as in the case of many historical forts or Japanese shrines. In other instances, any change might be deemed by the custodians to be inappropriate, especially in relation to sites of spiritual or religious significance.

Sustainability considerations also relate to the amount and type of use that is permitted before the intrinsic values being conserved are threatened (Marquis-Kyle and Walker 1992; Pearson and Sullivan 1995; ICOMOS 1994; Silva 1994; Cantacuzine 1995). Such considerations apply to both tangible and intangible assets. As discussed in Chapter 12, fragile sites regardless of their tourism appeal must be managed carefully. In some cases, prohibiting visitation or placing strict limits on the number of visitors will be an essential management activity to conserve the asset. Likewise, only culturally appropriate uses must be permitted. The challenge for asset managers to insure that such actions occur is discussed in Chapter 11.

Stakeholders

Stakeholder issues are a common theme that runs through this book. As such, they will not be discussed in great detail in this section other than to identify some issues that must be considered. Cultural heritage managers recognize that key stakeholders include host communities or cultural groups that live near a heritage asset or are attached to it culturally, schools and universities that use it as a resource, government heritage authorities that may be responsible for managing it, and commercial users, such as the tourism industry.

Most Heritage Assets Have Multiple Stakeholders

One of the great challenges in managing any cultural or natural asset is the need to mollify many stakeholders. On the surface, stakeholder consultation seems like a rather straightforward process. There is often an assumption that the number of stakeholders is limited to traditional owners and user groups on the one hand and the tourism industry on the other. In reality, most assets have multiple stakeholders with differing degrees of connectivity to the asset, differing levels of legitimacy in being considered as a stakeholder, and, also, widely differing viewpoints about how assets should be managed. In addition, there is often a history between stakeholders with formal or informal alliances being formed that may mitigate against easy resolution of issues.

Consultation with Stakeholders Helps Define Their Needs

Stakeholder consultation often plays a defining role in the successful development of management strategies. It is for this reason that consultation—true consultation, is now recognized as an integral part of the management planning that permeates the entire process from initial discussions to ongoing management of assets.

An External Stakeholder May Have Greater Control Over the Asset

A further stakeholder issue that is especially relevant to tourism is that an external stakeholder may, in fact, have more power over how the asset is managed and presented to the public than the owners of the asset. As discussed in Chapter 11, whoever controls the message disseminated about the asset sets the tourists' expectations and ultimately exerts a tremendous influence on how the asset is used. Numerous examples can be seen around the world where asset managers seem unable to stem the tide of inappropriate tourism uses, even though they ostensibly control the asset.

CULTURAL HERITAGE MANAGEMENT AND TOURISM

Cultural tourism has a major influence on how the presentation of cultural heritage is planned. In the developed world, its influence is most evident as cultural heritage management becomes more mature and aware of uses and users other than those traditionally covered in conservation planning. This awareness, however, may not always lead to an easy relationship, as tensions can emerge resulting from the different needs of tourism and conservation. The situation is especially critical in developing countries, where mass tourism occurs before suitable cultural heritage management legislation is enacted. Unless tourism is controlled, significant damage can occur from overuse, misappropriation of cultural property, souveniring, and the illegal trade of artifacts.

The cultural heritage management sector's traditional lack of power often makes it vulnerable to tourism, especially when governments regard these assets as potential revenue generating resources. Heritage rarely receives much of the revenue generated by tourism, even though these assets may act as primary attractions. It is important, therefore, that a balance is kept between tourism use and CHM conservation objectives. Decision makers need to have reasonable expectations of the amount of tourism potential an asset has and how to achieve that potential in a socially and culturally responsible manner.

Tourism Needs Are Not the Only Consideration in CHM

Tourists are just one of many possible user groups, and the needs of tourists, therefore, are just one of the many considerations that must be made when determining how to manage and present cultural heritage assets. In some instances, such as with museums and art galleries, the needs of the tourist will be similar to those of other user groups, apart from the possibility of translation. In many other instances, however, the needs of the tourist will be substantially different than those of other user groups. Different levels of knowledge about the asset, different interests in the asset, different cultural backgrounds, and different expectations may mean that that presentation of an asset for local users may be inappropriate for tourists and vice versa. The pursuit of tourism, therefore, requires a conscious management decision and the need either to shape the presentation differently or to target only tourists whose needs are compatible with local users.

Tourism Is an Important, but Not the Only, Use of a Heritage Asset

Likewise, while tourism may be recognized as important use of the asset, it is rare that tourism will be the only use consideration. Again, decisions about the compatibility of tourism and other uses, coupled with decisions about the most effective way to present the asset for different user groups, must be made.

NEGATIVE AND POSITIVE IMPACTS OF TOURISM

That tourism can have far-reaching impacts for the conservation and long-term management of cultural and heritage assets is axiomatic for most people from the developed world (Mercer 1996; Pearce 1995; Pearce 1996; Hollingshead 1996, 1999). Virtually every introductory tourism text contains at least one chapter discussing the social, cultural, and environmental impacts of tourism. This topic has also been the subject of extensive investigation in the academic literature. However, in regions that are undergoing rapid development and where an ethos of conservation has not been established, often surprising ignorance of the negative consequences of tourism exists. The attitude seems to be that the benefits of economic development outweigh any adverse costs such development may have. Such an attitude was common in the developed world forty or more years ago, when it too was undergoing the type of massive expansion seen elsewhere today. However, in hindsight, such an attitude is now seen as being shortsighted. As a result, a more balanced approach to tourism is advocated, acknowledging both its beneficial and detrimental effects on host communities and their cultures.

Clear-sighted long-term planning and management anticipates adverse impacts and develops programs to minimize or mitigate them. Following are just some of the impacts that tourism can have on tangible and intangible heritage assets. These lists were developed based on our observations of the nascent development of cultural tourism in many parts of Asia.

Negative Impacts

1. *Overuse by tourists:* This displaces local residents; causes overcrowding; creates parking, litter, and noise problems; and generally overburdens shared resources, such as water and fuel.
2. *Tourism dependency:* Large sections of the community become dependent on tourism at the expense of other industries, leading to loss of self-reliance and traditional-style activities.

3. *Tourist behavior:* Tourists can have an impact if they are not aware of, or chose to ignore, visitor etiquette at an attraction; lack of courtesy or sensitivity to local customs (e.g., insensitive dress or grooming); defiling sacred areas (wearing shoes in particular types of temples); drinking in public; taking drugs, etc.
4. *Unplanned tourism infrastructure development:* This involves altering the amenity of places for the community; altering the visual appeal and visitor experience for tourists.
5. *Limited beneficiaries:* Income flows to limited sectors of the community; high leakages; creation of divisiveness and discontent within the community.
6. *Loss of control over cultural property:* Communities and tradition bearers can lose control of cultural property (e.g., motifs used in their crafts and arts or even music) if it is not under copyright or special protective legislation.
7. *Physical deterioration of assets:* This occurs where there is

   - no commodification (e.g., site hardening) or resources to deal with it;
   - no way of monitoring such impacts to see if assets are at risk of permanent damage or loss (e.g., local events and festivals changed for tourists and at risk of losing their meaning and importance for locals);
   - no way of preventing the acceleration of natural processes of destruction such as soil erosion around an asset;
   - no control placed on tourism infrastructure development; and
   - no way of counteracting the influence of Western consumer culture (not just from tourism, because general modernization and globalization can be responsible, e.g., satellite television and computer and video games) on the behavior of locals, particularly young people, as they abandon traditional customs in favor of this culture.

Positive Impacts

1. The appropriate presentation of assets can assist the tourists' understanding of the need for the conservation and retention of important cultural heritage assets in general.

2. Opportunities can arise to develop local economies to be more entrepreneurial and self-reliant.
3. Revenue from tourism can be directed to local infrastructure improvement.
4. Reinvigoration of traditional culture can occur.
5. Cultural exchange with tourists can lead to greater tolerance of cultural differences in multicultural societies.
6. Revenue from tourism can be reinvested in documentation, planning, and management of heritage assets. This is important for the sustainability of assets that attract heavy visitation.

Tourism and Conservation Requirements May Sometimes Clash

Tourism requirements may clash with conservation needs. In the past, a conscious trade-off has occurred whereby conservation values were compromised for tourism or tourism values compromised for conservation. The inherent weakness of such a strategy has now been recognized. Rather than trading off values, the management task now is to seek a balance between tourism and conservation. Having stated this point, and given the seriousness of some of the negative impacts of tourism, it is the author's belief that conservation values should drive the process.

Tourism Revenue Reinvestment Is an Important Goal for Most Cultural Heritage Managers

One of the challenges facing conservation managers is that many of their assets are not viable commercial entities. What revenue is generated may cover operating costs or may simply reduce the need of the subsidy required to keep the asset operational. Creativity is required to search for revenue streams above and beyond standard entry fees and sales of souvenirs. In some jurisdictions, a fee is levied against the accommodation sector, with revenues going toward conservation. In addition, visitors themselves may be willing to contribute directly to conservation in ways other than through gate entry fees. Research by Duan and Duan (2000) suggests that most visitors are agreeable to some form of direct contribution.

CONCLUSION

The principles of cultural heritage management can be used as a guide to the underlying workings of this sector. They also provide a useful counterpoint to discussion of how tourism works, which was presented in Chapter 3. The challenge for cultural tourism is how to integrate the commercial need of tourism with the substantially different social objectives of cultural heritage management.

Chapter 5

Tangible Heritage

INTRODUCTION

Tangible heritage includes all assets that have some physical embodiment of cultural values such as historic towns, buildings, archaeological sites, cultural landscapes and cultural objects, or items of movable cultural property (UNESCO 2000a). From a management perspective, such assets are thought of as having an advantage over much that is intangible—their condition and integrity are easier to assess, and scale can be more accurately measured. Even so, tangible heritage is vulnerable to a wide range of processes that can damage or destroy the asset and its cultural values. Tourism is one of many stressor agents that can either accelerate destructive natural processes or encourage development and modifications that damage sites or compromise authenticity (Bowes 1994; Rosenbaum 1995; Wager 1995a; Wang 1999; UNESCO and Nordic World Heritage Office 1999; World Monuments Watch 2000).

This chapter introduces a number of issues relating to the management of tangible heritage. The fundamental stages in the conservation planning process for tangible heritage assets are outlined, followed by a discussion of how conservation priorities are set for different types of asset. The importance of evaluating cultural significance and its meaning for setting conservation and commodification goals is also dealt with and this leads into a discussion of authenticity and use. Finally, the issues of access to fragile assets and the role of stakeholders in the conservation process are investigated.

PROCESS-DRIVEN CONSERVATION OF TANGIBLE CULTURAL HERITAGE

The tangible heritage evaluation and conservation process is driven by a series of international protocols housed in codes, charters, or guidelines, which are endorsed by all members of the heritage community. Most often, they are based on the ICOMOS Venice Charter (1964) or its regional variations (ICOMOS 1994; Australia ICOMOS 2000). The Brussels Charter on Cultural Tourism (1976), which was recently updated, is another charter that is likely to be adopted widely (Sugaya 1999; Brooks 2000).

The scope of heritage planning and the management of heritage places and their accompanying cultural property is complicated by the differing scales that must be considered. Planning measures can focus on anything from a single building to an entire historic town and its surrounds. Heritage planning tends to follow a four-step process that leads to the development of a site management or conservation plan and possibly a risk-preparedness strategy in case of fire, war, and disaster (ICOMOS 1993; Shackley 1998b; Stovel 1998). The following four stages are often broken down into intermediate steps for large-scale projects.

1. The identification, classification, and documentation of the heritage asset and its components within a defined area.
2. The assessment of the cultural values evoked by the physical fabric of the asset.
3. An analysis of the opportunities and constraints which will have a bearing on the production of a management policy that will in turn direct the conservation of the cultural values of the heritage asset. (This step will also include the production of a set of recommendations or full conservation plan with implementation timetable.)
4. The implementation of decisions and recommendations devised earlier in the process, including that of ongoing monitoring or detailed recording prior to removal of heritage asset. (Pearson and Sullivan 1995)

THE SCOPE OF TANGIBLE HERITAGE ASSETS

Heritage management regimes selected will vary with the nature of the asset. Three different classes of assets are discussed: buildings and archaeological sites; heritage cities, routes, and cultural landscapes; and movable cultural property and museums.

Buildings and Archaeological Sites

Buildings and archaeological sites are the most common types of tangible heritage to be documented. In the earliest stages of CHM, issues tend to revolve around fights to save structures and sites from destruction. In later stages, though, use and reuse issues dominate as heritage professionals devise conservation management priorities with assistance from historians, urban planners, and others. Tourism needs are usually not uppermost in the documentation process unless the site has outstanding values or has come to be a spontaneous tourist attraction in its own right. However, developing appropriate visitors programs for heritage places open to the public should be an integral part of conservation planning (Pearson and Sullivan 1995; Shackley 1998b).

Heritage Cities, Routes, and Cultural Landscapes

Increasingly, it is recognized that cultural heritage management needs to adopt a communitywide or regional perspective, rather than focusing on individual buildings or sites (Rössler 1994; Titchen 1996; Van der Borg and Russo 1998) (see Photos 5.1 and 5.2). This field is still relatively new, however, and planning and management mechanisms for these heritage assets are still being devised. The development of towns and cities is controlled though town planning guidelines, bylaws, zoning structures, and policies that may include special regulations for heritage precincts or conservation areas (AHC 1998; English Heritage Web site 2000). This precinct approach works well providing they are discrete areas with clearly defined boundaries. However, in many cases, a more holistic approach is needed as valuable cultural assets often lie outside specially designated areas. It is for this reason that some cities are being designated as "historic cities" and managed with a more ground-up and sustain-

PHOTO 5.1. Pyramid of the Sun, Teotihuacán, Mexico

The scope of cultural heritage assets can vary from something as small as an arrowhead to assets as large as entire cities. The pyramid of the Sun, Teotihuacán, Mexico, is a massive structure but represents only a small portion of the total archaeological site (as shown in Photo 5.2), which at its height covered twenty-two square kilometers. The Pyramid of the Sun and the Moon, as well as the archaeological zone surrounding them, were inscribed on the World Heritage list in 1987.

able ideal in mind (Van der Borg et al. 1996; Cantacuzino 1995; Van der Borg and Russo 1998).

Traditionally, urban planners have controlled the planning and management process and, therefore, ultimately set priorities for historic precincts. Their decisions have occurred with varying amounts of cooperation from and participation by heritage professionals, individual property owners, and the general public. One of the desires of cultural heritage managers is to become more involved in the actual decision-making process of planning.

Cultural landscapes can also be managed by using a town planning approach. Municipal councils in Southeastern Australia and the United Kingdom, for example, have introduced planning controls to encour-

PHOTO 5.2. Model of the Layout of Teotihuacán, Mexico

An archaeological site museum was established recently in which this extensive model of the layout of Teotihuacán is displayed. Even though Teotihuacán is the most visited archaeological site in Mexico and a national symbol, it still suffers from a number of threats. Hence the World Monuments Fund has listed it on their Endangered Sites 2000 List with many other large-scale heritage places in developing countries. Conservation and visitor management of such places is a huge undertaking which requires funding from systematically collected tourism revenue and/or philanthropy. The World Monuments Fund notes that the physical fabric of the asset is at great risk, as well as the aesthetic integrity—in part from new commercial construction. Providing development buffer zones around such large conservation areas is a problem for historic cities as well. A recent grant may establish a conservation policy and help leverage further government support for managing the site. However, permanent conservation and tourist management programs are still needed (World Monuments Fund 2000).

age the conservation of cultural elements in natural areas (AHC 1998: 79; English Heritage Web site 2000). Cultural landscapes can now also be designated as World Heritage Areas as a result of recent changes in the listing criteria. Linear landscapes and heritage routes are now considered a special type of cultural landscape with their own management needs (Rössler 1994). These routes include cultural, economic, and communication corridors of long-standing use (e.g., the Silk Road, African slave routes, and canals in Canada).

The documentation of cultural landscapes and heritage routes is in its early stages, placing most countries in the first phase of CHM (i.e., inventorying and identifying phase) as far as management priorities are concerned. But the same routes are already being used by the tourism sector, heightening the challenge to manage them carefully and effectively. Heritage routes in particular are potentially a very marketable type of asset given the interest in following in the footsteps of ancient travelers (Rosenbaum 1995a,b). Indeed, they are so popular that tourism marketing organizations and rural communities are working closely to create artificially designed networks between heritage places to encourage tourist use (Kerstetter, Confer, and Bricker 1998; Anonymous 1999a; du Cros 1999).

Movable Cultural Property and Museums

Movable cultural property, which includes any type of portable heritage object or artifact, is an extremely vulnerable type of asset. It can be damaged physically, sold on the black market, or its intangible values and meaning can be destroyed. Sometimes meanings are lost as the original location, social context, and age of the asset are not recorded. Objects without any provenance or context are unlikely to have much meaning unless something permanent marks them as being from a certain context (e.g., a manufacturer's mark or signature). Movable cultural property is also extremely vulnerable to souveniring practices by visitors.

As a result, the management priorities of movable cultural property differ from other heritage assets. Policies for such assets usually require them to be placed in some type of setting such as museums, galleries, and libraries. Sometimes objects may be housed in their original setting, such as agricultural tools in a historic barn or in private and public collections where they have been removed from this setting. To be displayed, many objects go through commodification by being "conserved" (work that is carried out by a materials conservator to improve or stabilize their physical condition), displayed, and interpreted within a building or structure. Accordingly, some objects can easily form part of a tourism product. The design of management priorities for movable cultural property that is still in a historic or archaeological context often involves both museum specialists and site management specialists. Interpretation and overall management may be covered by recommendations in site management plans.

Many museums place a high priority on commodification of their collections to help visitors absorb educational messages about their cultural values (Wallace 1994; Weil 1994). In its raw state, movable cultural property was once considered "history defaced, or some remnants of history that have escaped the shipwreck of time" (Bacon in Cumming, Merriman, and Ross 1996: 9). A more recent attitude is that it is no longer "history defaced but history clarified" as museums emphasize research, interpretation, and communication as important parts of their collection management and exhibition policy (Cumming, Merriman, and Ross 1996: 17; McDonald and Alsford 1989). At the time of writing, many countries are in a frenzy of museum-related development associated with one or more of the following: urban or cultural renewal, adaptive reuse, and/or tourism development policies. How well all these museums can continue to satisfy and educate visitors now that they are in competition with many types of electronic media alternatives remains to be seen.

CULTURAL SIGNIFICANCE OF HERITAGE ASSETS

The best type of definition of cultural significance is one that is all embracing, such as that promoted by the Australian Heritage Commission and the Australian chapter of ICOMOS. The cultural significance of an asset comprises "its aesthetic, historic, scientific, or social value for past, present and future generations" (Australia ICOMOS 1998: 3). Some of the key criteria used to evaluate the cultural significance of heritage for the purposes of listing on registers of three other countries (the United States, Canada, and England) are listed here for comparison.

United States National Register of Historic Sites Criteria. Listings on this register are made once it is ascertained that "the quality of significance in American history, architecture, archaeology, engineering, and culture is present in districts, sites, buildings, structures, and objects that possess integrity of location, design, setting, materials, workmanship, feeling, and association" (U.S. Department of the Interior 1995).

United States National Historic Landmark Criteria. Same as above except such listings must possess *"exceptional value or quality* in illustrating or interpreting the heritage of the United States . . . and *possess a high degree of integrity* of location, (etc.)" (U.S. Department of the Interior 1993).

Canada National Historic Sites Criteria. "Subject under consideration will have a nationally significant impact on Canadian history, or will be deemed to represent a nationally important example or illustration of Canadian human history." Furthermore, "a site, structure or object may be designated by virtue of an association with a nationally significant aspect of Canadian history, provided that the association in itself is sufficiently important for the site to merit a designation of national historic significance." There are subcriteria produced by Parks Canada for evaluating different types of tangible cultural heritage such as archaeological sites, historic districts, parks and gardens, cemeteries, and schools (Parks Canada 1994: 68).

English Heritage Criteria for Historic Buildings Register. "*Architecturally important* to the nation because of their architectural design, decoration and craftsmanship, or represent particular building types and techniques, or have a significant plan form (this incorporates an aesthetic value); *historically interesting,* illustrating important aspects of the nation's social, economic, cultural or military history; *historically associated* with nationally important people or events; important because of a *group value* involving an architectural or historic unity or plan" (Marleesh Pty. Ltd. in Australian Heritage Commission 1997: 77).

English Heritage Conservation Areas Criteria. "The special character of these areas does not come from the quality of the buildings alone. The historic layout of roads, paths and boundaries; characteristic building and paving materials; a particular 'mix' of building uses; public and private spaces, such as gardens, parks and greens; and trees and street furniture, which contribute to particular views—all these and more make up the familiar local scene. Conservation areas give broader protection than listing individual buildings: all features, listed or otherwise, within the area are recognized as part of its character" (English Heritage Web site 2000).

Basic criteria for assessment of significance include an asset's rarity, research or teaching potential, representativeness (is it a good example of its kind?), visual appeal, evidence of technical or innovative processes, and associations with special individuals, cultural prac- tices, or spiritual beliefs. In determining representativeness, most as- sessments must consider an asset in comparison with others of a simi- lar kind locally, regionally, or nationally. Selection of items for World Heritage listing also considers cultural and/or natural values, with more emphasis being placed on outstanding or unique heritage places (UNESCO World Heritage Centre 2000). In this type of comparative analysis, time is also spent judging how the asset sits in relation to other places in terms of integrity (how complete or intact it is), design or style (if architectural), its physical condition, and significance to the local or indigenous community. A statement of significance is then produced, which is the basis for outlining the cultural values of the heritage asset (AHC 1998). The statement should be succinct, clear, and comprehensive, and assist in setting the priorities for the management and commodification of the asset.

AUTHENTICITY

Authenticity is perhaps the one area in cultural heritage manage- ment and conservation planning in which lively debate has resulted in a noticeable broadening of opinions. The usage of the term "authen- ticity" or "authentic" has changed markedly over the past 200 years in European language both inside and outside cultural heritage man- agement circles (Larsen 1995b; Lowenthal 1995). Hence, the con- cept of "authenticity" is, and deserves to remain, in state of flux (Jokilehto 1995; Lowenthal 1995). The word is of Classical Greco- Roman etymological origin and was used initially to indicate a sense of a true, sincere, or original element in a historical context. By 1849, it was defined as meaning, "that is authentic, which is sufficient to it- self, which commends, sustains, proves itself, and hath credit and au- thority from itself" (Fitzgerald in Jokilehto 1995: 19).

The Passion for the Authentic

As the concept of heritage gained currency, the idea of being able to guarantee authenticity became vital when evaluating assets. Art- works, rare books, and other examples of material culture were sub- jected to scrutiny in various ways, so that they could be affirmed as genuine. During the eighteenth and nineteenth centuries in Europe, authenticity became part of an emerging approach to the conservation of artworks and historical monuments (Jokilehto 1995). Maintaining historical authenticity in building restoration works was promoted strongly by Englishmen John Ruskin and William Morris.

With the advent of increased mass production and a greater homogeneity of material culture in the twentieth century, the focus of much conservation work shifted to the preservation of mostly preindustrial heritage. The resulting treatment tended to emphasize the importance of maintaining the original fabric of the heritage asset (or one phase of development) with as little intervention as possible and sometimes at the expense of the overall significance or meaning (Jokilehto 1995). Later additions to buildings were torn down, so that it could be returned to its "authentic" state. More recently, though, conservation practice has emphasized the importance of acknowledging something from all phases of historical development of many types of heritage assets (e.g., that a Civil War battlefield site was also once a farm or a Native American camp) and efforts are now being made to conserve the entire fabric of a place and not its original structure.

The core management issue for authenticity, however, is that any changes to the fabric of the place should be recorded both before and after action or intervention is taken. Any action should be made only in line with an existing conservation plan policy (Bell 1997: 40-50). Finally, ongoing monitoring of the physical condition of the heritage place and success of conservation measures should continue in a regular manner, which is also documented. This information is important for regular reviews of the conservation or site management plan and its policy, which should occur at regular intervals (of not more than ten years apart).

Testing for Authenticity

What is authenticity? The Venice Charter notes that an asset should be "imbued with a message from the past, the historic monuments of generations of people remain to the present day as living witnesses to their age-old traditions" (ICOMOS in Petzet 1995: 85). The 1972 World Heritage Convention further affirmed this approach as it is concerned about "richness of authenticity" and required that nominations pass a test in the degree of authenticity of their design, material, workmanship, and setting (UNESCO World Heritage Centre 2000, Operational Guidelines, Article 24b.i). Function is also sometimes included as a de facto category. However, the application of the test proved difficult as the World Heritage Committee encountered problems because of the vagueness and embedded cultural assumptions in the criteria. In 1992, it decided to revise the notion with assistance from ICOMOS and funding from several national governments (Petzet 1995; Larsen 1995b).

Another View from the East

The Nara Conference on Authenticity, held in the ancient Japanese capital in 1994, allowed Japanese and other non-European practitioners to share their views on conservation philosophy (Larsen 1995a). The term *authenticity* does not always have a counterpart in non-European languages, particularly Japanese. The two closest translations are *genuineness* and *reliability*. Several factors have influenced Japanese and other Asian philosophies regarding the management of cultural heritage. The first factor is the difficult nature of Asia's physical environment and the tendency to build using wood. Physical deterioration of the built environment has meant that structures require increasing maintenance. Another factor is the religious views some cultures hold, such as animism (sacredness of the surrounding environment), which means that people are more likely to think in terms of the mortal life span for shrines. Structures that were built to house such deities are considered also to be "mortal," that is, to have their own life cycle. It is also important that these structures are regularly renewed, so as not to be made unclean by death.

Japanese builders, in particular, developed a unique reconstruction system for such shrines that enables all structures within a temple complex to be renewed every twenty years. This work is carried out with strict attention to traditional methods; at one shrine, as many as sixty-one reconstructions have occurred since it was first founded circa 600 AD (Ito 1995). It is a case of intangible heritage associated with the fabric being its essence or main indicator of authenticity, not the fabric of the structure itself. The conference produced the influential Nara Document on Authenticity, which has become the basis of much revision of conservation practice around the world in this area. The main features of the document are the revised principles on understanding and managing authenticity in a way that takes into account Eastern as well as Western viewpoints. It also makes some important points about heritage and cultural diversity, which had not been made in previous charters (ICOMOS 1994).

Other Considerations

Two other factors have caused cultural heritage managers in Western countries to pause for thought when considering authenticity issues. One factor is the emerging understanding in some countries of the social and sacred value of some heritage assets—that is, their significance beyond that of their historical or aesthetic value for communities and individuals. Another factor is having to set the conservation of heritage assets against the backdrop of sustaining cultural identity and diversity. The latter deals with issues of scale, not just of site types (building, town, and heritage route) but also of management policies, which must accommodate assets with a plethora of cultural values (Domicelj 1995). Hence, authenticity has been linked to approaches, such as cultural mapping, that recognize the cultural heritage perceptions of diverse communities and ensure an inclusive study of all elements. Again, these need to be flexible enough to receive input from community cultural heritage mechanisms or consultation processes (Galla 1995).

TOURISM, AUTHENTICITY, AND COMMODIFICATION

Where does this leave us in relation to tourism, which, on the one hand, promotes "authentic" experiences and, on the other hand, needs to commodify assets by turning them into consumable products? Questions arise: How much commodification can occur before an asset ceases to be authentic? Moreover, as discussed in Chapter 3, the tourist may want an authentic experience but may not want to be confronted by reality. Thus, the discussion of different views of authenticity leads us to add the view of the visitor or tourist. Most often people experiencing a heritage attraction for the first time are assailed with its "feeling value" or apparent authenticity. Even when little is known or understood about the monument, object, or site, it will convey a sense of history, aura, or the trace of something almost nostalgic (Walle 1993; Petzet 1995; Sharples, Yeoman, and Leask 1999; Wang

1999). This sentiment has led some people to argue that assets can undergo near total transformation and still retain their authenticity as far as many tourists are concerned. The architectural compromise of preserving the façade of historic buildings designated for redevelopment has its roots in this belief. Again, the view that authenticity is relative makes us understand this strategy as a compromise given only that saving the whole building would increase its "feeling value."

Authenticity also seems to include a cultural element. The patina and subliminal feeling that many tangible heritage assets provide is difficult to fake at theme parks. Many visitors from Europe would consider these places to be less than authentic. However, visitors with an Eastern background of heritage, such as Japanese and Singaporean tourists, would see most theme parks' levels of authenticity as acceptable. Some Chinese visitors would even consider the newness of the attraction as commendable and the proper way to commemorate historical cultural values. How far a cultural theme park goes in trying to satisfy both markets is a dilemma that should be solved in the early stages of planning as it could be difficult and expensive to change direction later on.

Use of Assets Should Be Culturally Appropriate and Sustainable

How we use and treat the past have been major topics of debate in the past two decades. They raise issues such as who decides the use and management of heritage assets. It is a debate that cultural tourism professionals are affected by as much as their counterparts in cultural heritage management. According to a number of heritage analysts (Bickford 1983; Lowenthal 1985; McBryde 1992; Temple 1988; Warren 1989; Spearritt 1991; Kaplan 1994; Tunbridge and Ashworth 1996; Ashworth and Tunbridge 2000; and Orbasli 2000) such a debate is very important for understanding cultural identity and also a crucial part of any conservation plan for key heritage attractions such as World Heritage sites (ICOMOS 1993: 15).

Contemporary society uses the past in the following ways: as a commodity (particularly in tourism); to control, confirm, or confront present beliefs; for leisure, education, and profit; and for articulating national pride or group identity. Museums and heritage movements in many countries often ascribe to the latter use in the production of "national pasts" or specific historical narratives. Since the end of the nineteenth century such a use was not incidental to the formation of nation-states (Bennett 1993: 235) and is also known to drive the national heritage tourism policies of some of these nations (Sofield and Li 1998; Goudie, Khan, and Killen 1996).

More specifically, the compatible use or reuse of tangible heritage assets that are part of the built environment is a significant issue for the sustainability of their cultural values (ICOMOS 1993). Buildings that are abandoned or that continue to be left vacant are at risk of physical decay through lack of maintenance or risk destruction through vandalism or fire. Finding an appropriate use that will enhance (or at least not detract from) the cultural values of a structure or neighborhood will also add to its tourism potential (ICOMOS 1999). Accordingly, a heritage asset can be badly affected by uncontrolled, insensitive, and speculative development that may be proposed for or around it (ICOMOS 1993: 15). For instance, some private developers of visitor accommodations will try to take advantage of the close proximity of a heritage asset to maximize the view from their constructions. Where possible, such incursions into the setting of an important asset should be discouraged. If they cannot be ruled out completely, developers should be encouraged by urban planners to include some measure of sensitivity of design in the architectural style of the construction.

Inappropriate activities or even unnecessary repetition of themes and motifs can also lead to an area or structure being trivialized and also the culture that is associated with it (Cuattingguis 1993). It is unfortunately the case that such trivialization occurs as part of the development of mass tourism, and the historic character of heritage attractions can become seriously compromised by it. This is why cultural heritage managers of World Heritage sites in particular are being strongly urged by ICOMOS and UNESCO to undertake tourism and urban planning that is broader than only what is needed for the asset itself. Attention must also be given to the nature and use of the environment and space adjacent to or part of the setting of such an asset to sustain its cultural values (ICOMOS 1993; UNESCO World Heritage Centre 2000; ICOMOS 1999) (see Photo 5.3).

PHOTO 5.3. Malacca, Malaysia

Cultural insensitivity can damage the cultural value of an asset. In Malacca, located in southern Malaysia, as in other destinations, large numbers of tourists and the failure to manage sites effectively can exert adverse impacts on historic sites. In this case, graves, some dating back to the sixteenth century, are being desecrated by people selling artwork.

VISITOR ACCESSIBILITY TO TANGIBLE HERITAGE ASSETS

Not all tangible heritage assets should be made accessible to tourists. In later chapters, we discuss this issue from a tourism product perspective. The interest in this chapter, however, is from an asset perspective and its ability to withstand intense use levels. The management priorities for heritage places exisit on a use/conservation continuum (see Figure 5.1). For instance, heritage places that require

FIGURE 5.1. Management Option Continuum

Management Policy

Conservation   ⟵——————⟶   Commodification

strict attention to conservation measures to reduce visitation impacts will be placed near the conservation end of the continuum. Alternatively, heritage places with high tourism potential that can absorb heavy visitation will be placed at the opposite end. Inevitably there will be some heritage places that need attention to both and these will appear in the middle of the continuum (du Cros 2000).

Exceptions to this principle include assets that may be remote from centers of high population or that lack appropriate infrastructure to aid visitation. Other fragile assets could suffer if exposed to visitation, being incredibly fragile (see Photo 5.4); for instance, the rock paintings in the caves in Lascaux, France, where visitors are directed to a reconstruction as an alternative (Brooks 1993). Some heritage assets cannot be viewed or talked about outside certain circles to retain aspects of sacredness that are part of the conservation of their intangible heritage values (Truscott 1994). Information on many of these as-

PHOTO 5.4. Rock Art, Cederberg Ranges, Republic of South Africa

Some assets are too fragile to encourage tourism. Ancient rock paintings in the Cederberg Ranges in South Africa are extremely fragile and could be destroyed if tourism is encouraged. Instead, these sites may be best preserved for scientific research, as is the case with this group of archaeologists.

sets may be presented instead in a range of other ways including CD/DVD technology, education kits, documentaries, or publications.

CONSULTATION AS AN IMPORTANT ELEMENT OF THE MANAGEMENT PROCESS

Defining who stakeholders are and what they expect is important for setting the priorities in the conservation process (Hall and McArthur 1998). As with most conservation practice, to understand the needs of stakeholders, the issue of cultural value must be revisited or stakeholders must be consulted at the time of its initial assessment. Australia ICOMOS also notes that "the cultural significance of a place is embodied in its physical form or 'fabric,' its setting and contents, in associated documents, its uses, or in peoples' memory and associations with the place" (Australia ICOMOS 1998: 3). Understanding cultural significance and how it ties socially constructed meanings to the physical is at the basis of dealing with community stakeholders. Aside from cultural values, other factors are usually addressed in the conservation planning process such as the owner/managers needs and resources, reasons for potential risk, current physical condition, and likely future impacts.

It also becomes apparent that one stakeholder can overrule the views of others or dominate in discussions of conservation or commodification priorities (Bahaire and Elliot-White 1999). This stakeholder may be the owner of a freehold title heritage asset and not the cultural heritage manager or tourism sector representative. If not handled carefully, the impact on the asset could detract from its value for conservation or tourism. For instance, private owners are given tax incentives or the opportunity to transfer development rights to encourage them to retain buildings and conduct regular maintenance. In CHM cultures where sustainability is important, continued community involvement and incentives of this kind appear in more general urban planning policies (Van Borg and Russo 1998; AHC and TCA 1999; du Cros 1999). Issues about maintaining authenticity, in terms of what kind of intervention is required to conserve the physical fabric and its cultural values, need to be discussed. In setting commodification priorities that can affect both fabric and cultural values, tourism can be a much more powerful stakeholder than the host community or the heritage manager. How an arrangement can be reached among all these stakeholders on this important issue is the subject of the final chapter in this section.

Chapter 6

Intangible Heritage
and Its Management

INTRODUCTION

Intangible heritage is traditional culture, folklore, or popular culture that is performed or practiced with close ties to "place" and with little complex technological accompaniment. Put more simply, if tangible heritage assets represent the hard culture of a community, its places, and things, then intangible heritage assets represent its soft culture, the people, their traditions, and what they know. This description incorporates aspects of the UNESCO's definition of oral culture and intangible heritage as "folklore (or traditional and popular culture) [that] is the totality of tradition-based creations of a cultural community, expressed by a group or individuals, and recognized as reflecting the expectations of a community in so far as they reflect its cultural and social identity" (UNESCO 1998: 5). It includes, among other elements, language, literature, music, dance, games, mythology, rituals, customs, handicrafts, architecture, and other arts. In addition to these examples, account should also be taken of traditional forms of communication and information (UNESCO 1998).

Intangible heritage requires the presence of traditional culture bearers to give it life. Consequently, the cooperation and participation of "folk" are prerequisites for the presentation of real intangible heritage. Likewise, the setting or cultural space is important, for intangible heritage is intrinsically linked to a place or context. Removing the heritage asset from its context may affect its authenticity.

As with tangible heritage, the assessment of the significance of intangible heritage is crucial to planning for its management and the setting of conservation priorities. In an ideal world, it would be carried out in the documentation, registration, and/or archiving stage before a management policy is devised. Promotion of its cultural values to the wider community by appropriate dissemination or display would also be an important part of any management plan. As a result, responsible marketing and commodification by the tourism sector should also be an important element of any conservation strategy.

Intangible heritage raises a number of interesting issues for the tourism sector. At a simplistic level, it is an important tourism asset as it enables the tourist to gain a deeper understanding of the destination being visited. It is manifested through live performances, festivals, events, storytellers, and local markets. Indeed, tourists often talk about "absorbing" the local culture as their means of consumption.

Questions can be raised, however, about whether the cultural experiences tourists consume are forms of intangible heritage or are something else. Also, the link between true intangible heritage management and tourism is more tenuous than it is between tangible heritage and tourism. Tourism's commodification needs may mean that little of the "culture" tourists consume is indeed representative of authentic intangible heritage. Given, for example, the criterion of little use of complex technology, a sound and light show or costumed animation at a theme park would not be considered intangible heritage, while a display of traditional dancing might be. Likewise, the criterion of location means that indigenous performances in theme parks and cultural centers may not be considered authentic representations of intangible heritage.

This chapter introduces the reader to the concept of intangible cultural heritage and how it relates to tourism. Because this field is still relatively new, much of what is discussed has been developed only in the past few years. Using the analogy from Chapter 4, the management of intangible heritage in most countries is at the early stage of the cultural heritage management framework (inventorying, documentation, and evaluation), with much debate going on about what to do next.

RECOGNITION OF INTANGIBLE CULTURAL HERITAGE MANAGEMENT

Japan was the first country to recognize the value of intangible cultural heritage, and it remains one of the few countries to legislate its protection. Its Living Human Treasures program began in 1950. This program allows "living national treasures" or "holders of important intangible cultural properties" to be identified individually or collectively. Although legislation does not necessarily bring with it greater protection or invigoration of intangible heritage, it does provide a basis for a more general recognition of the role of special individuals as "transmitters of traditions" (Larsen in Nishimura 1994: 179; UNESCO 2000a,b). It is not unusual that this role also includes measures to promote and invigorate such traditions where they may be under threat from modernization or globalization.

The Korean Cultural Properties Protection Act of 1962 allows for a similar category of heritage protection. It was enacted in response to the realization that rapid modernization following the Korean Conflict was producing a reduction in interest in traditional skills and crafts. The law has been amended several times and clearly sets out the role of local and national government authorities in preserving intangible cultural properties (Korean National Commission 2000: 12). In 1995, Korea had listed 167 individual holders and fifty holding organizations (UNESCO 2000b).

Other programs that recognize the "elite" of tradition bearers operate in the Philippines, Thailand, and France (UNESCO 2000b). In addition, UNESCO has established a listing and award system for intangible heritage. Its biannual proclamations of "Masterpieces of Oral and Intangible Heritage" honor the most popular and traditional cultural activities or popular and traditional forms of expression. The awards project was formally adopted in November 1999 and is based on an idea put forward by a meeting of Moroccan and Spanish intellectuals in Marrakech 1997. The "Masterpieces" are selected by a nine-person international jury (UNESCO 1998, 1999).

Elsewhere, the recognition of intangible heritage operates on a more ad hoc basis, often driven by political activism of indigenous groups and other parties. In North America, Australia, and New Zealand, for example, efforts to recognize the importance of living indigenous cultures have included cultural festivals, lobbying for indigenous languages to be taught in schools, and disseminating information through various media, including the Internet. Cultural revitalization and education of younger generations are key outcomes sought from such programs. Tourism can be a key benefactor as well as an important initiator of this process, with interest by outsiders being recognized as providing the motivation and economic rationalization for indigenous communities to rediscover their own culture (Jafari 1996).

Since 1989, UNESCO, the United Nations Educational, Scientific, and Cultural Organization, has played a leading role in promoting intangible heritage conservation through the adoption of the Recommendation on the Safeguarding of Traditional Culture and Folklore. This document draws the attention of the world's decision makers to the importance of intangible heritage in enabling different cultural groups to assert their cultural identity, allowing humanity to maintain its cultural diversity (see Photo 6.1). It provides a generalized overall framework for identifying and preserving this form of heritage. The following summarizes the core elements of this policy.

Identification and Inventory: This will require that governments conduct, support, or encourage surveys on regional, national, and international levels for gathering information to be fed into regional and global registers administered by folklore institutions or organizations. This work would require

- the establishment of identification and recording systems to assist or complement those that exist in carrying out this objective, and
- the coordination of classification systems used by different institutions to produce a standard typology with a general outline and regional classifications.

Conservation: In the first instance, this concerns the hard culture documentation and storage of intangible heritage to give researchers and tradition bearers access to data, enabling them to understand the process through which tradition changes. The dynamic character of such heritage cannot always be directly protected; intangible heritage that is transformed into hard culture is still vulnerable to abuse or theft and should be effectively protected (see *Protection*).

Preservation: Basic steps are outlined in the UNESCO recommendation for measures to guarantee the status and economic support for intangible heritage both in the communities that instigate it and beyond. These steps include providing educational and research opportunities that are of particular importance in cases where tradition bearers and cultural groups are under pressure of various kinds, such as the increasingly pervasive aspects of a more politically, economically, or culturally dominant group.

PHOTO 6.1. Gay Pride Parade, San Francisco, California

Intangible heritage includes many different elements. Annual Gay Pride Parades that occur in many communities (here in San Francisco) are an expression of that heritage. Some of the parades are very well established and are becoming part of the cultural identity of such places, particularly in the case of San Francisco and Sydney. They are also major tourist attractions for both the domestic and international markets, appealing to tourists of all sexual orientations.

Dissemination: This section recommends that measures be taken to disseminate intangible heritage for increased understanding and respect; and for the groups for which it forms a part of their cultural identity. This action should be undertaken only with close reference to the conditions outlined in the next point.

Protection: Intangible heritage comprises the intellectual cultural property and, as such, should be protected in a manner similar to other intellectual property. Copying and commercial use of such heritage is of concern to the tradition bearers and owners, who would like to be in greater control of such processes; such processes are important because they can have a direct bearing on cultural identity. The other rights associated with intangible heritage include those of the

- informant, in the area of privacy and confidentiality;
- collector, by caring appropriately for any collection or documentation that has been gathered in a systematic manner of such heritage; and
- archive, by allowing it to monitor the use of such materials.

International Cooperation: Cooperation is sought between different nation-states to ensure that development and revitalization programs for intangible heritage are carried out appropriately and in a timely and systematic fashion. It calls for exchanges of relevant information and expertise while encouraging such states to provide opportunities for projects previously recommended. It recommends that necessary measures be taken to safeguard intangible heritage from acts likely to

- diminish its value,
- impede its dissemination, and
- damage it, e.g., armed conflicts, occupation of territories, public disorders of other kinds, and natural dangers.

INTANGIBLE HERITAGE ASSETS— MANAGEMENT AND TOURISM ISSUES

The preceding discussion shows that intangible heritage is more than just folklore and cultural expression. In fact, intangible cultural heritage management includes nationally proclaimed elites or "living human treasures," less well-recognized performers and artisans, and, finally, traditional custodians and religious figures.

Living Human Treasures

The management challenges for living human treasures have been discussed previously. These individuals or groups of individuals play a major role in promoting continuity of intangible cultural heritage and are recognized as being nationally or internationally significant cultural custodians. From a tourism perspective, though, they are a rather limited asset. The absolute number of living human treasures is finite; they are treasured for different reasons than their use as tourist attractions, and they are not typically performers. Thus, tourism cannot, nor should it, rely on these people as performers to entertain masses of visitors who may know little about the culture they are visiting.

Performers and Artisans

Conversely, performers and artisans using traditional methods or modes of cultural expression are of great interest to the tourism industry. These people are not recognized formally but still play a key role in the maintenance of traditions. Performers and artisans represent "living" cultures or living links to past cultures (see Photo 6.2). Many of these people live in developing countries or are part of indigenous groups. They often welcome tourism as an opportunity for cultural exchange and celebration of their survival.

One management strategy being employed to protect this type of intangible heritage is to establish institutes, cultural centers, music halls, parks, or museums that performers and artisans can be encouraged to frequent. Such a management action provides a number of benefits for the artisans themselves, as well as for the traveling public. These venues form a focal point for people who may be dispersed over a large geographical area. Moreover, the value of what they do and know is recorded and can be reaffirmed. These centers can also double as tourist attractions where visitors can observe traditional performances or work practices being undertaken in an authentic setting. In addition, these venues provide revenue generation opportunities for tradition bearers either through gate entry fees or the sale of

PHOTO 6.2. Bun Festival, Cheung Chau Island, Hong Kong

Intangible heritage, often embodied for tourism consumption in festivals, is of equal importance as tangible heritage, though a less well-examined aspect of cultural heritage management. This element of CHM encompasses the traditions, lifestyles, and habits of residents, as expressed in the "floating children" parade as part of the Bun Festival in Cheung Chau Island near Hong Kong. The festival has been an annual event for many years and is just now becoming a tourist attraction with the consent of the islanders.

goods and services. Successful venues have been created all around the world, focusing on such diverse features as pottery and local crafts in West Africa and Cantonese opera performances in a new heritage museum in Hong Kong (Adande 1995; Koffi 1995; Diarrassouba 1995; Hong Kong Leisure and Cultural Services Department 2000). The following case study is just one example (based on Paige and McVeigh 1999: 20-22).

Case Study:
New Orleans Jazz National Historical Park

Legislative Background

A resolution was passed in U.S. Congress in 1987 designating jazz music a national American treasure. The National Parks Service later carried out a resource study to investigate the best way to preserve and commemorate New Orleans jazz. As a result of the study's recommendations, Public Law 103-433 was passed in 1994, which established the New Orleans Jazz National Historical Park. A general management plan was then devised for the site.

Cultural Significance

The historical development of New Orleans ensured a multicultural society that hybridized a number of different musical traditions in a way that did not occur anywhere else. As each new ethnic group arrived, it added another element to this active musical environment and other cultural traditions (e.g., festivals and cuisine). At the turn of the century, a synthesis began to develop that was to become New Orleans jazz, and this was performed in many places including clubs, community halls, street corners, and during parades. Not only did this activity become part of the city's leisure and recreation but it also embodied growing social linkages between many different aspects of society. These included mutual aid and benevolent societies, brass bands, and the Mardi Gras Indians. These organizations have demonstrated a continuity of tradition by being just as involved in jazz-related activities today as they were one hundred years ago.

Major Management Issues

The legislation for establishing the park directed that it should provide the visitor with live jazz interpretation, information about jazz-related activities elsewhere in the city, and a broad range of educational programs. Community consultation and participation was vital to the management of the park and related activities. The park also serves as an archive for information volunteered by community groups regarding the history and development of jazz within each particular neighborhood or community group. Getting the balance right between visitor needs and community expectations is the most important issue for the park's management and the ongoing sustainability of New Orleans jazz.

Summary of Management Policy

The management plan guides how jazz can be preserved and interpreted to the general public in line with local community participants' views and visitors' needs.

Custodians and Religious Figures

Many tourism products involve exposing visitors to special knowledge or traditions that may be secular, sacred, or a mixture of both. Holders of that knowledge and its associated tangible heritage often see themselves as custodians of the knowledge first, with participation in the presentation of the knowledge for tourists as having a lower priority. The challenge is how to value and subsequently use this special knowledge. Increasingly, indigenous custodians are being asked to comanage places with significant tangible and intangible values, especially if those places hold important spiritual significance to traditional owners. As the case study of Uluru-Kata Tjuta National Park in Australia shows (McKercher and du Cros 1999; Parks Australia 1999), comanagement involves understanding and respecting traditional values. Management actions may involve closing sacred sites to public visitation and imposing strict use guidelines on other areas.

Growing interest in learning something about indigenous culture also places greater pressure on these custodians to share their knowledge with visitors. Whether to share knowledge, what knowledge to present, how to present it, what stories to tell, and who presents it therefore become important management considerations. These questions can be answered only after thorough consultation with the custodians and tradition bearers. Some information that may generate strong tourism interest may be too culturally sensitive or culturally inappropriate to present, in spite of its potential appeal. Likewise, management principles suggest that any information must be presented by the custodians directly or through an interpreter to ensure that the material presented is correct and is offered in the proper context, in a culturally sensitive manner. It is inappropriate to have bus drivers/tour guides present intangible cultural heritage without close association with and monitoring by custodians and tradition bearers.

Case Study:
Uluru-Kata Tjuta National Park (Ayers Rock/Tourist Icon)

Legislative Background

The current Uluru-Kata Tjuta National Park was created after amendments to the Aboriginal Land Rights Act (Northern Territory), 1976, and the National Parks and Wildlife Conservation Act, 1985, allowed it to become unalienable freehold title held by the traditional owners. The title was vested in the Uluru-Kata Tjuta Land Trust to be leased by a specially constituted Board of Management combining elements of the Anangu Aboriginal community and Parks Australia.

Cultural Significance

Uluru (Ayers Rock) and Kata Tjuta (the Olgas) are both key sacred sites in traditional law or *Tjukurpa* of the indigenous Anangu Aboriginal community, who are the traditional custodians of this scared site. It is also one of the few World Heritage cultural landscapes (i.e., has both natural and cultural values as part of its listing). Ayers Rock, Uluru's alter-ego, is a postwar tourist icon and potent cultural symbol for non-Aboriginal Australia—so much so that a visit to it is irrevocably linked with undertaking "the climb." Its perceived recreational value has become part of the site's social significance for this section of society and many overseas visitors.

Major Management Issues

The joint managers, the Anangu and Parks Australia, aim to reduce the social and environmental impacts on intangible and tangible heritage assets, specifically educating visitors to elect not to climb in accordance with the wishes of Anangu tradition bearers (see Photo 6.3). Problems generally lie for the board with the persistence of perceptions outside the park amongst the general public and tourism sector regarding its recreational use. A cultural center was established by the board to raise awareness about Aboriginal culture in 1995. It is still not quite fulfilling the board's and Aboriginal community's hopes that it will encourage visitors to forsake "the climb" in favor of more culturally sensitive activities.

Summary of Management Policy

The board has just completed a new management plan that emphasizes educational use above recreational use. It is stated that the practice of Tjukurpa must still come first. There are plans to ensure that the cultural center may yet become better utilized by a greater number of visitors; whether this will influence their preconceived beliefs has yet to be proven. Many visitors, particularly those from overseas, seem to arrive with a strong desire to experience Uluru more as a leisure experience with the climb and activities at the nearby resort without wanting to absorb much about its intangible heritage. The problem may lie with the marketing and branding of this well-established attraction.

AUTHENTICITY AND CULTURAL SPACE

Does removing an intangible asset from its context or setting affect its authenticity? Such a question must be framed within the context of the idea of *cultural space*. Cultural space refers to a place in which popular and traditional cultural activities are concentrated but also generally characterized by a certain periodicity (cyclical, seasonal, calendar based, etc.) or by an event (UNESCO 1998: 32, Section 3.5.5 1(c)). Intangible heritage management principles suggest that the integrity of the cultural place plays an important role in presenting an authentic experience.

PHOTO 6.3. Uluru, Central Australia

Sometimes the actions of tourists come in conflict with the wishes of traditional custodians. At Uluru in central Australia, traditional Aboriginal owners request visitors not to climb the world's largest monolith to little avail. A sign posted at the start of the climb asking people not to climb and to participate in alternative activities is ignored by almost all visitors.

Cultural space does not necessarily have to be a heritage place. It could be the usual place of performance, an associated object, collection, or landscape. For festivals, it could be the streets of city or a religious structure or complex. The association between intangible heritage and cultural space could be based in the past as well as the present. One example of a past association would be a storyteller, bard, or acrobat presenting in a street or square that still evinces continuity with the past. Such a place could be considered an appropriate cultural space for diplaying intangible heritage (regardless of its current physical character).

Is the experience still considered to be authentic if that storyteller is moved to another part of the city? Can the experience be authentic if the storyteller presents the same story in a different country? Can these cultural spaces still be considered authentic settings for his or her tales? Does the tourist care? These and other questions have been the subject of recent debate among cultural tourism analysts who question whether international festivals that feature different indigenous performers presenting intangible heritage, removed from its cultural space, are harming its authenticity (ICOMOS 1999). Cultural purists argue that such a fundamental change in venue makes it impossible for the intangible heritage to remain authentic and relevant. They are also concerned that such performances cross the line from education toward entertainment.

Others feel that such events are innocuous and argue that these displays should be regarded as performances. They accept that the physical context cannot remain unchanged but that the beauty, intensity, and significance of the performance can remain relevant to the audience. The festival concept provides cultures involved with an opportunity to create greater awareness and respect for their intangible heritage both at home and abroad.

TOURISM AND CHANGES TO INTANGIBLE HERITAGE

By its very nature, tourism imposes changes on intangible heritage presented for tourist consumption. Limited time budgets, lack of a deep understanding of the cultural context, and the desire to be entertained mean that most presentations of intangible cultural heritage assets will tend to be somewhat superficial. Is this necessarily a good or bad thing? Again, the answer depends on the perspective.

Culture is not a static concept. Over time, every culture changes, sometimes radically, sometimes imperceptibly. At stake is the rate of change, the purpose of change, the instigator of change, and its relationship to the context of the core values of the culture. Significant adverse impacts can be felt if the rate of change is too swift or abrupt. Similarly, if change is imposed from the outside for the benefit of outsiders, with few benefits to the asset holders, the merits of such change must be questioned. In America, Hopi Indians, the Madison Treaty Rights Support Group, and other community groups are concerned about "wannabe" Native Americans exploiting their culture and trivializing it for profit. In response, they have set up Web sites and lobbied the federal government to institute cultural property and copyright protection laws (Readings on Cultural Respect 2000; Dambiec 2000).

On the other hand, if the community can control both the absolute amount of change and the rate of change, adverse effects can be minimized. Commodifying intangible assets for tourism use need not be a negative thing if the commodification is controlled by the asset holders and if the content is still understandable. Converting traditional secular activities into performances may produce a number of positive social and economic benefits for the community. Moreover, if these performances are presented in their own venue, their net impact on extant traditions and activities can be minimized.

CULTURALLY APPROPRIATE AND SUSTAINABLE USE OF ASSETS

Having stated this, though, assets must be used or presented in a culturally appropriate manner. Many examples come to mind when intangible heritage and its use by contemporary society are considered. The past for some is something to be cast off as soon as possible so that they can move on avoiding its "dead hand" on their shoulder (du Cros 1996). For others, it is a source of comfort away from hectic modern life. For instance, Bennett (1993: 231) describes the historic precinct of The Rocks in Sydney, Australia, as a place where it is possible to feel "the past insinuate its presence into the rhythms of daily life, marking it off from the present—the hurly burly of city life—as a zone of tranquillity."

Indigenous groups, likewise, rely on aspects of their intangible heritage to connect them with their cultural identity. More than any other at the moment, these groups are under pressure from external economic, social, cultural, and political forces. Issues such as intellectual property rights, the misappropriation of cultural assets for profit, and abuse from inappropriate use in tourism promotion, development, and copyright issues are a concern for most indigenous groups. Intangible heritage, particularly in the form of oral culture and local knowledge, is becoming increasingly important in the environmental management side of sustainable development.

As part of the move toward sustainability, it is also becoming crucial to the preservation of intangible heritage that ways are found to deal fairly with living practitioners and cultural groups who own the intellectual property rights to intangible heritage. Keeping control of certain aspects of the cultural identity through intellectual property rights has become closely linked with the ultimate survival of some of these groups, particularly indigenous minorities (Dambiec 2000). Not only does the loss hurt them economically, but it also undermines much of their self-esteem. Such diminishing respect can leave them vulnerable to general discontent that leads to addictions and other social vices. It can also give the impression that they are no longer culturally or politically active (and therefore vulnerable to further cultural raiding and other types of abuse). Sustainability in this context would mean that cultural equity is therefore closely linked to political equity for many of these groups, as they are still negotiating their relationship with others in relation to land and tangible cultural management issues. The preservation of intangible heritage is therefore of great significance to them in this process.

STAKEHOLDER CONSULTATION IN SETTING MANAGEMENT PRIORITIES

Working with stakeholders is an important part of setting conservation and commodification priorities in the new partnership-style planning process advocated by many governments (Hall 1999). A consultation and planning process that involves host communities and particularly the tradition bearers is required. To be truly successful, it should be one that will be appropriate to the mode of decision making of the host communities or tradition bearers associated with the knowledge. Such decision-making processes can also be influenced by tradition and aspects of the intangible heritage itself.

Historically, tourism planning has been less sensitive to consultation than other activities, such as park management planning (Birkhead, De Lacy, and Smith 1992). To achieve a balance between education and entertainment, conservation and commodification, a more holistic focus is needed in the way the planning processes are managed. The understanding of cultural identity, rate of change, and its impact on authenticity and the appropriate use of intangible heritage are all issues that should be discussed in all stages of the planning with all major stakeholders involved.

Chapter 7

Cultural Tourism Products—
A Regional Perspective

INTRODUCTION

Tourism is driven by attractions. Attractions are the demand generators that give the customer a reason to visit a destination and, further, usually form the central theme for the visit. Ideally, they should be experiential, unique, exciting, one-of-a-kind encounters that appeal to the target market (EPGC 1995). No destination can succeed without a suitable breadth and depth of attractions, first to draw the tourists and second to retain them in the region for long periods. Simply stated, attractions act as the catalyst for the provision of all other tourism products and services. Without them, limited tourism development will occur.

Cultural tourism assets are ideally suited to be developed as tourism demand generators. They encompass the unique features of a place which reflect its culture, history, or environment, and, by their experiential nature, promote the rich tapestry of cultural traditions, ethnic backgrounds, and landscapes (Copley and Robson 1996; Blackwell 1997). Cataloging an area's cultural or heritage assets is an important first step in evaluating the cultural tourism potential of a destination (NTHP 1999). It is, however, only the first step, for a fundamental difference exists between a cultural or heritage asset and a cultural tourism attraction.

The important second step is to transform these assets into products that can be consumed by tourists. A unique asset, culture, or building is not a tourist attraction unless its tourism potential is actualized by enabling its consumption. This step is resisted by many cultural heritage managers because they feel this transformation must invariably compromise the cultural values being conserved. This threat is real, but risk can be minimized through proper management. Indeed, it is better to adopt a proactive approach by transforming the asset yourself into the type of product desired than to let others with no connection to the asset do it.

Thus, understanding how cultural tourism works as a discrete activity, separate from but related to cultural heritage management, involves developing an understanding of what products are. Chapters 7 and 8 examine cultural tourism products. In particular, Chapter 7 looks at the general concept of products and examines the product mix at a regional level. It discusses the concept of a product and how the array products at a destination can collectively provide desired tourism experiences. Chapter 8 examines the process that individual assets must go through to become cultural tourism products. It examines what makes a product attractive to tourists and discusses how products can be presented for tourist consumption.

Before beginning this discussion, let's review some features of tourism. It is important to remember that destinations pursue tourism largely for economic and social benefit. They do this by promoting their wide array of community assets as products to be experienced by the visitor. It is also important to remember that, apart from purpose-built attractions, the "tourism industry" plays a unique role as facilitator of experiences, rather than experience provider. In the past, these two elements (experiences and facilitator) operated in a somewhat parasitic relationship; the facilitators relied on the experience providers to bring people to the region, then exploited them, and returned little. Increasingly, though, we are realizing that the convergence of tourism and cultural consumption is not coincidental (Richards 1996a) and that tourism and culture must function in a symbiotic manner for their mutual benefit. Cultural tourism represents the result of wider social changes by which culture provision is becoming commercialized. In many ways, culture is being molded successfully for tourist consumption through the development of such products and experiences as tourist arts, festivals, and purpose-built theme parks targeted at tourists (Craik 1997).

PRODUCTS

It would seem self-evident that, if tourism is about the consumption of products and cultural tourism involves the consumption of cultural products, it would be important to develop an understanding of what a product is. Marketing theory defines products as "anything that can be offered to a market for attention, acquisition, use, or consumption that might satisfy a need or want" (Kotler and Turner 1989: 435). The key concept here is *consumption that satisfies a need or want.* In other words, people do not buy products for the sake of the product itself; they buy them for the benefits they provide or the problems they solve (Lewis 1984). Accordingly, products can be described simply as solution providers for real or latent problems. These solutions are packaged into something tangible that the person can consume.

If you think about it, it makes sense. Why do we buy toothpaste? All toothpastes are pretty much the same, as is the tangible product offered to consumers. So, why do people prefer different brands? Because different toothpastes are positioned in the market to provide different solutions to real or imagined problems, be they the need for whiter teeth, cavity prevention, fresher breath, a nicer smile, or a better sex life. Products succeed because their manufacturers know the benefits they offer to target markets and have devised the products accordingly (Lewis 1984). The success of a product, therefore, depends on the ability of the producers to understand the needs of the consumer and then to shape the product accordingly. Any discussion of products, therefore, must always occur from the perspective of the consumer.

Thinking Conceptually of Products

Products exist conceptually at three levels: (1) core, (2) tangible, and (3) augmented. The *core product* is the most important feature for it describes the core benefit or solution provided by its consumption. It therefore answers these questions: What personal needs is the product really satisfying? What benefits does the product offer me? No product can succeed unless these questions are answered clearly and succinctly. Of course, the beauty of adopting a marketing approach to product development is that the core problem being solved can vary widely, even for largely similar products. This variation enables different providers to position their product uniquely in the marketplace according to the benefits being promoted. This strategy is so successful, using the toothpaste example, that the consumer believes each brand has different attributes that serve very different needs.

The *tangible product* represents the second conceptual level of a product. It represents the physical manifestation of the core product that facilitates the need satisfaction. In short, it is the physical product or service that is purchased. It is the historic fort that is entered, the battlefield site that is visited, the museum that is seen, the cultural tour that is joined, or the festival that is attended (see Photos 7.1 and 7.2). But, remember, the tangible product is *not* the core experience provided. It is the means by which the core need can be satisfied. This is a difficult concept for many people to appreciate because most are so attuned to purchasing tangible products that they do not think about the deeper needs being satisfied. Indeed, one of the powerful features of cultural tourism is that its tangible products subliminally signal an expected experience so effectively that people will respond to the product without thinking about why. A fort signals history and struggle; an art gallery signals beauty; ruins signal the deep past, etc.

Tourism products must be shaped to satisfy the needs and wants of the consumer. Designing the tangible product to deliver a certain type of experience enables the attraction both to meet visitor expectations and to control the experience. The failure to do so can result in an asset being overwhelmed by tourists, as is the case at the Royal Palace in Bangkok that attracts over 10,000 visitors a day. Remedial management actions are needed to control tourists and minimize impacts.

The third element is the *augmented product*. Augmented products provide additional features above and beyond the tangible product that add value and facilitate easier satisfaction of the core need. It could be something such as a free shuttle to and from the hotel, the provision of umbrellas for rainy days, a complimentary souvenir at the end of a tour, or a money-back guarantee.

Satisfy Consumer Needs First

Today, contemporary marketing and business management philosophy argues that first you must understand what the market wants and then devise products that satisfy those wants (Aaker 1995; Brown 1997; Hiam 1990). This lesson is being learned slowly by the tourism industry. Large players, such as major casino and resort chains, now

PHOTO 7.1. Exterior of Royal Palace, Bangkok, Thailand

PHOTO 7.2. Tourist Control Measures at the Royal Palace, Bangkok, Thailand

Tourism products must be shaped to satisfy the needs and wants of the consumer. Designing the tangible product to deliver a certain type of experience enables the attraction to set visitor expectations and control the experience. The failure to do so can result in an asset being overwhelmed by tourists, as is the case at the Royal Palace in Bangkok pictured above. The palace attracts over 10,000 visitors a day, causing crowding and posing a threat to the fabric of the attraction and the quality of the visitor experience. In these situations, remedial management actions, through signage, etc., are needed to control tourists and minimize impacts. Such actions are reactive in nature, however, and are designed to address the symptoms of overuse rather than its causes.

realize they are selling hospitality and entertainment rather than a room and food (Rowe 1996). Likewise, some nature-based tourism operators realize that they are not selling wildlife viewing opportunities but rather a set of personal benefits ranging from a chance to learn about fragile ecosystems to a chance to help save the planet (Hawkins 1994; Weiler and Richins n.d.).

Although the idea of three conceptual levels of a product is simple in theory, in practice, many people in the tourism industry or new to tourism have difficulty adopting a marketing strategy when considering their own product offerings and, consequently, have difficulty appreciating the differences between their core product and its tangible manifestation. The result is that many tourism organizations are quite ignorant of the real reasons people purchased their tours (McKercher and Davidson 1995). As a result, they develop products and then try to push them onto unwilling users, instead of building products to the market's needs and using them to pull tourists.

The problem seems to be acute in the cultural tourism sector where, traditionally, there has been great resistance to thinking of cultural and heritage assets as products. Many cultural heritage resource managers, however, focus their attentions on the tangible asset they manage, without appreciating the core product they offer to visitors. This focus is understandable, given that few have studied business and that most managers are charged with protecting and conserving tangible assets rather than providing tourism experiences. But if the decision is made to allow people to visit an asset, consumption of a product will occur. It is better to appreciate what product is being consumed and to manage the experience accordingly than to ignore this fact.

It may seem crass to suggest this, but cultural assets should be treated no differently than toothpaste when considering how to actualize their tourism potential. Tourism is the quintessential example of a sector that must adopt a marketing approach to products; by its very nature, it sells dreams and experiences that satisfy the consumer's needs, wants, and desires. People participate in cultural and heritage tourism to have an inner need satisfied, regardless of whether the individual is seeking a deep or shallow experience. People do not go to Civil War battlefield sites to look at an empty field with a monument, which, in many instances, is all the tangible product that remains. Instead, they go to gain an appreciation of American history, to visit hallowed ground, to honor the memory of those soldiers who fought and died (Galagher 1995), to connect to one's own cultural roots, to marvel at the incredible waste of war and loss of life, or even to attempt imagining how they would react if they were placed in a similar circumstance.

BENEFITS OF ADOPTING A MARKETING APPROACH TO PRODUCT DEVELOPMENT

The use of a marketing approach to asset management provides a number of benefits for cultural heritage managers, whereas the failure to do so presents a number of threats to the sustainability of the asset. By understanding why people visit, the experience can be shaped to better satisfy their needs in a manner that is compatible with the wider cultural heritage management goals of the asset. A significant number of visitors to cultural or heritage tourist attractions will be fundamentally ignorant of the cultural or heritage significance and meaning of the asset. Rather than viewing this as a problem, it can been seen as an opportunity to shape the presentation of the asset (the tangible product) to influence the message being received (core product).

Although assets serve the needs of tourists, it does not mean that the tourist has the right to do anything he or she wants. Nor does it mean that all tourists should have the equal rights to visit; indeed, quite the opposite is true. The marketing approach enables the asset managers to define the core product on their own terms and, in doing so, identify and target the desired type of visitor. In this way, the asset is presented in a manner that makes it most appealing to the desired type of user and less appealing to undesired visitors.

Adopting a marketing approach may involve prohibiting some activities, but this can be done in such a way that it adds value to the asset. Explaining why something is not allowed may actually accentuate the experience being consumed. It has been our experience in Australia, for example, that most tourists respect the request of traditional Aboriginal owners not to visit sacred sites. Informing visitors why a site is closed to the public serves to enhance the overall experience, as it emphasizes the spiritual significance of the place being visited and also reinforces the desire of many cultural tourists to act in an appropriate manner.

Conversely, thinking of the asset as a tangible product and not considering the core feature can result in the loss of control over the asset and, ultimately, in its unsustainable use. Two related issues come to play. First, if an asset is well known, people will want to visit it, regardless of the amount of marketing or de-marketing done. If the experience is not shaped to satisfy the visitors' needs, or if those needs are not known, then the tourists will shape the experience themselves to satisfy their own needs. In other words, they will define the asset according to their own core needs and consume it accordingly, even if it is quite different than the desires of the asset managers. Given that most visitors will be largely ignorant of the asset and its deeper meaning, a greater chance exists that their actions will be inappropriate, more out of ignorance than malevolence. If the tourist cannot be managed effectively, how can the asset be managed in a sustainable manner?

Similarly, if the asset is positioned vaguely in the marketplace, or if the tourist is unaware of the positioning strategy used, a greater likelihood exists that the wrong type of tourist will visit the asset. By the wrong type, we mean the type of tourists whose needs are incompatible with the needs satisfaction provided by the asset. Many of the social impacts noted in tourism are a function of well-meaning but largely ignorant tourists, seeking to have their personal needs satisfied in a manner that impinges adversely on the host community. Alternatively, the failure to appreciate the tourism significance of an asset and the concomitant need to transform it for tourism consumption could result in the unappealing presentation of the asset, resulting in lower visitation levels, lower satisfaction levels, less repeat visitation, and fewer financial returns.

The same product may satisfy the core needs of different users whose goals may be incompatible. Ashworth (1999), for example, illustrates that people imagine different places in the same location. As a result, each user may have different expectations and experiences. In some cases, this is not a problem, providing that the core needs of each group are compatible. A historic site can be presented in a way that satisfies a wide spectrum of visitors whose only difference may be their level of engagement.

In other cases, the disparity between the needs of different users may be problematic. It may be an honorable goal to appeal to as many users as possible; it may even be written into the mandate of publicly owned assets. In practical terms, though, no product can be all things to all people. Trying to satisfy everyone is a sure recipe for satisfying no one. Instead, it is better to target clearly defined compatible users and to shape the experience around their needs. Others can visit, but only under the terms set for the primary user. If a cultural or heritage asset exists primarily for the benefit of the local residents, for example, it cannot be easily transformed for tourism use without alienating the primary user.

HIERARCHY OF ATTRACTIONS

Not all cultural tourists are the same. So, too, must it be recognized that not all cultural tourism products are the same. Some will be of great interest to the visitor and will draw visitors from great distances. Others will have limited interest, while many more will have little or no appeal to tourists. Tourism theory recognizes that a clear hierarchy of attractions exists in most destinations and that this hierarchy is defined by the degree of compulsion the tourist feels to visit them (Leiper 1990). The more powerful the demand-generation capacity of the attraction, the greater its ability to draw visitors from great distances. Lesser attractions may provide activities for visitors at a destination but do little to draw them to it. Attractions can, therefore, be an intrinsic part of a trip and a major motivator for selecting a destination; or they can be an optional, discretionary activity engaged in while at a destination (Mill and Morrison 1985; McIntosh and Goeldner 1990; Bull 1991; Jordan 1999).

Three types of attractions have been identified: *primary, secondary,* and *tertiary.* Primary attractions are so important to most destinations that they play a critical role in shaping their image and in influencing visitation (Mill and Morrison 1985). But, again, not all primary attractions are equally strong demand generators. Some have the ability to draw visitors from a greater distance than others. The greater the distance the consumer is expected to travel, the more distinctive and unusual the attraction must be. People will travel long distances to consume truly unique experiences but are unwilling to invest the effort, expense, and time needed to consume common ones.

The purchase decision, or degree of compulsion felt to visit, becomes increasingly discretionary as one moves through the attraction hierarchy. Secondary attractions may be locally significant tourist attractions. They complement the tourism experience and may be very popular in their own right but do not influence the decision to visit the destination. Visits to tertiary, or the lowest-order, attractions are typified by low-involvement purchase decisions and are also largely convenience based or occur by happenstance.

Ironically, the same attraction could act as a primary, secondary, and tertiary attraction simultaneously, depending on the tourists' different reasons for visiting. A simple example illustrates this point. Theatre tourism is booming globally (Hughes 1998). The theatre may serve as the primary attraction for those people who specifically buy theatre packages. Going to a show thus becomes the primary motive for visiting a city, with the theatre the venue for consumption of the primary attraction. Others may be in town for other reasons but have planned to include a night at the theatre as one of the many things they will engage in while on vacation. For these people, theatre tourism is a secondary attraction. For others still, the theatre may be a tertiary attraction. They may be visiting for unrelated reasons and happen to walk by the box office just as it opens. On the spur of the moment, they decide to purchase tickets for that night's show. These people had not planned on going to the theatre but decided to anyway.

Most cultural tourism attractions fall into the category of secondary or tertiary attractions. Many people would dispute this assertion, pointing to a number of well-known global cultural, heritage, and arts tourism icons. But when the total array of cultural tourism assets is considered, these places represent a disproportionately small minority of assets.

DEVELOPING CULTURAL TOURISM ATTRACTIONS

A number of strategies exist to develop cultural heritage assets into cultural tourism attractions.

- Building a primary attraction
- Bundling lesser attractions together to create a themed set of attractions that collectively constitute a primary attraction
- Creating tourism precincts

- Developing linear touring routes or heritage networks
- Using events

Building

Building a primary attraction is the dream of most community leaders. Some communities will do it successfully, but many do not have the resources, innate tourism appeal, proximity to major markets, or themes around which an attraction can be built. Purpose-built primary cultural tourism attractions tend to be built along one of two themes: tourismification of the extant yet previously undeveloped heritage assets or building of purpose-built cultural or heritage theme parks. Opportunities exist to develop extant heritage assets, such as forts, penal colonies, abandoned mines, ghost towns, historic precincts of cities, and abandoned industrial assets into attractions. This strategy has certainly been used to great effect in many parts of the world (Rudd and Davis 1998; Sletvold 1996; WTO 1995; Costa and Ferrone 1998). Where such extant assets do not exist, an opportunity exists to purpose build heritage theme parks. Upper Canada Village, located in Ontario on the shores of the St. Lawrence River, is a recreated rural village circa 1860 using authentic buildings that were relocated when the St. Lawrence Seaway was built in the 1950s. Reconstructions of forts, such as Old Fort William in Thunder Bay, Ontario, or the reconstruction of "typical" rural communities into heritage theme parks (Sovereign Hill in Australia) are other examples where a more commodified experience is provided.

The costs associated with converting extant assets into tourism attractions and then securing ongoing funding for essential conservation work, coupled with the marginal economic returns if the location is isolated, are often too prohibitive for the private sector. Indeed, many of these places are developed without the sound financial and business plans that are demanded by private-sector developers. The provision of this type of primary attraction is often seen as a role for the public sector or not-for-profit community-based organizations. Their development is rationalized based on the broader community benefits they provide (attachment to the past, educational opportunities, employment, economic stimulus) or through their role as catalysts for private-sector tourism development, including accommodation, shopping, and food services. Such developments are supported providing that the net social benefits and/or the net economic activity generated is seen to outweigh the financial costs of subsidizing their operation.

The private sector, on the other hand, is more likely to invest in purpose-built theme parks that have a heritage flavor (Jones 1998; Jones and Robinett 1998). The decision to enter this sector is based on business reasons, with profit and financial viability driving most decisions. Developers can choose an ideal location, rather than having to work with an extant structure that may be off the beaten track. They can purpose build facilities to cater to the tourist's needs and, also important, structure the experience in such as way as to maximize its appeal and optimize revenue generation opportunities. Although they are clearly less authentic in many ways, purpose-built attractions provide a better quality tourist experience than extant facilities.

Bundling

Bundling is a more realistic and cost-effective option available to many communities. It is defined as the provision of separate products and services to buyers as a package or bundle (Aaker 1995; Brown 1997). This approach is used commonly in business where different products are grouped together to create a more appealing new product that benefits both the consumer and the individual suppliers. An example of bundling is the combination of skis, bindings, boots, and polls to create a one-priced ski package. The components are manufactured by different suppliers but are bundled by the retail operator to create a new, more appealing, easier-to-purchase product.

Bundling is common in tourism, with the packaged tour representing a prime example. Airfare, accommodation, ground transport, and a variety of other services are combined to create a new product. Bundling, within a cultural tourism context, typically involves combining a variety of similarly themed products and experiences and promoting their collective consumption to the visitor. This strategy encourages visitation throughout a destination and not just to one or two assets. In this way, the economic benefits of tourism are dispersed more widely. More important, bundling helps create a theme for a place, creating a stronger sense of destination for the tourist by invoking many places with similar meanings.

Precincts

The development of cultural tourism precincts represents an extreme form of bundling. Theater, museum, historical, and ethnic districts provide a number of direct benefits both to the consumer and the provider. Concentration creates a critical mass of products that facilitates easier use by the tourist. In turn, larger tourist numbers provide enhanced business opportunities for ancillary attractions and service providers. In addition, strong consumer demand provides a powerful economic reason to protect and conserve heritage areas. It is the commercial tourist appeal of historic precincts in large cities that provides the needed economic argument to foster conservation of heritage places. Indeed, the tourismification of cultural resources opens new perspectives for historic cities (Ashworth 1995). Of course, a risk exists that overcommodification and standardization of assets for tourism consumption could damage the integrity of the asset (Jansen-Verbeke 1998).

Linear or Circular Tours/Heritage Networks

Opportunities also exist for destinations with similar or complementary cultural assets to work cooperatively for their mutual benefit (Morrison 1998). The creation of linear or circular touring routes linking different communities provides another low-cost option for many destinations. Increasingly, regional communities are realizing that, collectively, the sum of their cultural assets has greater tourism appeal than the individual assets within a community (Rosenbaum 1995a; Stocks 1996). Bundling diverse attractions into a themed touring route creates an appealing primary attraction. Moreover, the array of linear touring routes that can be developed is limited only by the imagination of the person putting together the tour.

The California Cultural Tourism Coalition, a partnership between the arts communities and travel industry in Los Angeles, San Francisco, and San Diego, launched a collection of thirteen themed self-drive itineraries that takes visitors on, as the promotional material states, exotic urban and rural ventures through theaters, museums, galleries, ethnic communities, festivals, historic assets, architecture, restaurants, and shops (Anonymous 1999a). Each itinerary targets a separate theme, including routes that highlight various ethnic themes (such as African-American heritage, Latino culture, and Asian culture), historic themes, science and natural history, workers and museums, architecture, and cultural tours.

Festivals

Festivals and events are de facto, short-duration primary attractions. Again, festivals serve to concentrate a wide array of activities into a condensed time frame, creating a critical mass of products for tourist consumption. Moreover, festivals and events enjoy a strong opportunity of becoming de facto-branded products or of linking into well-known de facto brands, and, in doing so, fostering positive brand associations. A jazz festival is branded as a jazz festival and will appeal to jazz lovers.

CONCLUSIONS

This chapter adopted a generic overview of products within a cultural tourism context. It described what products are and emphasized the need to consider them always from the perspective of the user, looking at the benefits or solutions they provide. We then discussed how a marketing approach to product development can benefit cultural heritage assets by ensuring a desired message is sent to a desired set of users and, alternatively, ensuring that undesired users are discouraged from visiting. Not all cultural tourism products are the same. Using the attraction's hierarchy model, we discussed how different attractions have different levels of appeal and how, through the use of innovative techniques, attraction sets can be combined to create appealing cultural tourism products.

Chapter 8

Commodification, Environmental Bubbles, and Cultural Tourism Products

INTRODUCTION

The previous chapter discussed the concept of products at a destination-wide level. This chapter discusses the development of cultural tourism products at an organizational or operational level. The conversion of a cultural asset into a cultural tourism product necessitates the transformation of that asset into something that can be consumed by the tourist. This process is normally achieved through some level of modification, commodification, and standardization of the asset. In doing so, it makes abstract experiences concrete. Although commodification has been identified as one of the great threats to extant cultural facilities, from a tourism perspective it is an essential and beneficial aspect of the tourism process that provides a wide array of benefits for the tourist, the commercial tourism industry, and the asset itself.

Consumption of tourism experiences has been canvased widely in the tourism literature for almost forty years (Boorstin 1964; MacCannell, 1973; Cohen 1972, 1979), with much of this commentary decrying tourism as a destroyer of cultures and as a denigrator of cultural assets. It is still common to read comments such as this one, written in the early 1970s: "If tourism becomes a success, it would become a cultural tragedy" (Hanna 1972 as cited by Picard 1995: 65). Fortunately, more people are beginning to appreciate that tourism is actually a partner in cultural heritage management (Boniface 1998; ICOMOS 1999; AHC and TCA 1999).

CONSUMPTION—STRANGENESS VERSUS FAMILIARITY AND THE ENVIRONMENTAL BUBBLE

The origins of the debate over the consumption of tourism experiences can be traced to early tourism sociologists. They sought to explain the social reasons for travel and the type of tourism experience people were either seeking or getting. American sociologists, in particular, were concerned about the contrived and illusory nature of the human experience. They felt that people were no longer experiencing reality in their lives; instead, they were being presented with a series of pseudoevents. Mass tourism was seen as being a prime example of how American life had become overpowered by pseudoevents and contrived experiences (Boorstin 1964). Modern tourists were portrayed as being passive onlookers who were isolated from the host environment and local residents. Some felt they were victims of an all-powerful tourism industry that forced them to stay in tourist ghettos and controlled their experiences. Others felt that tourists preferred to be ghettoized, choosing to disregard the real world around them. The end result was contrived tourism experiences that surrounded the visitor in a thicket of unreality (Boorstin 1964).

These assertions had some validity. The industry sought to retain tourists on site for as long as possible to maximize revenue-generating potential; but the tourists themselves were also willing accomplices in this situation for they tended to have much more in common with fellow tourists than with the host community. Urry (1990) identified a number of features of tourism that explain why tourists prefer their own company.

- Tourism represents a change from normal routines, where accepted behavioral norms do not apply and where tourist behavior differs markedly from normal behavior.
- Tourism involves a short-term residency at a destination, with short-term visitors perceiving and using destinations in very different manners than permanent residents.
- The places visited offer a distinct contrast with the tourist's normal world, and, thus, normal social conventions can be temporarily discarded.
- Mass tourism in itself represents a socialized form of travel where the group replaces the individual.

As short-term casual visitors, who may have no great affinity for the destination region and who view it as a place to pursue activities they would normally not pursue at home, at an intensity not normally pursued at home, their actions will be expected to be different from those of the host community. For example, their pursuits might be more intense, as evidenced by excessive alcohol consumption and sexual behavior, or less intense, as evidenced by more relaxed standards of personal hygiene and a break from the person's accepted social norms.

Cohen (1972) explains this behavior from the perspective of "strangeness" versus "familiarity" by looking at the extent, variety, and degree of change from normal life tourists seek or are capable of seeking in their various contacts with the host community. The degree to which strangeness or familiarity prevails in the tourist's activities determines the nature of the tourism experience, as well as the effects he or she has on the host society. Although all tourists are to some extent strangers in the host community, different tourists have different abilities to engage that strangeness. Some tourists, those Cohen describes as explorers and drifters (or in his later categorization [Cohen 1979] as experiential, experimental, and existential tourists), travel explicitly to engage themselves as fully as possible in the alien environment. Most tourists, though, are interested in experiencing only limited degrees of strangeness and novelty. This large group of tourists has been labeled by Cohen (1972) as institutionalized or individualized mass tourists (or later [Cohen 1979] as recreational and diversionary tourists).

Recreational tourists want or need to experience the novelty of a destination in an enjoyable yet nonthreatening way. They do this by enveloping themselves in their own environmental bubble. The environmental bubble is essentially a social or cultural safety blanket that surrounds the tourist with the known or familiar, enabling the person to sample the unfamiliar while not being overwhelmed by it. Different tourists have different abilities to cope with strangeness and therefore require different environmental bubbles. Some will be incapable of traveling without all the creature comforts of home and thus will demand a huge environmental bubble before travel to unfamiliar places becomes possible. Others will eschew the norm and will seek purposefully experiences that force them out of their comfort zones.

The idea of strangeness versus familiarity relates to the level of perceived risk a person is willing to accept. Risk theory argues that people adopt a number of strategies to reduce risk to a tolerable level, either by reducing the amount at stake (reducing that which the person hoped to gain or reducing penalties for failure) or by increasing the degree of certainty that no loss will occur. Risk is especially relevant for international tourists, for virtually all of their purchases will be new buys (Mitchell and Greatorex 1990). Not only that, but many products that are particular to the host region or host nation may never have been seen before, heightening the potential risk of an unsatisfying experience. Although this adds to the richness of a holiday, it also adds to the risk of purchase. Mitchell and Greatorex (1990) ascertain that this lack of familiarity coupled with the general newness of the environment being visited is likely to cause consumers to have increased risk perception. Providing an environmental bubble is one means this risk can be reduced to a tolerable level.

Plog's (1974) categorization of tourists, along a normal bell curve behavioral continuum based on the amount of change they can withstand, helps develop this idea further. *Allocentric tourists* are found at one end of his continuum. They are interested in experiencing as much change and strangeness as possible in the tourist experience. Allocentrics travel to sharpen their perspectives of the world, for educational or cultural motives, or for learning and increased appreciation. They seek to change, personally challenge, and eschew, as much as possible, any form of environmental bubble.

At the other extremity are *psychocentric tourists*. These people are reluctant tourists who can withstand the least amount of change from their home environment. Psychocentrics travel to familiar places or to places that they have seen or read about. Travel is possible only if they surround themselves with a large environmental bubble. This group rarely travels internationally, takes few risks, and may even find travel to unfamiliar domestic destinations or to visit novel experiences unappealing.

The vast majority of tourists fall somewhere between these two extremes. Plog labeled them *midcentric tourists*. Midcentrics travel primarily for relaxation, pleasure, for a change of pace, or for escape. They are attracted to destinations because of their glamour or beauty and are often motivated to travel to have sensual indulgences satisfied. These people seek some level of change when they travel but, because they are traveling for pleasure and recreation purposes, want change only to the point that it does not impinge on their ability to enjoy their vacation.

Most travelers are not adventuresome drifters who want to take the destination of their choice as it is presented to them. These people exist, but they are a clear minority (Jackson 2000). Instead, most people travel for pleasure, escape, or for personal benefits. Indeed, some people are now questioning if the typical midcentric tourist is more closely aligned to psychocentrics, in terms of wanting a highly controlled experience that highlights satisfaction over change (Jackson 2000; Jackson et al. 2000). Being rational consumers, they wish to maximize the potential for an enjoyable experience while minimizing the risk of an unsatisfactory one. The provision of an appropriate environmental bubble will achieve that goal.

Participation in adventure tourism activities illustrates this point. Commercial activities that emphasize the thrill aspect of an activity or that facilitate ease of participation are more popular than activities that require high skill levels or great physical exertion. White-water rafting provides a thrilling adventure in a large environmental bubble (large rafts, guides, many participants). It is a much more popular consumer activity than a small environmental bubble activity such as white-water canoeing, where the individual's ability to successfully negotiate rapids depends directly on that person's skill levels. By the same token, a large environmental bubble activity such as downhill skiing or snowboarding is more popular than a small environmental bubble activity such as cross-country skiing.

Cultural tourism is no different, except that the environmental bubble tends to address intellectual and emotional risk factors rather than physical concerns. Participation rates in cultural tourism experiences are enhanced when an environmental bubble is provided that facilitates easier consumption of the product. The examples of bundling, concentrating use, creating precincts, and festivals cited in the previous chapter are all forms of environmental bubble construction that reduce the risk of having an unsatisfying experience while at the same time facilitating greater use levels.

How Strangeness versus Familiarity Affects Product Delivery

Strangeness versus familiarity is an interesting sociological concept, but it means little unless a link can be made between it and the delivery of tourism products. At a practical level, strangeness reduction makes a product more accessible and, therefore, easier to consume. Indeed, to a very real extent, much of the process of tourism product development involves some form of strangeness reduction. Strangeness reduction is often denigrated in the tourism literature (Belk and Costa 1995; Mason 1996; Urry 1990), but it plays an essential role in transforming a cultural heritage asset into a cultural tourism product. Hughes (1998), for example, observes that both the tourist and the arts industries have standardized their product to satisfy consumer demand and enable effective signification to the consumer. Similarly, museums combine consumption activities with personal experiences that appeal to a larger number of people from different backgrounds (Tufts and Milne 1999; Prideaux and Kininmont 1999).

Minimal strangeness reduction may involve nothing more than signage or directional arrows. The provision of multilingual guides who can place the assets in some context represents a stronger form of strangeness reduction. The creation of purpose-built spaces, such as museums, where the visitor can experience and celebrate society's past and form a sense of its cultural identity represents an even greater form of strangeness reduction.

Packaged guided tours, encasing an experience in a large environment bubble, is an extreme form of strangeness reduction. Some people see them as low-contact, brief, and shallow experiences that provide a means to experience a foreign culture safely, in comfort, and without having to alter customary living patterns (Belk and Costa 1995). That may be true; but they are also immensely popular, suggesting that travel within a large environmental bubble is the only way many people may be able to gain any foreign tourism experience. The provision of a large environmental bubble is the very reason why tourists purchase packaged tours because it allows an individual to experience strangeness safely, not in spite of it.

Purpose-built cultural theme parks represent another type of extreme environmental bubble formation by creating themed spaces offering a safe, controlled, and controllable environment (Craik 1997) (see Photo 8.1). Indeed, Craik (1999) elsewhere argues that tourists often prefer recreated sites for their ability to provide a guaranteed, enjoyable tourism experience. The demand for more purpose-built artificial tourism environments is one of the dominant emerging trends in tourism (Jones 1998). This point is not lost on theme-park operators. A report on the future of theme parks in international tourism (Jones and Robinett 1998) notes that they are increasingly becoming a symbol and showcase for regional culture but warns of the risks that by being too serious about "cultural" tourism the parks may cease to be fun. It stresses that consultants must counsel their clients continually that a theme park's primary objective is entertainment

PHOTO 8.1. Cultural Theme Park Outside Seoul, South Korea

Strangeness reduction can increase access, especially if large-scale tourism is desired. An extreme form of strangeness reduction that is very effective is the development of cultural theme parks, such as this one outside Seoul, South Korea, where visitors can be exposed to traditional cultures in a nonthreatening environment. Cultural theme parks, though often derided as lacking authenticity, represent a practical and often desirable means of introducing visitors to local cultures, maximizing the economic returns of tourism, and also minimizing its sociocultural impacts. Tourists know they are entering a tourist space. Performers know that they are providing a show for the visitor.

and that it is the entertainment "sugar" that makes the learning and culture "pill" work (quotation marks as per original, pp. 9-10).

Considered another way, commodification, standardization, and modification represent a form of value adding that increases the value of the experience for the tourist, thus enabling the operator to increase the price that can be charged to consume it. Apart from reducing strangeness and making the products more accessible, these actions serve a number of other purposes for the tourist, the tourism industry, and the asset itself. The benefits of strangeness reduction are summarized in Table 8.1.

Reducing strangeness provides a number of real benefits to the tourist in terms of reduced risk, enhanced enjoyment, certainty about the experience, the ability to place the experience within a known cultural context, and, ultimately, to provide greater confidence in the product being consumed. The tourism industry and the attraction itself benefit by the standardization, modification, and commodification of its products to achieve efficiency in operations, reduce costs, and to provide some certainty of experience. Also important, strangeness reduction broadens the market base, making it more accessible to a larger number of consumers. If it is done in a sensitive manner, commodification will serve to satisfy the needs of disparate groups of visitors from those seeking a deep experience to those visiting for purely pleasure/sightseeing reasons.

CREATING CULTURAL TOURISM PRODUCTS OR ATTRACTIONS

What needs to be done to transform a cultural heritage asset into a cultural tourism product? All successful cultural tourism attractions seem to share some common features:

- Tell a story
- Make the asset come alive
- Make the experience participatory
- Make the experience relevant to the tourist
- Focus on quality and authenticity

Each of these features is interrelated but will be discussed separately. Of course, this discussion is predicated on an appreciation of the

TABLE 8.1. Benefits of Standardizing, Modifying, and Commodifying Cultural Tourism Products

Benefits to the Tourist	Benefits to the Tourism Industry	Benefits to the Cultural Heritage Asset
Safety/Risk Reduction		
Increased safety, reduced physical risk while traveling	Control the actions of the visitor	Control the actions of the visitor
Greater personal and psychological security	Control experience that reduces real risk	Control experience that reduces real risk
Optimize use of time	Optimize limited time use by showing highlights	Optimize limited time use by showing highlights
Overcome inhibitions or distractions that may hinder participation	Make the product more accessible	Make the product more accessible
Thrill over skill (make it accessible)		Greater ability to manage the asset by controlling tourist actions
Highlight novelty of experience		
Observe without experiencing in an uncomfortable way		
Easier to consume, lower-involvement purchase decision		
Satisfaction/Experiential		
Explain key message or core benefit more easily	Explain key message or core benefit more easily	Explain key message or core benefit more easily
More confidence in buying a packaged, known product	Value added by being able to charge for knowledge and skill	Value added by being able to charge for knowledge and skill
Guarantee a quality experience as often as possible, thus enhancing customer satisfaction	Guarantee a quality experience as often as possible, thus enhancing customer satisfaction	Guarantee a quality experience as often as possible, thus enhancing customer satisfaction
Ease of consumption	Ease of consumption	Ease of consumption
Facilitate consumption of more experiences	Ordered, predictable experience	Ordered, predictable experience
Satisfy latent need by actualizing the product	Provide experiences demanded by the visitor	Provide experiences demanded by the visitor
Overcome cultural distance problems		

TABLE 8.1 *(continued)*

Benefits to the Tourist	Benefits to the Tourism Industry	Benefits to the Cultural Heritage Asset
Ability to place the experience within the visitor's own frame of reference		
Business Considerations		
	Efficient processing of clients and the ability to process more clients	Efficient processing of clients and the ability to process more clients
Cheaper	Achieve economies of scale in product delivery	Achieve economies of scale in product delivery
Wider market appeal	Make the product accessible to more people	Make the product accessible to more people
	Enhanced profitability, increased income, and reduced costs	Enhanced profitability, increased income, and reduced costs

realities of how tourism works, as discussed in Chapter 3. If an underlying appreciation of what tourism is; what drives tourism; the geographical factors that influence the success of a destination; the appreciation of the hierarchy of attractions; and the realization of where the asset fits in that hierarchy and the presence of suitable infrastructure, support facilities, and additional activities is lacking, no amount of transformation will produce a viable tourism product.

Tell a Story

Cultural and heritage tourism places have been described as destinations with a story, with cultural tourism described as the process of telling that story (Cass and Jahrig 1998a). This is an oversimplification of cultural tourism, of course, but it illustrates how some tourism people regard it. The story may be told in many ways and at many levels so that the consumer can choose which level he or she wishes to engage the place. Cultural assets have little meaning on their own unless their context or, for want of a better word, their story can be conveyed. The world is full old buildings. The world is full of museums. The world is full of evidence of historical or prehistoric occupation by ancient peoples. For the most part, these have little meaning to tourists whose knowledge of local history and culture may be minimal. Weaving a story around a place, a tangible asset, or an intangible asset instills that asset with some meaning, bringing it to life and making it relevant. It also creates consumer interest in hearing that story firsthand. Telling a story also provides signals as to how the tourist should interpret or use the asset. What stories are selected to be told also provide signals about what activities are acceptable or unacceptable at that asset.

Make the Asset Come Alive

Telling a story makes the asset come alive and this makes discovering it more exciting for the tourist (Tilden 1977). The United States National Trust for Historic Preservation states in its excellent booklet about how to succeed in heritage tourism (NTHP 1999: 13), "The human drama of a history is what visitors want to discover, not just names or dates. Interpreting assets is important, but so is making the message creative and exciting." Being entertained is an important part of most experiences. Having an enjoyable experience enhances visitor satisfaction but also, equally important, creates opportunities for learning either directly or indirectly. If the tourism experience is enjoyable and engrossing, the visitor will be motivated to spend more time at the attraction, which will enhance his or her chance of consuming it at a deeper level. If, on the other hand, the presentation is dry and alienating, the visitor will not engage the asset in any meaningful manner.

Make It a Participatory Experience

Tourism by its very nature is an active, participatory experiential activity. The very nature of the physical plant of most cultural tourism attractions, such as museums, festivals, historic assets, cultural assets, and arts centers, should encourage participation. These experiences can be enjoyed best by wandering through the attraction and by engaging it at a personal level. Providing opportunities to do so enhances the experience for the visitor.

Make It Relevant to the Tourist

Few people would argue with the first three points. However, it is important to appreciate who the story is being told to, for whom the asset is made to come alive, and who will engage the asset. Cultural tourism attractions are first and foremost tourism products, and products exist to satisfy the needs, wants, and desires of consumers. As such, they must be made relevant to the person who will be consuming the attraction (see Photo 8.2). That is, they must be presented in such a way that they relate to the tourists' knowledge and frame of reference.

The challenge is both to control the image and to foster an image that will appeal to the desired type of visitor. Because of their status in the tourism hierarchy, and because of the nature of the tourism distribution system linking the consumer to the product, many cultural tourism attractions are many steps removed from the tourist when the decision is made to visit a destination. The result is that the message

PHOTO 8.2. Archaeological Site, Kingdom of Tonga

Good cultural heritage management practice is not necessarily good tourism practice! Presentation of assets must be relevant to the tourist and also easy for them to consume. Here, in the Kingdom of Tonga, good cultural heritage management practice at an archaeological site has been transformed into a poor tourism attraction. Large sections of a heritage report are reproduced word for word in interpretive material. The sign is too long and is difficult to read, alienating tourists rather than attracting them. This is a classic example of the failure to appreciate the needs of the tourist when designing interpretive material.

the tourist receives may be quite different from the message the attraction owners or managers would like the tourist to receive. This issue is explored in greater detail in Chapter 9.

Focus on Quality and Authenticity

Finally, a focus on quality and authenticity should be axiomatic considerations for any cultural tourism attraction. Cultural tourists are upscale, well-educated, well-traveled, and sophisticated visitors who are looking for a unique and interesting experience. Although their knowledge of specific assets or specific cultures may be limited, they are still far more culturally aware than ever before. Further, as more and more communities realize the potential of cultural tourism, competition for the cultural tourist dollar will intensify. A sophisticated tourist offered many choices will select the best value option, combining quality and price. The days have well and truly passed where low-quality experiences can satisfy the gullible tourist.

TACTICS

Transforming the asset into a tourist attraction involves constructing or fabricating it to make it appealing and relevant to the tourist. Especially for assets designed for mass consumption, the story must be simple and singular in its theme to comply with accepted advertising procedures (Bird 2000). This process creates a number of challenges for asset managers and is also a source of much controversy over the presentation of culture for tourism consumption (Palmer 1999; Rojek 1997).

Much cultural and heritage tourism serves a covert and, in some cases, an overt role in creating or reinforcing national myths, cultural symbols, and ethnic identities. As Palmer (1999: 317) indicates, "The nationalistic messages of the heritage tourism must, therefore, have an impact on how individuals within that nation conceive of their personal identity and, by the same token, how the nation and its people are perceived by others." Thus, for example, national historic assets and monuments tend to promote those mythic events that were central to the formation of the core national story. Alternatively, cultural tourism assets promoted by minority cultures tend to highlight their unique features or differences from the core culture, illustrate how minority cultures have remained vibrant against overwhelming odds, or promote alternative histories that are relevant to these groups but may contradict the better known core history.

The cultural tourist is motivated to hear this story, whether it is to reaffirm a connection to a core or minority culture, to reaffirm stereotypical attitudes of the core or minority culture, or to reject core and minority cultural values. It is for this reason that the cultural tourism experience must be carefully manufactured. Indeed, as reprehensible as it may sound, the manufacturing of experiences typically involves distortion, myth, and fabrication in the social construction of tourist assets to ensure that the message is received. Rojek (1997) illustrates how this is used effectively at Nazi concentration camp sites, especially in light of the success of the movie *Schindler's List*.

This issue touches on the much broader issues of whose history is presented, power and power relationships in culture, cultural hegemony, the ownership of the past, and the whole issue of national mythmaking. Nonetheless, the reader must be cognizant that tourism does not work in isolation of the broader sociopolitical context of the destination region. Notwithstanding these comments, commercial viability, and not politics, is the operator's primary concern. A number of tactics are available to transform a cultural asset into a consumable tourism product:

- Mythologize the asset
- Build a story around the asset
- Emphasize its otherness
- Show a direct link from the past to the present
- Make it triumphant
- Make it a spectacle
- Make it a fantasy
- Make it fun, light, and entertaining

The tactic or tactics chosen will depend on a combination of factors relating to the physical and the emotional characteristics of the asset, the desired cultural heritage management goals, the desired experience to be provided, and the existing knowledge or level awareness of the asset and the tourist. Clearly these factors are interrelated, for the physical and emotional characteristics of the asset will influence how it is managed. By the same token, the existing knowledge or level of awareness by visitors influences their behavior, which may influence directly or indirectly management activities. Well-known assets or assets that have a strong position in the consumer's mind will predispose the visitor to an expected experience and, thus, to expected behavior. The expectations for the known assets will be much lower, while tourist behavior will be less predictable at places that fall outside of the visitor's normal frame of reference.

Mythologize the Asset

Mythologizing an asset transforms it from the mundane to the extraordinary and converts a physical asset into a place of spiritual or secular significance. Two tactics are available in mythologizing a asset: tying it to existing myths or creating a new myth. The first option is easier, for national myths tend to be known and are often focused around precise geographic locations. It is, therefore, easier to create an association between a place and an existing strong myth. A number of communities in Texas, for example, are linking their destinations to the state's core myths as the home of the Wild West. San Antonio is targeting the cultural tourism market with a strategy named in 1999 as "Beyond the Alamo" (Richelieu 1999), while Fort Worth runs cattle drives down the streets of Cowtown (Wood 1999).

Creating new myths is difficult unless some form of mass media promotion of the myth occurs or unless the destination has undergone a paradigmatic social or political shift away from existing myths. Mythmaking is still very much in evidence, for example, in postcolonial countries and postcommunist countries, where it is in the best political interest of governments to create new national myths that establish new identities that are distinct from their former identities. The process of new mythmaking is evident in countries such as the "new" postapartheid South Africa. Robben Island, the penal colony where Nelson Mandela was jailed for twenty-eight years, has been converted into a cultural pilgrimage asset to witness the place where the struggle to free South Africa was focused (see Photo 8.3). Mandela's cell has assumed the status of a sacred site within Robben Island.

PHOTO 8.3. Robben Island, Near Capetown, Republic of South Africa

Robben Island, near Capetown, is the prison where Nelson Mandela was incarcerated for almost a quarter of a century. It has become a popular and important tourist attraction in postapartheid South Africa. In many ways, Robben Island is now being presented as something akin to a "sacred site." The content of the story presented to visitors and the manner in which it is presented also appear carefully crafted to create a new national myth that is relevant to contemporary South Africa.

The tour that most people take presents a selective history of the island, focusing on the apartheid era, while rarely mentioning its earlier history. Tour guides are former prisoners. They talk of the solidarity among all prisoners and the hope they shared while imprisoned. One guide stated that the prison was more like a university, with the prisoners acting as teachers educating the white guards. A highlight of any tour is the cell once occupied by Nelson Mandela, which is in the process of being converted into a shrine.

Build a Story Around the Asset

Alternatively, if the place does not have the potential to be mythologized yet is interesting nonetheless, it is possible to build a story around it that will make a visit enjoyable. The story may be based on historic fact or may be based on a fictional character. It matters little, just as long as it is a good, enduring story. *Anne of Green Gables,* the classic children's tale by Lucy Maude Montgomery, is set in Prince

Edward Island, Canada. This is a typical example of a cultural tourism destination that has grown up around a story (Squire 1996). Although Anne never existed, the story of the red-haired orphan has captured the imagination of much of the world. Anne's fictional home, Green Gables, is the focal point of a thriving tourism industry on Prince Edward Island that includes a resort, golf course, restaurants and souvenir sales. Likewise, rural communities in Virginia are capitalizing on the *Coal Miner's Daughter* theme to show their links to Appalachia and country music, while fictional settings for television shows have become popular tourist assets in cities throughout America (e.g., various spots in Chicago and New York).

Emphasize Its Otherness

A third tactic available is to emphasize the otherness of a place in terms of the tourist's frame of reference. This tactic is used in domestic tourism destinations to highlight differences from the core culture. Multicultural tourism, also known as ethnic tourism, is gaining wide popularity in America and elsewhere (Cass and Jahrig 1998b). Indeed, in the early 1990s, the United States Travel and Tourism Administration and the Minority Business Development Agency launched a joint economic initiative to increase awareness of minority historical and cultural tourism destinations (Doggett 1993). The rationale was partly to generate economic and business development opportunities but also to foster cross-cultural understanding. The approach used with international tourists is to highlight how different the culture of a destination is from the tourist's core culture. In doing so, however, it is important that tourists can relate the experience to their frames of reference.

Show a Direct Link from the Past to the Present

History comes alive when a direct link between the past and present can be established. Heritage theme parks are popular tourist destinations because they show a direct link from a region's historic origins to its current status. The presentation is often idealized or fictionalized, concentrating different historical eras or events into a confined space. They are popular, however, because they allow the tourist to consume a wide array of experiences designed specifically for them at one venue.

Make It Triumphant

Making a place triumphant or extraordinary sets it apart from other, more common places. If the place can be made triumphant, then visiting it assumes more importance than if it is seen to be common. Literally hundreds and thousands of battlefield sites exist around the world. The ones that stand out, though, tend to be those places where turning points in wars occurred (Waterloo, Hastings, Quebec, Bull Run, Bunker Hill). What assets people are aware of and therefore want to visit are those that are most spectacular, either in terms of their historical impact or in terms of sheer human carnage. Parks Canada, for example, commemorates certain historical events as part of interpreting the cultural significance of its historic parks and heritage places it manages for visitation.

Ironically, places illustrative of defeat, failure, or incredible human suffering can achieve a similar status, providing their scale is exceptional. Here, size or historical significance does seem to count. Little Big Horn is spectacular because of the sheer scale of the defeat suffered by General Custer. Nazi death camps have achieved status as cultural tourism attractions partly because of the scale of the atrocities committed by Hitler but also because of the triumph of the human spirit in surviving such horrendous conditions. To succeed, however, these places are usually presented in a manner that conveys the horror of the past within a contemporary context that is peaceful and hopeful. Thus, for example, battlefield sites are presented in a peaceful serene manner, even though they were the scene of terrible bloodshed.

Make It a Spectacle

Cultural festivals succeed because they create a spectacle. Subcultures are thriving in virtually every city, yet most people are unaware of them unless there is some reason to focus attention on them (Cass and Jahrig 1998b). Much ethnic tourism relies on this maxim. Festivals and events serve the purpose of concentrating attention into a finite time frame as well as creating a critical mass of activities to convert the event into a spectacle (see Photo 8.4). Making something a spectacle implies that the person will have a special experience while

PHOTO 8.4. A-Ma Temple, Macau SAR

Lunar New Year is a time for celebration throughout much of Asia. For many tourists, the spectacle of the season, as seen here at the A-Ma temple in Macau, is in itself part of the attraction. Lunar New Year celebrations are a total sensory experience involving sight, sound, touch, taste, and smell. The tourist is overwhelmed by the sight and noise of the fireworks, the smell of incense, the taste of the smoke, and the visual sensations of the holiday period.

attending, and also important, implies that those who do not attend will miss out on something special. Live music is available in most large cities every night of the week. Yet a music festival turns attendance at live concerts into a special event.

Make It a Fantasy

The popularity of castles and stately homes as cultural tourist attractions has as much to do with the fantasy element as it does with the physical presence of magnificent buildings. Transforming fantasy into reality, even if that reality is experienced in a fleeting and vicarious manner, is an important element in the cultural tourism experience of a large number of people who are motivated to participate for entertainment and escapist reasons. Purpose-built theme parks, historic assets, and historic week creations of the events of allow people to speculate what it was like to live back then.

Make It Fun, Light, and Entertaining

Finally, cultural tourism does not have to be oppressive. We have already shown that the majority of people who visit cultural and heritage tourism attractions are not seeking a deep learning experience. Many are looking to be entertained; many others may be simply looking for something interesting to do as an incidental activity in their vacation. Making the cultural experience fun, light, and entertaining is important for many tourists; it is still possible to get some important points across about the asset's importance or cultural significance.

CONCLUSIONS

Far from denigrating places, the standardization, modification, and commodification of cultural assets plays a vital role in facilitating tourism consumption. Indeed, transforming cultural assets into cultural tourism attractions provides a number of benefits for the tourist, the tourism industry that facilitates use, and of the asset itself. Most tourists travel for pleasure, to seek strange and different experiences, but only to the extent that they are nonthreatening. Commodifying experiences encourages safe consumption. In doing so, it adds value to the tourism industry, enabling products to be sold. Developing the asset around the tourists' needs enables the asset managers to control the experience and to better impart the desired message. Successful cultural tourism attractions share some common features and also adopt common strategies to present their products.

Chapter 9

The Cultural Tourism Market: A Cultural Tourism Typology

INTRODUCTION

Who are cultural tourists? On the surface, this question seems straightforward, but, as with everything to do with cultural tourism, the issue is enmeshed in layers of complexity. Just as no two cultural tourism products are exactly the same, no two cultural tourists are exactly the same. However, groups of cultural tourists do share similar behavioral characteristics, allowing us to categorize them into broad classes. Five types of cultural tourists are identified in this chapter.

WHO ARE CULTURAL TOURISTS?

As recently as fifteen years ago, cultural tourism was thought of as a small niche market. Today, if the figures are to be believed, cultural tourism is firmly established as a mainstream, mass tourism activity. The World Tourism Organization, for instance, estimates that cultural tourism accounts for 37 percent of all tourist trips and that demand is growing by 15 percent per annum (Richards 1996c). Based on its estimate of 650 million international trips taken each year (Sugaya 1999), about 240 million international trips can be attributed, at least in part, to cultural tourism. Antolovic (1999) reports that 70 percent of all Americans traveling to Europe seek a cultural heritage experience, and about 67 percent of all of visitors to the United Kingdom are seeking a cultural heritage tourism experience as part of their trip, but not necessarily as the main reason to visit the United Kingdom. A study by an American shopping center developer reported that about 40 percent of international visitors to the United States engaged in cultural tourism (Anonymous 1998; Kemmerling Clack 1999). Nearly half of all American domestic travelers, almost 65 million people, participated in some type of cultural or heritage tourism activity, such as visiting a historic site or museum, or attending a musical arts or other cultural event in 1996 (Kerstetter, Confer, and Bricker 1998; Miller 1997a; Craine 1998; Kemmerling Clack 1999). In California, 45 percent of overseas visitors went to historic sites (Anonymous 1999a). About 90 percent of Canadians are interested in visiting heritage sites, including Aboriginal sites (Campbell 1994). Even in more remote areas such as the Australian island state of Tasmania, more than 60 percent of all tourists visit cultural heritage sites or restored buildings (TVS 1995).

Cultural tourists are portrayed as an attractive and easily differentiated market segment, which explains some of the excitement about this phenomenon. Research based primarily in America or on Americans traveling to Europe suggests that cultural tourists are older, better educated, and more affluent than the traveling public as a whole (Richards 1996c; DKS 1999; Kerstetter, Confer, and Bricker 1998; Formica and Uysal 1998; Craine 1999; Prentice, Witt, and Hamer 1998; Kemmerling Clack 1999). Women constitute an important part of this market (Bond 1997; Silberberg 1995). Further, cultural tourists are frequent travelers who tend to stay longer at a destination, spend more while there, and join in more activities than other tourists (Anonymous n.d.; Miller 1997a,b; Anonymous 1999b; Silberberg 1995; Richards 1996b; Blackwell 1997; DKS 1999; Kemmerling Clack 1999). A small but growing number of voices, however, says that cultural demographic and trip profile characteristics are unreliable indicators of cultural tourists (Prentice, Witt, and Hamer 1998). Our own research in Hong Kong, as well, shows that demographic and trip profile characteristics are useful in differentiating American cultural tourists from other American tourists but are not reliable in differentiating cultural tourists from other countries from non–cultural tourists.

Importantly, macrodemographic shifts suggest that this market will continue to grow. Aging baby boomers, who are the biggest single growth market in tourism in general, are also recognized as the largest potential market for many cultural and heritage tourism attractions (Dickinson 1996; Sugaya and Brooks 1999). As people age, they become more interested in their cultural roots, in things historic, and in developing a greater understanding of the past (Lowenthal 1985; Dickinson 1996). Indeed, the over-fifty market and seniors are felt to hold the greatest potential for growth in cultural tourism (Dickinson 1996).

Likewise, a direct correlation has been shown between education level and interest in such activities as cultural and heritage tourism. The desire to learn about things beyond one's own backyard, to learn about alternative lifestyles and cultures, and to experience different things is directly related to educational levels. As Coathup (1999) illustrates, a better-educated global population is motivated more to travel for cultural enrichment and self-enlightenment. Therefore, as education levels rise, so too should demand for cultural tourism activities.

Are These Figures Reliable?

How reliable are the figures currently being promulgated so widely about the size and, therefore, implied importance of the cultural tourism market? Does a figure such as the one promoted by the WTO indicate that 37 percent of tourists are motivated to travel largely for cultural tourism reasons? Or does it mean that 37 percent of travelers, regardless of their reasons for traveling, will participate in a cultural tourism activity sometime during their trip? The answer is important for tourism marketers, destination managers, the travel industry, and asset managers, for there is a substantial difference between primary trip purpose and participation rates.

The use of any definition of tourist implies or is felt to infer strongly primacy of purpose. Labeling someone a *business traveler,* implies that their primary reason for visiting a destination is to conduct business. Likewise, calling someone a *VFR tourist* (visiting family and relatives) suggests that this person chose a destination primarily to visit friends and relatives. So too would one think that primacy of purpose is implied when the label *cultural tourist* is applied. Being a cultural tourist, to most people, means that cultural tourism plays a key role in the selection of a destination and in activities pursued while at the destination. It further implies that the person is motivated to travel for cultural tourism reasons and will seek deep experiences while traveling.

But that is not the case. Virtually all of the figures presented above document participation rates in cultural tourism activities and not centrality of purpose. A cultural tourist is defined as someone who visits a named cultural or heritage attraction, a museum, art gallery, historic site, goes on a cultural or heritage tour, attends a festival, sees a live performance, or participates in some other defined activity at some point during their trip, regardless of the reason for visiting the destination. None of these studies assesses main trip purpose or how important cultural tourism was in the decision to visit a destination.

Tourists participate in a wide variety of activities when they travel. Some activities relate directly to the primary purpose of the visit, but most of them do not. A business traveler may do some duty-free shopping before returning home. Would you label that person a shopping tourist? Probably not, unless the person felt the label applied. Would you label a tourist who has a bottle of wine with a meal as a wine tourist? Again, probably not, even if the wine was very nice. Would you call a convention delegate who attends a reception in an art gallery a cultural tourist? Probably not. Yet that is exactly what happens with cultural tourism. Because someone participates in a named activity, that person is labeled as a cultural tourist with all the connotations such a label implies.

In reality, participation in many cultural tourism activities may represent nothing more than an incremental activity that completes the trip experience. Why does there appear to be a relationship between cultural tourism participation, length of stay, and first-time visitation? Is it because a destination's cultural assets motivate people to stay longer or to visit in the first place? Either may be the case. Is it because long-stay visitors have more time to participate in a greater number of activities, including cultural activities, while first-time visitors generally tend to participate in more activities than repeat visitors? Is cultural tourism a cause or beneficiary of longer stays and first-time visits? This question cannot be answered unless the critical issue of centrality is resolved.

Destinations promote their cultural highlights as part of the bundle of attractions offered to recreational tourists who may be visiting for other reasons. Cultural tourism, for example, has been promoted as an incremental activity that wine tourists can pursue while in Spain (Gilbert 1992). Likewise, Sugaya suggests (1999), "It would not be uncommon to find travelers with Ubud, the cultural center of Bali, on their itinerary as well as the beaches [which is their main reason for visiting Bali]" (Sugaya 1999: 3). Indeed, conference and incentive travel planners promote cultural tourism strongly as a novel form of entertainment that offers a break from the main business of the trip (Anonymous 1999c; Giles 1995; Schweitzer 1999). In all these cases, cultural tourism represents an element of a visit but not the main reason for the visit.

A TYPOLOGY OF CULTURAL TOURISTS: RECOGNIZING DIFFERENT SHADES OF CULTURAL TOURISTS

For many if not most tourists, a visit to a cultural or heritage attraction represents a discretionary or secondary trip activity and not the main reason for travel. Ecotourism provides a strong example, for this been one of the hard lessons learned from the ecotourism sector. Just because someone visits a protected area at some point during a trip does not make that person an ecotourist in the truest sense of the term (Acott, La Trobe, and Howard 1998). Instead, it is now recognized that many shades of ecotourist exist, ranging from the archetypal deep ecotourist, representing a small fraction of the total market, to the very shallow ecotourist, whose actions are more akin to the mass tourist (Acott, La Trobe, and Howard 1998). Each of the different types has substantially different needs and demonstrates quite different behavior.

The same situation applies in cultural tourism, where a divergence of cultural tourist types exists. Some cultural tourists will be motivated to visit primarily to consume a region's cultural or heritage assets and will seek a deep cultural experience when doing so. Others may be equally strongly motivated to visit but may have a qualitatively different experience. For many others, cultural tourism will play a progressively smaller role in the decision to visit a destination. Indeed, cultural tourism may play no part in choosing a destination, even though some tourists may visit cultural tourism attractions.

Five types of cultural tourists are identified in this book, based on the importance of cultural tourism in the overall decision to visit a destination and depth of experience. The types are presented graphically in Figure 9.1. The horizontal axis reflects the centrality of cul-

FIGURE 9.1. A Cultural Tourist Typology

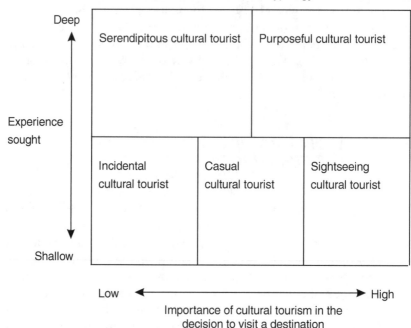

tural tourism in the overall decision to visit a destination. It recognizes that the role cultural tourism plays in the decision to visit a destination can vary from the main or only reason to visit to playing no role in the decision-making process, even though the tourist may still participate in some cultural tourism activities. The vertical axis represents depth of experience. A range of experiences exist, varying from deep or meaningful cultural experiences to entertainment-oriented or largely recreational cultural experiences.

The Centrality Dimension

It is axiomatic, or at least should be, that not all cultural tourists are alike. Any typology of cultural tourists must recognize the centrality or primacy of cultural tourism in the decision to visit a destination. For some people, the chance to gain a cultural or heritage tourism experience will drive the travel decision. Others may plan to have cultural tourism experiences as an important but not central part of the trip. Others still will not preplan visits to cultural or heritage attractions, but will still, nonetheless, visit some sites while they are traveling.

Empirical research is beginning to confirm the intuitive understanding that different types of cultural tourists exist (Anonymous 1999d). A study of cultural resources in the province of Ontario, Canada, for example, identified four discrete types of cultural tourist (Silberberg 1995). At the core are those people who are greatly motivated by cultural tourism. A second segment includes those people who are motivated in part by culture, while a third group involves people for whom culture is an adjunct to another main trip motivation. The study also identified a fourth group that the author labeled "accidental cultural tourists." Accidental cultural tourists do not intend to go to cultural attractions or events but at some point during the trip visit cultural tourist attractions. As the name suggests, attendance is accidental rather than planned.

In a similar manner, the European Association for Tourism and Leisure Education (ATLAS) cultural tourism project identified a difference between *specific* and *general* cultural tourists (Richards 1996c). Specific cultural tourists are those people who traveled specifically to visit the cultural attractions. For them, the attraction was important or very important as a motivation for their choice of destination. They were found to make multiple attraction visits during their stays and, consequently, multiple decisions about what to see. They were also found to be more frequent consumers of cultural attractions than other groups. Using this definition, approximately 9 percent of tourists to Europe could be defined as specific cultural tourists, substantially lower than the 70 percent reported by Antolovic (1999). By contrast, general cultural tourists, who represented the majority of cultural tourists, placed far less importance on cultural tourism in their overall destination decision-making process.

In the United States, the Pennsylvania Department of Conservation and Natural Resources recently commissioned a study of heritage tourism (DKS 1999). An estimated 26 percent of leisure travelers to Pennsylvania participated in heritage activities during the trip. The study team identified three discrete groups of heritage tourists: core heritage travelers (47 percent of the sample), who indicated that heritage tourism is a very important factor in their decision to visit Pennsylvania; moderate heritage travelers (39 percent), who suggested that heritage tourism was a moderately important factor in the decision to visit Pennsylvania; and low heritage travelers (14 percent), who felt that heritage tourism was not an important factor in the decision to visit but who still visited heritage attractions during the trip. Core heritage travelers accounted for about 12 percent of all leisure visitors to Pennsylvania in 1997 but spent a disproportionately high 25 percent of tourism expenditures.

Depth of Experience

Centrality is only one dimension that must be considered when developing a typology of cultural tourists. The other dimension is depth of experience. It is also becoming increasingly evident that different types of tourists seek different benefits from the attractions they visit (Prentice, Witt, and Hamer 1998; Kerstetter, Confer, and Bricker 1998; Sharpley 2000). Increasingly, understanding vacation destination choice involves developing an understanding of the motives for visiting a destination, or, in other words, the personal benefits sought by visiting. Benefit segmentation is recognized as an important way of defining markets effectively which will lead to more effective product development and promotional activities (Moscardo et al. 1995).

It is commonly assumed that centrality of purpose equates to depth of experience, for one would assume that people traveling specifically for cultural tourism purposes would seek a deeper experience than those traveling for other reasons. But this assumption may not be true in all cases, as an individual's capacity to have a deep experience is affected by a wide array of factors, including time availability, prior knowledge, cultural affinity for the asset, education level, and other issues. Thus, two people traveling, ostensibly, primarily for cultural tourism reasons may end up having quite different experiences at the same attraction.

Stebbins (1996: 948) uses the concept of *serious leisure* to explain this phenomenon. He defines serious leisure as the "systematic pursuit of an amateur, hobbyist, or volunteer activity sufficiently substantial and interesting in nature for the participant to find a career there acquiring and expressing a combination of its special skills, knowledge, and experience." To Stebbins, the cultural tourist is akin to a hobbyist, whom he defines as someone who has a profound interest in a topic and who exhibits a certain level of skill, knowledge, conditioning, or experience in pursuit of the hobby. Although cultural tourism may be a major motivation for travel, Stebbins identifies two very different types of hobbyist cultural tourists. The generalized cultural tourist makes a hobby of visiting a variety of different assets and regions. Over time, this cultural tourist acquires a broad, general knowledge of different cultures. The specialized cultural tourist, on the other hand, focuses his or her efforts on one or a small number of geographic sites or cultural entities. This tourist repeatedly visits a particular city or country in search of a deeper cultural understanding of that place or goes to different cities, regions, or countries in search of exemplars of a specific kind of art, history, festival, or museum.

Timothy (1997) addresses the issue of depth of experience from the perspective of the individual's connectivity to an asset. He identifies four levels of heritage tourism attractions: world, national, local, personal. He suggests that tourists have different levels of connectivity to each type of asset and, therefore by implication, have different depths of experience depending on which type of asset is visited. World heritage attractions may draw large masses of tourists that may invoke feelings of awe but probably do not invoke feelings of personal attachment. By contrast, national, local, and personal sites engender progressively stronger feelings of personal connectivity and likely facilitate different depths of experiences by the visitor.

Others (Waller and Lea 1999; McIntosh and Prentice 1999), building on MacCannell's (1973) work, suggest that authenticity or the perception of the pursuit of authenticity may influence depth of experience. McIntosh and Prentice (1999), in particular, explored the relationship between perceived authenticity gained by tourists and their emotive processes with attractions' settings. They found that the depth or the quality of the depth of the experience visitors had with British socioindustrial cultural heritage attractions depended both on the individual thought processes when visiting these attractions and the resultant perceived levels of commodification. Three distinct psychological processes were identified from visitors' reported experiences: reinforced assimilation, cognitive perception, and retroactive association.

FIVE TYPES OF CULTURAL TOURISTS

Combining the two dimensions produces five possible types of cultural tourists.

1. The *purposeful cultural tourist*—cultural tourism is the primary motive for visiting a destination, and the individual has a deep cultural experience (see Photo 9.1).
2. The *sightseeing cultural tourist*—cultural tourism is a primary or major reason for visiting a destination, but the experience is more shallow.
3. The *serendipitous cultural tourist*—a tourist who does not travel for cultural tourism reasons, but who, after participating, ends up having a deep cultural tourism experience.
4. The *casual cultural tourist*—cultural tourism is a weak motive for visiting a destination, and the resultant experience is shallow (see Photo 9.2).
5. The *incidental cultural tourist*—this tourist does not travel for cultural tourism reasons but nonetheless participates in some activities and has shallow experiences.

All five types of cultural tourists can be found at any one time in a destination. The mix of tourist types will vary from destination to destination depending on the destination itself, the asset being visited within the destination, and the origin of the cultural tourist. The overall awareness of the destination and its repute as a cultural tourism node will influence the type of visitor drawn to it. Not only will well-known cultural or heritage destinations attract larger numbers of cultural tourists than lesser-known destinations, they are also more likely to attract more purposeful cultural tourists, cultural sightseers, and casual cultural tourists. Tourists will make a point of visiting such places because of their cultural or heritage renown. Whether these tourists seek a deep or shallow experience is open for debate. As Boniface and Fowler (1993) suggest, just because an asset is well known does not mean it is known well. Some of these visitors will visit for no other reason than to gain the personal status of having visited the destination or to take another photo for their collection. Many visitors will be fundamentally ignorant of the destination or will visit with such limited knowledge that it will be impossible for them to

PHOTO 9.1. Sasenji Temple, Kyoto, Japan

PHOTO 9.2. Hangzhou, China

Some cultural tourists are more serious than others. Attractions should be developed to cater to the type of cultural tourist sought and to provide different levels of engagement for different types of cultural tourist. A purposeful cultural tourist studies more about an ancient temple in Kyoto, Japan (Photo 9.1), while a casual cultural tourist is photographed sightseeing at a temple in Hangzhou, China (Photo 9.2).

have a deep experience. Others, however, will seek and enjoy a purposeful cultural tourism experience.

Lesser-known cultural tourism destinations are likely to attract either purposeful cultural tourists or incidental, casual, and serendipitous cultural tourists. The purposeful cultural tourist will seek the cultural attributes of a destination. This type of person is akin to Stebbin's (1996) specialized cultural tourist. Incidental, casual, and serendipitous cultural tourists, on the other hand, will visit for other reasons yet will take in some of the area's cultural heritage attractions. Most will have a shallow experience—partly because of ignorance about the place's culture and also partly because cultural tourism is a peripheral component of their trip.

By the same token, different sites or attractions within a destination will attract different types of cultural tourists depending on the intensity of experience and the effort required by the individual to gain a satisfactory experience. Museums and art galleries, for example, are more likely to attract purposeful cultural tourists. Streetscapes, historic buildings, and cultural tourism attractions emphasizing fun rather than experiences (including historic theme parks) are more likely to attract people seeking a shallower experience.

Likewise, the categories are not exclusive to any one type of tourist. Depending on the trip taken and the motivation for travel, one person could be identified as all five types of cultural tourist. A person traveling explicitly to visit an art gallery could be labeled as a purposeful or sightseeing cultural tourist. By the same token, the same person taking a family vacation that includes a cultural element may also be labeled a casual or incidental cultural tourist, depending on the importance of cultural tourism factors in the decision to visit a destination. The same person traveling on business who visits a museum and has a deep experience may be labeled, legitimately, a serendipitous cultural tourist.

The mix of cultural tourists at any one destination will also be influenced by the origin of those tourists. For international visitors, the greater the cultural distance between the host culture and the traveler's own culture, the greater the likelihood that the destination will attract purposeful cultural tourists (McKercher and Chow 2001). McIntosh and Goeldner (1990: 257) define cultural distance as "the extent to which the culture of the area from which the tourist originates differs from the culture of the host region . . . the higher the cultural distance between particular origin and destination areas, the more an allocentric person may wish to travel to that destination."

Domestic travelers, on the other hand, are more likely to seek cultural tourism experiences when the places they visit reflect greater cultural proximity. The closer the cultural or heritage attraction is to the core values of the domestic traveler, the greater the likelihood that it will attract the purposeful cultural tourist. Cultural tourism destinations or cultural tourism attractions that reflect durable national ideals or the collective core values of the nation will likely draw more purposeful or sightseeing cultural tourists then assets of lesser value.

Although all types of cultural tourists may be found simultaneously at any one destination or asset, it is important to appreciate that each type will visit the asset for different reasons and will seek different experiences. Cultural tourism is about seeking a sense of place or endowing a place with meaning, but people can imagine different "places" in the same location (Ashworth 1999). This creates interesting management challenges for both asset managers and destination marketers, for their challenge is to make the asset or destination appealing to and relevant for different users.

TESTING THE MODEL: HONG KONG AS A CASE STUDY

The tourist typology was developed from a study of cultural tourism participation in Hong Kong that was conducted in late 1999 that involved a survey of 2,066 departing visitors from six countries: China, Taiwan, Singapore, the United States, the United Kingdom, and Australia. One-third (33.3 percent) of visitors surveyed participated in some form of cultural tourism activity at some time during their visit, a figure that is comparable to the World Tourism Organization's estimate of global cultural tourism. Participation rates varied widely, however, according to the country of origin, with Westerners being one and one-half to two times more likely to participate in cultural tourism than Asian visitors. Americans and Australians were the largest consumers of cultural tourism products, with 41 percent and 39 percent participation rates, respectively.

As shown in Figure 9.2, a majority of Hong Kong's cultural tourists (58 percent) stated that cultural tourism reasons played little or no

FIGURE 9.2. Cultural Tourists in Hong Kong

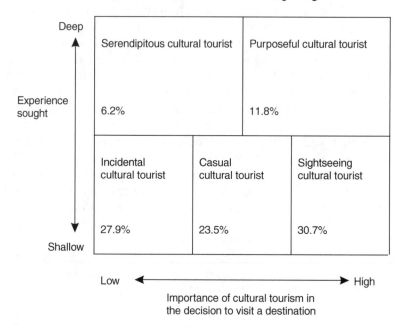

role in their decision to visit Hong Kong. These people still participated in some form of cultural tourism activity, with most of them
having a shallow experience that can be described mostly as sightseeing, photography taking, or learning only a little about Hong Kong's
culture and heritage. By contrast, only about 42 percent of cultural
tourists surveyed indicated that cultural tourism reasons played an
important role or were the main reason they came to Hong Kong.
Even among this group, sightseeing cultural tourists, those who consumed many experiences at a fairly shallow level, outnumbered purposeful cultural tourists by a factor of 2.5 to 1.

Based on raw participation rates, one could assert that 33.3 percent
of tourists to Hong Kong are cultural tourists of some description.
But, on closer inspection, only about 10 percent of all tourists surveyed indicated that cultural tourism played a significant role in their
decision to visit Hong Kong, and only 4 percent of all tourists could be
classified as purposeful cultural tourists—people highly motivated to
travel for cultural tourism reasons who have a deep experience.

Little Difference in Profile of Cultural Tourists

The five types of cultural tourists displayed few significant differences in either their demographic profile or trip behavior, supporting the assertion that these factors are not reliable indicators for cultural tourism (Kerstetter, Confer, and Bricker 1998; Prentice, Witt, and Hamer 1998). Among the few differences noted were that people who identified cultural tourism as playing a more important role in their decision to visit Hong Kong (sightseeing and purposeful cultural tourists) were more likely to be first-time visitors and were also more likely to be members of packaged tours than other cultural tourists. People who identified cultural tourism as playing a lesser role in their decision to visit (serendipitous and incidental cultural tourists) were somewhat more likely to be business travelers or independent tourists.

Significant Differences in Behavior

However, significant differences were noted in the behavior among the different groups. The purposeful cultural tourist was the greatest consumer of museum experiences in general, and was also the greatest consumer of fine arts museums, art galleries, and pottery museums. This type of cultural tourist also chose to visit lesser-known temples and heritage assets. In addition, the purposeful cultural tourist immersed himself or herself in the local culture by going to the many markets scattered throughout Hong Kong.

The sightseeing cultural tourist, on the other hand, was more interested in collecting a wide array of experiences rather than pursuing any one activity in any depth. The quantity of experiences consumed mattered more than the depth of any one experience. This tourist was mostly likely to visit icon attractions and was also most likely to travel widely throughout the territory. Sightseeing and absorbing the streetscape were popular activities reported.

By contrast, incidental cultural tourists visited convenience-based attractions in tourist nodes that were easy to consume and not particularly emotionally or intellectually challenging. For example, the incidental cultural tourist was most likely to visit the Space Museum to see the IMAX cinema or to visit heritage theme parks. The incidental cultural tourist also avoided visiting temples and other religious assets.

The casual cultural tourist exhibited behavior that was largely similar to that of the incidental cultural tourist, except that this person was more amenable to visiting temples and some of the outlying areas. The casual cultural tourist also appeared willing to engage sights more intensely than the incidental cultural tourist, but less intensely than the purposeful cultural tourist. The behavior of serendipitous cultural tourists is the hardest to describe. Discovering something new or unusual about the destination or visiting an attraction with a new or different twist provides the pleasurable experience.

IMPLICATIONS FOR CULTURAL TOURISM

The realization that cultural tourism may represent an ancillary activity for many tourists has significant implications for destination marketers and product developers. Further, the realization that different types of cultural tourists exist with different needs should affect the development and delivery of cultural tourism products and services. Cultural tourism participation may be a mass-market activity, but the core or purposeful cultural tourism market is still a small, niche market. Most mainstream or mass cultural tourists participate in a range of activities largely as subsidiary element of a visit and not as a core activity. Promoting cultural tourism, therefore, may serve to complete a trip experience. But promoting cultural tourism as the main reason for visiting could be counterproductive for all but a few destinations that possess outstanding cultural or heritage assets.

Business opportunities in this sector are likely more limited than the raw participation rates would suggest. Here, ecotourism provides a guiding example. The true size of the commercial ecotourism market, those people who are willing to pay full market rates for quality ecotourism experiences, is only a small fraction of the number of people who visit protected areas, resulting in limited business opportunities (McKercher and Robbins 1998). We feel the same situation applies here. People may participate in cultural tourism activities, but we doubt their willingness to pay a sufficient tariff to make many of these activities commercially viable, unless the product appeals to the mass market cultural tourist who is seeking an easy to consume, enjoyable experience.

The recognition that different types of cultural tourists exist also has product development implications. The purposeful and sightseeing cultural tourists, those people who are motivated largely by cultural or heritage tourism reasons, will explore a destination area seeking experiences. But cultural tourism represents only an adjunct to the trip for incidental, casual, and serendipitous cultural tourists, who constitute the majority of participants. For them, consumption decisions will be based largely on convenience and ease of access. These people will seek experiences in tourism nodes or in shopping precincts but will not venture widely for other experiences.

Similarly, the majority of cultural tourists seem to seek a fairly shallow, easy to consume experience. After all, they are on vacation and are looking for a break from their everyday routine. This means that products must be developed in an appropriate manner for the target audience. This is the theme of the next two chapters.

Chapter 10

Gatekeepers

INTRODUCTION

Knowledge is power. Whoever controls the knowledge imparted to the visitor wields a tremendous amount of power over how the cultural tourism asset is ultimately used. The role of information in conceptualizing a place is well recognized (Dann 1996 as cited in Ryan 2000). It creates an impression of what an asset has to offer and, also important, provides insights into how experiences are to be consumed. Information, therefore, also signals types of behavior that are deemed to be appropriate or inappropriate on-site.

Knowledge exchange is a reciprocal process involving both the product and the tourist. It is accepted that one of the roles of cultural tourism attractions is to impart a desired message to visitors. But this message can be conveyed effectively only if visitors are amenable to it. Likewise, whether well formed or nebulous, tourists usually have certain expectations about what a place has to offer or what the experience will be. Thus, for effective communication, the message must match the consumer's expectations and the consumer's expectations must match the message. In short, understanding visitor expectations is essential in developing effective communication programs (Belland and Boss 1994).

Dissonance is likely to occur if the message is disseminated at the wrong level (e.g., if the consumer's expectations are firmly set on one type of experience prior to arrival and another is offered; if the consumer's mind is closed; if the message involves changing established mind-sets). The results can range from mild disappointment to significant value clash over the role, meaning, and use of cultural assets.

Ideally, the cultural asset should control directly the flow of information to tourists. In doing so, the asset can exploit this knowledge to its own benefit by setting appropriate expectations of what type of experience will be offered and, in doing so, ensuring that the desired type of person is most likely to visit. In practice, however, the asset often has little real control over the type, quality, and veracity of information imparted to the visitor, for it is the last stop on the information chain for most visitors, rather than the first. Instead, knowledge dissemination is vested in a large number of intermediaries or gatekeepers, as we refer to them, that act as an information filtering or relaying medium between the organization and its audience (Seaton and Bennett 1996). Some cultural heritage managers appreciate that the tourism industry and media, in particular, if not given guidance may inadvertently wrongly position the desired heritage experience (Whytock 1999).

Who are these gatekeepers? They comprise all potential intermediaries who advise tourists about travel plans; they are also sources of tourism information consulted by tourists when choosing a destination. They include the commercial travel trade, local tour guides, destination marketing agencies, producers of travel guidebooks, and even family and friends. Nine different classes of gatekeepers are discussed in this chapter. No doubt more exist, but these are the key players involved in informing the visitor about the place. Each gatekeeper gathers information, processes it, and then retransmits it either to other gatekeepers along the communication chain or directly to the traveler. Information forwarded by gatekeepers to the prospective tourist may be selectively modified and the message changed to suit the gatekeeper's own needs, to suit the gatekeeper's perceptions of the traveler's needs, or simply out of ignorance.

The more gatekeepers involved, the greater the likelihood that the message will be presented in a simplified, commodified, or inaccurate manner. The cultural values for which the attraction is known may also be trivialized or presented in a simplified manner to gain the attention of the consumer. At every gatekeeping stage, some control over the information disseminated is lost, which, in turn, means some loss of control over the asset. The inability to control the information imparted means that the asset loses the ability to ensure that the desired message is sent to prospective visitors in a desired way, which, in turn, means a loss of control over how the asset is portrayed and a loss of control over what type of experience can be expected. In short, the inability to control the knowledge flow results in a loss of power over how the asset will be used.

It is difficult to condemn someone's behavior as being inappropriate if the person is acting in a way that has been signaled strongly in promotional materials, by travel agents, or by word of mouth. Thus, in spite of the expressed wishes of the Aboriginal custodians and national park managers, most tourists still go to Uluru (Ayers Rock) in Central Australia expecting to climb, because that is the message conveyed in most tourist brochures (McKercher and du Cros 1998). Likewise, can you condemn tourists who purchase antiquities that may have been looted from archaeological sites when destinations in the developing world promote themselves as havens for antique buying? Can you condemn visitors to the Ainokura district in Japan for failing to show respect for residents who live in the village, for thinking it is just another sightseeing-oriented tourist attraction (Otake 1997)? Can you condemn tourism for being nothing more than a series of superficial photo opportunities, when that type of behavior is encouraged so strongly by tour guides (Urry 1990)? No. In all cases, the tourists are acting in a rational manner based on the information supplied to them by the gatekeepers.

USING CULTURAL AND HERITAGE ASSETS TO BRAND A DESTINATION

Cultural and heritage assets usually feature prominently in destination-branding strategies, for they represent a community's unique features that evoke strong emotional ties between the tourist and the destination. The reason organizations embrace branding is that it is a source of competitive advantage (Aaker 1995; Bharadwaj, Varadarajan, and Fahy 1993). The reason destinations do it is to differentiate themselves from their competitors (Evans, Fox, and Johnson 1995) and to "own" a prominent place in the consumers' minds (Ries and Trout 1986; Bonn and Brand 1995; Jarrett 1996; Chacko 1997). Branding has also been shown to increase use among foreign visitors for it reduces the perceived risk of consuming an unknown product (Mitchell and Greatorex 1990; Dodd 1995).

Creating the right brand associations are especially important when the product being offered is of an aspirational or self-gratifying nature (Selwitz 1998) as is the case with most tourism experiences. Positive brand associations are developed by bundling tangible (product) and intangible (experiential) attributes associated with the brand to meet the guests' needs and wants (Dev, Morgan, and Shoemaker 1995). Within a destination context, these attributes reflect the array of activities available at the destination that complement the overall position sought by that destination.

The features being branded must be presented as a single-minded product to make the brand work effectively (Chacko 1997). Within a tourism context, this task is achieved by commodifying a destination's attractions and bundling them into themed products. These themes, however, are usually developed by public- or private-sector tourism marketing agencies and not by the owners/operators of the attractions being promoted. If the custodians have not been consulted widely about how their asset is positioned in the marketplace, and if this positioning strategy is inimical with their own needs, conflicts can arise.

Partnerships form a large part of the concept of sustainable tourism as a means of overcoming these real issues (UNESCO and Nordic World Heritage Office 1999). To some extent, partnerships work well, providing that the power balance among partners is roughly equal and their goals are compatible. In these cases, the asset can exert some control over how it is used. However, if the power balance is unequal or if the goals of different stakeholders are incompatible, the dominant player may exert its influence to achieve its goals, at the expense of the subservient player. This issue is especially relevant if the commodification occurs by second and third parties that have no direct association with the tangible or intangible asset being promoted. If it is in the best commercial interest of the tourism industry to promote a different message, it will do so.

Standardized Products—Simplified Messages

The realities of tourism come into play here. For the most part, the average length of stay at any destination can be measured in days or even hours. To maximize the return from tourism, tourists are encouraged to consume as many experiences as possible during their stay. Revenue maximization can be achieved only if experiences can be consumed quickly and easily. The benefit is heightened enjoyment but at a cost of loss of depth of experience. This reality is the antithesis of cultural tourism which seeks to foster reflective learning opportunities that can often be achieved only by engaging assets deeply.

The commercial travel trade is a willing conspirator in this commodification process. The travel distribution network sells "commissionable product" through its network of intermediaries. In almost all cases, "commissionable product" involves the creation of a tangible product for sale by agglomerating visits to a number of sites with transport and interpretation. The new product must be packaged in a way that guarantees a certain quality of experience. Such a guarantee can be provided only if the product is standardized (see Photo 10.1). Again, the winner becomes sightseeing while the loser becomes depth of experience.

Time constraints, coupled with the need to process visitors efficiently, mean that the message must be simplified, often to nothing more than a children's story. Tour guides pour soap down a geyser in New Zealand to ensure it erupts promptly at 10:30 every morning illustrating the story of how it was discovered by accident over 100 years ago by a sleeping sheep herder. Well-meaning tour guides giving a tour through the Royal Palace Compound in Bangkok are often more interested in pointing out ideal photo opportunities rather than telling the story of the Palace. Tourists are more interested in the "Coconut Man" (a man who can peel a whole coconut with his bare hands) on the Cook Islands rather than in the story of how his Polynesian ancestors first discovered the islands (see Photo 10.2). Tour guides in San Francisco stop their buses in Chinatown for photographs of Chinese graffiti without imparting anything about the history of Chinatown or Chinese immigration.

It is also recognized that tourists' ability to comprehend cultural assets is variable. Goulding (1999) reminds us that individuals negotiate the meanings of sites and approach them on their own terms. Ryan (2000) further adds that tourists use signs and symbols differently to create their own meanings. It is well documented that both the nature of information search and the type of information needs that people have is variable and usually incomplete (Fodness and Murray 1997; Vogt and Fesenmaier 1998; Stewart and Vogt 1999), meaning that individuals' abilities to negotiate the meanings of sites will also be highly variable. Thus, no guarantee exists that the message will be received in the desired manner by the visitor.

PHOTO 10.1. North Island, New Zealand

An extreme form of product standardization, providing a highly commodified, superficial, short-duration photo experience. Tourists are attracted to visit this geyser because it erupts each morning at precisely 10:30. They are not told the geyser is activated by pouring soap down its funnel in full view of the audience a few minutes beforehand. The geyser dutifully erupts on schedule and visitors take their photos. Almost everyone leaves the scene within ten minutes of the eruption. In the end, the visit provides a good photo but ultimately an unsatisfying experience. Tourists are expecting to see a geyser erupt naturally as implied by the promotional literature. Yet on arrival, they are witnesses to a highly contrived experience.

PHOTO 10.2. "Coconut Man," Cook Islands

An example of cultural tourism as entertainment. The "Coconut Man" at the Cook Island Cultural Centre peels a coconut with his bare hands. This type of experience works very effectively as a cultural tourism attraction offering entertainment-oriented experiences rather than deep learning. The "Coconut Man" performs his trick for the tourist, while the master of ceremonies discusses the importance of coconuts in Polynesian culture. This live show also complements the more static cultural displays available at the attraction, providing a variety of experiences for the tourist.

The purposeful cultural tourist (the person who travels primarily for cultural tourism reasons and who has a deep experience while at the destination) will likely be interested in seeking as much information about the place being visited as possible. Indeed, high-knowledge holders are likely to be the most intense information seekers (Johnson and Russon 1984, as cited in Vogt and Fesenmaier 1998). The other types of cultural tourists identified in this book will likely engage in a far narrower information search. The serendipitous, incidental, and casual cultural tourists, for example, regard cultural tourism as a secondary activity and as such will likely not be highly motivated to seek information widely prior to arrival. Even the sightseeing cultural tourist, who ostensibly travels for cultural tourism reasons but has a rather superficial experience, does not exhibit evidence of having conducted a deep information search. As such, this person is also likely to be reliant on the gatekeepers described in this chapter for much of their knowledge about destinations.

From the perspective of the asset, the tourist visit represents the culmination of the information quest process that may have involved a number of gatekeepers who shaped the meaning of and expectations established for the attraction. The amount, quality, and accuracy of this information will determine (1) the appeal of the asset as a possible place to visit, (2) how tourists will be predisposed to negotiate its meaning, and (3) how tourists will use and thus behave at the asset. At a destinationwide level, this information will also influence which places the person chooses to visit.

Thus, the ability of the asset managers to convey a desired message will be influenced by the amount of information or misinformation the tourist brings to the experience. If they can reach an open, uncluttered mind, they have a chance to educate the tourist in a desired manner. If, on the other hand, the tourist's mind is already cluttered with information that may not be appropriate for the asset, and if the person's mind is closed to new ideas, the attraction managers will have little chance to impart new information. The first task becomes one of undoing misinformation and not imparting new knowledge.

This task is done effectively at Alcatraz island in San Francisco. On arrival, visitors are greeted by a park ranger who asks a series of questions about tourists' knowledge of the island and why it is part of a national park (see Photo 10.3). In a very gentle manner, the guide debunks a number of myths (the Birdman of Alcatraz did all his

PHOTO 10.3. Alcatraz, San Francisco, California

Undoing the work of gatekeepers. Vistors are greeted on arrival at Alcatraz near San Francisco by park rangers who explain that Alcatraz was nominated as a national park. They then survey visitors about their knowledge of Alcatraz. Much of the introduction is devoted to debunking a number of myths that have evolved around the island and its prison.

experiments in Leavenworth prison and not at Alcatraz; he was a psychopath and not the sympathetic figure portrayed in the movies; prisoners were criminals and not movie stars or folk heroes; the island is not at all like it is portrayed in the movies—there is no lower lighthouse and no series of tunnels) and discreetly reminds the visitor why the island is nationally significant (its military history is the reason it is proclaimed part of the national park, not its history as a prison; the Native American occupation in the early 1970s was a socially and historically significant event). In this manner, the rangers strive to dispel some of the Hollywood myths about the place with the hope that visitors can appreciate it for what it is and not what its image is.

Likewise, the more fundamentally ignorant the visitor is about the cultural significance of the asset prior to arrival, the less likely asset managers will be able to impart its true importance during a short visit. We have observed that the greater the cultural difference between the tourist and destination, the less likely the tourist is to engage the attraction at a deep level. We are not sure if this is a function of lack of interest or lack of ability. In extreme cases, the tourist will focus on something trivial but starkly different as a means of trying to place the experience in some type of perspective. It is almost as if looking at the place in its totality is too overwhelming. Such a person will focus on, for example, the humor of a ceramic statue that presents a caricature of a Chinese deity rather than trying to learn something about that deity. When we eavesdrop on conversations between tourists or between tourists and guides, conversations tend to revolve around marveling at how different elements of the place are from their own frames of reference, without seeking to understand those differences.

THE ROLE OF GATEKEEPERS
IN CONVEYING MESSAGES

The role of gatekeepers is well recognized in tourism in general (Middleton 1994; Bernstein and Awe 1999; McKercher 1998c) but has been explored rarely in cultural tourism (Prideaux and Kininmont 1999). Understanding who gatekeepers are, what role they play, and how, collectively, the message can be changed provides an understanding of how tourists form their expectations of places and consequently, how they use them. Seaton and Bennett (1996) identify two types of gatekeepers: *opinion formers* and *opinion leaders*. The former are generally regarded as being highly credible by virtue of their perceived expertise, while the latter are individuals who are close to the person and who share the same social network.

Nine different types of gatekeepers are identified in this chapter (see Figure 10.1). Each will be described briefly before their collective impact on the communication process is assessed. Clearly, not all of them will be relevant to all tourists in all instances. Many independent travelers will have no need for gatekeepers associated with the commercial travel trade. Likewise, others may use them selectively, seeking advice from a trusted travel agent, accessing a destination Web site and talking to friends or family members.

Four general features apply to the gatekeeping process. First, the greater the physical distance between the tourist and the destination, the greater the number of gatekeepers likely to be involved. The need to purchase airfare and accommodation from a distance often necessitates the use of a retail travel agent, which opens the prospect of purchasing a fully or partially packaged tour.

FIGURE 10.1. Gatekeepers Controlling the Information Flow Between the Asset and the Tourist

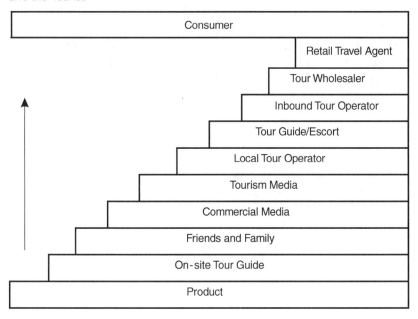

Second, the less the person knows about the place being visited, the greater the number of gatekeepers used or the wider the information search (Stewart and Vogt 1999). First-time visitors, for example, are far more likely to purchase local tours than repeat visitors and are also more likely to seek more travel information. Midcentric and psychocentric tourists are more likely to select some form of package tour if the destination is felt to be very exotic. Destination-naive visitors are most likely to use a travel agent (Snepenger et al. 1990).

Third, the less knowledgeable the tourist is about the culture or heritage of the destination, the more likely he or she will be to use the services of a gatekeeper to provide that information.

Finally, fourth, the more reliant the tourist is on the commercial travel trade, the greater the number of gatekeepers.

The Asset

The asset forms the starting point for this discussion. Direct communication between the asset managers and the tourist enables the desired message to be imparted unimpeded. The message sent is pure and is not polluted by any intervening source. Clearly, this is the ideal situation but occurs only rarely. Most visitors need to be made aware of the asset before they will visit it. This awareness-making process usually is the responsibility of destination marketers, tourism operators, or the travel trade. So unless the tourist stumbles upon the asset by accident or has restricted all information gathering to the asset's managers, it is likely that some other gatekeepers will have had some influence in the awareness-creation process.

On-Site Guide/Interpreter

The on-site guide represents the first knowledge gatekeeper who may modify the message. Studies have indicated that substantial differences exist in the ability of interpreters/guides to impart information effectively to visitors (Ryan and Dewar 1995). The visitor is reliant on the guide to make the asset come alive and tell its story. The ability to do so effectively is related directly to the guide's own knowledge of the asset, or lack thereof, the effectiveness of training programs, and also specific job descriptions. In some cases, the quality of the interpretation is excellent. Archaeologists, cultural heritage experts, art experts, and the like interact with tourists effectively and provide a high-quality experience. In other instances, though, the guides are little more than costumed performers who assume a persona. Moreover, well-meaning but ignorant staff may simplify the message and, in so doing, may reinforce stereotypical attitudes rather than foster real learning.

Friends and Family

Family and friends potentially exert a great deal of influence in the selection of and expectations for the use of cultural or heritage assets. They are known, trusted "experts," who have visited the place in question, and are, therefore, qualified to offer advice. Yet these people are likely to be just as ignorant about the cultural values of a region as the person seeking advice. Indeed, friends are often important but unreliable gatekeepers. If their visit was part of a short holiday, if they themselves are not knowledgeable about the cultural values of the place, and if they have not conducted adequate research, then their advice will be suspect.

Commercial Media

Travel-oriented lifestyle, *infotainment* and *edutainment* television shows, radio shows, and magazines are ubiquitous. These gatekeepers justify their existence as information sources for people planning to visit the destinations highlighted. But producers know that only a small percentage of their audience will ever travel to the destinations highlighted and most will consume the product vicariously as armchair travelers. As a result, these places featured tend to be presented as having spectacular scenery, idyllic spots, up-market resorts, and smiling natives. What cultural features are shown tend to be presented in a "Wow, isn't this spectacular!" manner or as part of a theme park attraction.

As a result, destinations are presented in a highly commodified manner, with their features presented as products to be consumed. This approach is acceptable and suitable if the product is a recreational, escapist experience. It does create problems, however, if the cultural or heritage asset does not promote itself for such consumption.

Tourism Media

Tourism promotional literature comes in two forms: material presented by destination-marketing organizations and material presented by independent media. Each plays a slightly different role. Information provided by destination-marketing organizations is designed to encourage visitation and further to stimulate heavy consumption while in the region. The area's assets are presented as products to be consumed. The message is usually simple and single-minded.

Independent media, such as the material produced by such publishers as Lonely Planet, Fodor's, or the AAA, and others have greater scope to present a more balanced and detailed overview of the destination. Background information on the cultural values of the destination are often included as are suggestions on appropriate behavior. But, like all other gatekeepers, these media have limited space to convey the message about the places being described, which means that the message must be condensed into its core features. In doing so, some of the richness of the asset must be lost. A commercial guide book might devote only a few column inches to a key attraction. For example, a well-known guide book on Washington, DC, devotes less than one column to the Vietnam Memorial. It contains a brief description of its physical layout and a few sentences about how controversial it is.

Local Tour Operators

Local tour operators take tourists on short duration tours (one-half to a full day) of the local area. They are normally independent businesses or local franchises of national tour companies. The operator provides transport, access to attractions, commentary, and may also include meals and a souvenir. The sector is dominated by bus tour operators offering generic sightseeing tours that may include cultural or heritage components. In recent years, some specialist tour operators have emerged that focus exclusively on cultural, heritage, or ecotours. These are typically small-scale operations that have limited market appeal. Their role is to offer the visitor a taste of the destination's sights and sounds. Most include a series of brief stops at key attractions or points of interest that preclude the visitor from doing much more than sightseeing, photography, or having a drink and using the toilet.

Described as cultural brokers, tour operators are recognized as playing a key role in both shaping the experience and in presenting material to tourists (Welgemoed 1996). But the most important qualification required to be a local tour operator/guide is a commercial bus license. It is rare to find a tour operator, especially one working for a large, mass tourism-oriented company, who possesses formal qualifications in history or cultural heritage management. Indeed most knowledge comes from the completion of a short in-house or external training program, the guide's own personal initiative, or from local knowledge.

Tour Escort

The tour escort accompanies a tour group for the duration of that group's visit to a country. Whereas the tour guide is responsible for the activities at one destination, the tour escort will join the group on arrival and travel with it for the duration of its stay in a country. The escort's primary role is to ensure that the tour runs smoothly and that any problems are resolved. But this person also plays a similar cultural broker's role as the local tour operator, setting the context for the places to be visited and providing continuity between places visited. By virtue of being a resident of the host country, the tour escort also assumes the mantle of "local expert." How (usually) he or she presents or interprets information influences the overall quality of the cultural experience the group receives.

But, again, like the tour operator, the escort is usually employed for reasons other than his or her cultural or heritage background. Unless this person is trained specifically, apart from on-site exposure the escort may have little real knowledge of places outside his or her normal home environment. As a result, this "expert," on whom the group relies, may not be particularly expert.

Inbound Tour Operator

The next group of gatekeepers constitute what is commonly refereed to as the travel trade. Their role is to link consumers to producers through various commercial arrangements. The inbound tour operator (IBO) assembles the land content of a visit for overseas wholesalers and travel agents. The role of the IBO, therefore, is akin to a small manufacturer that assembles components into a product. To succeed, the IBO must produce an attractive package and position it uniquely in the marketplace. Unless the tour package is themed around culture, an in-depth cultural tourism experience becomes a low-order goal.

Tour Wholesaler

The tour wholesaler assembles ground content with transportation to provide tangible products for sale through retail outlets. The ground content can be provided by the IBO; if the wholesaler is sufficiently large, it can do the assembly itself. The wholesaler's main role, therefore, is to supply product. Although some small, specialty tour wholesalers exist, for the most part these types of operations are high-volume, low-margin businesses that supply the mass market. They do this by providing a series of regularized, standardized, and commodified products that can be consumed efficiently, safely, and profitably.

Seeing many places or doing many things in a short period of time is more important than spending long periods of time at any one destination. It is common, for example, for tours of Europe to spend only two nights in Paris, including the arrival night after a full day's bus journey and a midafternoon departure after the second night. Thus, the tourist may spend as few as forty hours in Paris, including two nights' sleep. The result is that the experience provided must, by definition, be superficial, spending only small amounts of time at any one attraction.

Retail Travel Agents

Retail travel agents provide the direct connection between the tourist and the travel experience. Although the Internet is changing their role, travel agents still represent, arguably, the most important gatekeeper in the travel purchase decision-making process (Middleton 1994). Their stock and trade is knowledge, and it is that knowledge that they sell to clients. Their recommendations carry a great deal of weight in the final purchase decision. The travel agent represents the most accessible local expert who is a trained professional in satisfying their clients' travel needs.

But what many people do not realize is that the recommendations agents make may be influenced as much by agent self-interest as by clients' needs. Agencies work on very tight margins that are getting tighter all the time. To survive, they must sell profitable products. Profitable products are those that offer the highest commission rates or that are the most time-efficient to book. Cost considerations dictate that most retail travel agents will look first at mass tourism products provided by large national or multinational organizations. Few will seek small, specialty tour operators, who may offer the type of cultural tour people want unless the tour is specifically requested.

Agents acquire information on destinations from the material presented to them by tour wholesalers or, if they are lucky, by participating in familiarization tours offered by the wholesaler. As stated above, while they act as trusted sources of intelligence on destinations, their knowledge base is limited to products they sell and the message imparted to them by their suppliers. By their nature, therefore, they tend to view destinations as products and to view its assets as commodities to consume while at a destination.

EFFECT OF MANY GATEKEEPERS ON THE MESSAGE PASSED TO THE TOURIST

Each of the gatekeepers has a different geographic proximity to the asset (proximate to distant), different levels of contact with the asset (frequent to infrequent/never), different levels of awareness of it (may be aware or may never have heard of it before), different knowledge levels (high to none), and different reasons for wanting to impart certain information (to sell a product, to induce visitation, to impart knowledge). Moreover, the individuals involved at each gatekeeper stage will also have different interests, educational backgrounds, different jobs, different clients they must serve, and different professional obligations about how they portray the asset.

As a result, the focus, function, and information needs of each gatekeeper change significantly at different levels of the communication chain from the asset to the consumer. The closer the gatekeeper is to the asset, the more dominant cultural heritage management objectives become. On the other hand, the closer the gatekeeper is to the tourist, the more tourism product focused the gatekeeper becomes. Because of these different professional functions and different levels of knowledge, the type of message transmitted will likely be significantly different. The cultural heritage manager will be interested in imparting a message that promotes the cultural values of the asset. The tourism professional will impart a consumptive message as a means of helping close a sale.

The following features occur at each stage of the gatekeeping process:

- The asset loses control over the message that is conveyed and the manner in which it is conveyed.
- The desired message gets distorted as it is reinterpreted and re-presented by an increasing number of gatekeepers.
- The message gets simplified as the messenger becomes less aware of cultural heritage values and more aware of tourism products.
- The message gets conveyed in the cultural context of the potential visitor and not in the cultural context of the destination area.
- The message gets commodified to make it easier to convey it clearly to the consumer and to position the asset in a more appealing manner.
- Less important assets are ignored (those assets that gatekeepers deem to be secondary or tertiary assets), while primary attractions are highlighted.
- Expectations about being able to consume the product quickly increase, inhibiting expectations of a deep experience.
- The messenger becomes progressively less familiar with the product and is, therefore, less able to convey information in detail.
- The messenger becomes progressively less interested in the cultural heritage message and more interested in the tourism message.
- Potential visitors' expectations of the asset will change as a changed meaning is conveyed.
- Expectations about appropriate behavior onsite can be modified, which may result in inappropriate activities undertaken by the tourist.

The result is that by the time the visitor arrives on site, he or she may be expecting quite a different experience than the one being offered. That may be a minor annoyance in some instances, but, in other cases, significant problems can occur when masses of tourists arrive expecting to be able to act in a certain way yet are requested to act in a different manner. One of two things will happen: they will ignore the latter message, or they will stop coming. Neither option is particularly acceptable.

Chapter 11

Assessment

INTRODUCTION

The previous ten chapters discuss tourism and cultural heritage management issues affecting cultural tourism. They illustrate that both sectors largely function independently and in parallel, sharing assets but little else. The great challenge for cultural tourism is how to integrate cultural heritage and tourism management needs in a process that will result in a product that is appealing to visitors, while at the same time conserving cultural and heritage values. The buzzword is *sustainable cultural tourism.* But sustainability is such an abused and misunderstood concept that the word must be used with caution, for it has been used by different groups to promote completely opposing agendas (see McKercher 1993). To some, sustainability means economic sustainability, where heavy use of an asset can be justified as long as wealth is generated. Some adverse impacts are both expected and tolerated as sites are managed primarily for their use values. To others, sustainability has been used to promote an agenda opposing most uses, arguing that any use will invariably lead to its destruction. Management actions are imposed to discourage use, even if it is to the overall detriment of the viability of the asset.

In reality, sustainability is, or should incorporate, both use and conservation values in overall management activities. Such a statement, however, recognizes the complexity of managing cultural assets, the differing needs of stakeholders, differing levels of robusticity of assets, and their varied tourism appeal. Although it acknowledges that tourism and cultural heritage management must work in partnership, it also appreciates that this partnership need not always be equal. In many cases, cultural heritage management principles must take precedence, while tourism will play a secondary role. In extreme cases, where the asset is too fragile or where the asset has little market appeal, tourism may be actively discouraged. In other instances, tourism may be the lead consideration, with cultural or heritage management concerns being the lesser partner. Likewise, in extreme cases, such as at purpose-built theme parks or entertainment-oriented attractions, tourism may be the only consideration.

How to determine which sector leads and how to translate ideas into a working management plan or strategy are the topics of Chapters 11 and 12. Chapter 11 identifies a variety of tourism and cultural heritage factors that must be examined when assessing the tourism potential of assets and then deciding on management actions. The assessment must consider more than asset- or site-specific issues and must also look at macro or destinationwide issues. Chapter 12 discusses how the information gathered can be evaluated in a systematic manner to provide insights into how assets should be managed.

ASSESSING THE TOURISM POTENTIAL OF ASSETS

The assessment of the tourism potential of cultural or heritage assets is complicated, for it involves more than just an assessment of their market potential. Any assessment must also consider the robusticity of the asset or its ability to cope with visitors. Market assessments are most interested in determining whether the asset has those features that make it appealing to visitors and how the asset's potential can be converted into consumable products. The robusticity assessment, on the other hand, determines the more fundamental question of whether tourists should be allowed to visit and, if so, what levels of visitation can be permitted without compromising the asset's original intrinsic values.

It is proposed that this assessment be conducted from a macro to a micro level, beginning with the general and working to the specific. After considering aspects in a broader context, more specific issues need to be examined. These include the immediate setting of the asset as a place or cultural space, stakeholders to be involved, and considerations about people, skills, and financial resources associated with the asset. When these have been assessed, a more detailed analysis, such as the one suggested in Chapter 12, can take place to identify options for integrated planning and development of the asset or assets.

CONSIDERING THE WIDER CONTEXT

Tourism in general and cultural tourism in particular are linked closely to the broader social and political context in which they operate. If conditions are not favorable for cultural tourism development, regardless of how appealing the project may seem, its chances of success will be limited. No matter how good an idea is, if legislation prohibits certain types of development, it will not proceed. Likewise, if market conditions are not favorable or if the proposed product is incompatible with either the image of the destination or other products at the destination, then its chances of success are limited. To begin, then, a broader or destinationwide assessment must be undertaken. Table 11.1 identifies many factors that must be considered. They are grouped under three theme areas: the political or legislative context, cultural or heritage assets, and tourism activity within the destination. Factors that are relevant to both cultural heritage management and tourism stakeholders are identified, as well as a wide range of sector-specific concerns. Since most of these have been discussed elsewhere in this book, there is no need to go into great detail here.

Legislative/Political Context

Any tourismification of cultural heritage must work within a legislative or policy framework. The presence of international, national, and/or regional legislation and charters of principles will dictate, ultimately, how many tangible assets and sometimes intangible assets can be developed for tourism. Mundane pieces of legislation, such as zoning regulations and heritage building development controls, exert enormous influence over whether projects can proceed and what can and cannot be done to an asset.

It is also recognized that the debate about the merits of cultural tourism often has an overt political connotation. If tourism is supported politically and seen by the community as a whole as being beneficial, then support for projects will likely be forthcoming. If, on the other hand, animosity exists toward tourism, or if stakeholder groups object to the tourismification of assets, then it will be much more difficult to get proposals approved.

TABLE 11.1. Cultural Tourism—Looking At the Broader Context

Theme	Common Considerations	CHM Considerations	Tourism Considerations
Legislative/ political context	Existing legislative/policy framework Existence of conservation legislation Zoning/use by-laws and development controls/guidelines	Codes of ethics and conservation principles In-house heritage agency or departmental policies Heritage agreements with stakeholders	Political importance of tourism Support for tourism in the community
Cultural/ heritage assets	Quantum of cultural/heritage assets Spatial distribution of assets Importance/uniqueness of these assets (local, regional, national, international) Icon assets	Robusticity—ability to withstand visitation pressures Resources available to manage the above Need to restrict access to certain assets for conservation or stakeholder-related reasons	Critical mass of assets Ability to bundle awareness of cultural or heritage assets
Tourism activity at the destination	How the destination is positioned in the marketplace (and importance of cultural tourism in that positioning) Amount of other cultural or heritage tourism activity	How the management policy or regime associated with conservation of the asset integrates tourism needs along with those of other users Whether overall visitation is increasing and, if so, what planning and management are required	Amount of tourism activity Level of infrastructure, superstructure Sources of tourists (domestic/international, cultural distance) Tourist profile (length of stay, trip purpose, first or repeat visitor, demographic profile, etc.) Psychographic profile Competing tourism products Complementarity of products Prices Synergies (bundling, nodes, etc.) Distance decay and market access issues

Cultural/Heritage Assets

Community guides on cultural tourism suggest strongly that communities begin by cataloguing their assets to see what they have (NTHP 1999). The main purpose of cataloging, from a cultural heritage management perspective, is to ensure that a representative sample of the region's tangible and intangible heritage is conserved for future generations. The main purpose of cataloguing, from a tourism perspective, however, is quite different. Rather than being concerned about the intrinsic value of assets, the tourism sector is more interested in their use values.

Cataloging seeks to determine if a critical mass of assets exists and if common themes exist among them. In addition, the spatial distribution of these assets will offer insights into how they can be bundled into nodes, precincts, networks, or themed touring routes. Although a critical mass of assets is important, it is even more important to be able to identify *icon assets:* those assets that are truly unique or outstanding and will draw people to the destination.

Tourism Activity

As a discretionary activity, the success of most cultural tourism products or experiences is linked intrinsically to the overall performance of tourism at a destination. Therefore, a background analysis of tourism flows, the destination's current position in the marketplace, and an assessment of services and infrastructure plays an important role in determining whether opportunities exist to develop new products or expand existing ones. It is much easier to develop viable tourism products, cultural or otherwise, in recognized tourism destinations than in areas that have received little visitation.

It is also important to consider how the destination is positioned in the marketplace and whether that positioning is compatible with the development of cultural tourism. How the destination is positioned will influence not only that type of cultural tourism activity, but its scale and, equally important, the depth of experience provided. Again, greater opportunities exist to capitalize on the cultural or heritage tourism potential of destinations that are known in the marketplace for their heritage assets than for other assets. It is relatively more difficult to provide a deep historical cultural tourism experience at a destination such as Las Vegas, for example, than it would be in a place such as Philadelphia, partly because of how they are positioned in the marketplace. On the other hand, a destination such as Las Vegas may be ideal for a superficial, entertainment-oriented, highly commodified cultural tourism experience.

UNDERSTANDING THE ASSET IN ITS SETTING

The setting of the asset in its immediate surrounds, along with its developmental and sociocultural context, should be considered. Three factors come into play: the asset's physical setting within the region, physical access, and the sociohistorical factors that have led to its creation (see Table 11.2).

Sociohistorical Setting

It is important to understand the historical and social developments that led to the creation of the asset. Producing a tourism product that is divorced from the sociohistorical context is considered by the cultural heritage management community to be against the best interests of that asset. The setting that comprises its physical relationship to the surrounding landscape is also important for most clearly evoking associated cultural values. Hence, stories told by a storyteller are more evocative of continuity with the past if told by a tradition bearer in a "cultural space" (such as a market or street) than if they are used as video presentation background in a site cafeteria.

TABLE 11.2. The Setting

Theme	CHM Considerations	Tourism Considerations
Sociohistorical setting	Historical context	
	Continuity	
Physical setting within the region	Can the cultural values still be appreciated by the visitor?	Physical location within the destination
	Management and conservation considerations inherent in protecting the cultural values of the asset	Compatibility with surrounding facilities, structures
Access		Proximity to other cultural/heritage assets
		Location vis-à-vis tourism nodes

Physical Setting

The aesthetics of the setting need to be considered from a tourism perspective as well as from a CHM perspective. Attractive settings will enhance the quality of experience, while an unattractive or unsafe setting may diminish the tourism appeal. A number of urban heritage buildings, including much industrial heritage, are located in unattractive or unsafe areas. These assets may have important intrinsic value but are of little interest for tourists if their safety needs are not taken into account or if the setting is unappealing. Moreover, the compatibility of the tangible asset with its surroundings plays a role in enhancing the experience, helping to place the asset in context and assist in helping the visitor better understand its meaning and significance.

Access

Ease of access will play a role in determining use levels. As a general rule, the easier, more convenient, and more direct access is, the greater the potential for higher visitation. Alternatively, inconvenient or awkward access may act as a dissuader, unless the journey itself becomes part of the experience. In these cases, getting to the asset becomes a worthwhile goal in itself. Assets in close proximity and/or that are located conveniently close to tourism nodes are more appealing than solitary or remote assets. In the latter case, the tourist must overcome a perceived distance obstacle before visitation can occur. If the visitor perceives that such a journey would consume too much time for too little reward, if more attractive alternatives are available, and/or if interest in the assets is not sufficiently high to entice a visit, then visitor numbers will be limited.

ASSET SPECIFIC ISSUES: "PLACE" AND CULTURAL SPACES

Once these broader issues have been considered, the next step is to look at the specific asset itself. Table 11.3 identities the types of issues that must be examined. Tangible and intangible assets are identified in separate categories for the first time, as they are conceptualized differently by the cultural heritage management community. From a tourism perspective, though, similar issues must be considered.

TABLE 11.3. Focusing on "Place" and Cultural Space Issues

Theme	CHM Considerations	Tourism Considerations
Tangible assets	Physical state of asset and its robusticity How much of it is still intact—integrity Cultural values it evokes Visibility of the remains Uniqueness Good or bad example of its type The cultural values of the asset	Uniqueness Ability to shape, provide experience "Product" potential and ability to actualize that potential Its potential place on the attractions hierarchy Commodifying it sensitively to maximize visitor satisfaction without losing authenticity
Ownership/management	Presence/absence of a systematic management regime that allows for regular maintenance and monitoring of the asset at its most basic	Ownership structure (private, public, community) Purpose (private sector versus public sector) Presence/absence of a formal management structure and business plan
Intangible assets	Is tourism use of asset culturally appropriate? (e.g., access to sacred information) Marketing is conducted responsibly Design of the tourism product does not include elements that go against preserving the asset's cultural values Tradition bearers are not overwhelmed or adversely affected The cultural values of the asset are not changed to accommodate tourism needs	Its uniqueness Ability to shape, provide experience "Product" potential and ability to actualize that potential Its potential place on the attractions hierarchy How it complements or enhances the appeal of tangible assets being marketed Commodifying it sensitively to maximize visitor satisfaction without losing authenticity
Current and potential uses	What is its current use—public space, private space? Who are its current users? Education of the general public is the primary concern Use of asset to send a message about heritage conservation	Importance of tourism Number of similar/competing places and their level of development Its place on the attractions hierarchy and ability to shift places

Tangible Assets

The concept of "place" is useful for identifying issues associated with the integrated management and development of tangible assets, including archaeological sites, historic buildings, and precincts, as well as for movable cultural property or objects, such as artifacts, historic objects, or possessions. A place-specific examination of tangible assets considers the physical state of the asset, its robusticity, physical state of repair, and integrity, as well as its cultural values and significance. Part of this assessment is undertaken to determine the asset's state of repair to assess what must be done to it if visitation is to occur. In addition, the assessment is undertaken to determine if visitation by nontraditional or nonlocal users will impinge upon the cultural values it evokes. Tourism considerations are much more pragmatic. The tourism assessment will determine if the asset will be appealing to tourists and, if so, where it could fit in the tourism attractions hierarchy (primary, secondary, or tertiary attraction). This assessment will also determine what needs to be done to the asset, if anything, to actualize its tourism potential.

Intangible Assets

A somewhat different approach is required with intangible assets, though. The idea of "cultural space," first mentioned in Chapter 5, provides a useful means of examining this category of asset. The concept of cultural space allows all kinds of intangible assets to be associated with a traditional setting that enhances the interpretation and absorption of the asset's cultural values by the visitor. It also gives presenters of intangible assets a locus from which to control the visitors' experience and deal with any development and management issues. Again, the assessment will determine if tourism use is both acceptable and desirable, based on both a market perspective and a cultural analysis, and what can be done to the asset to convert it to a product.

Current and Potential Uses and Users

The key point to be taken into consideration when looking at current and future users is to determine if tourism use and tourists are compatible with existing uses and user groups. If they are, as in the case of many temples and religious sites that welcome all visitors, then fewer problems are likely to occur when the asset is commodified. If, however, tourism represents an invasive or potentially incompatible activity, then the merits of tourism must be reconsidered, or plans to manage the actions of tourists need to be developed.

STAKEHOLDER AND CONSULTATION ISSUES

Most cultural and heritage assets have multiple stakeholders, whose opinions must be considered. Table 11.4 lists the main types of stakeholders likely to have interest in cultural and heritage assets. Some stakeholders will of course have stronger concerns about an asset than others. Stakeholder consideration is recognized as an important part of the sustainable management of any asset developed for tourism (ICOMOS 1999; AHC and TCA 1999). The failure to consider the needs of stakeholders, including even minor stakeholders, can lead to conflict situations that can endanger the effectiveness of any management structure put in place. The omission of stakeholders from the consultative process means that their concerns will not be heard, and their legitimate concerns cannot be addressed from the outset. The consultative process is not a one-off process. For an asset to be truly sustainable, ongoing feedback from stakeholders must be encouraged so that emerging issues can be resolved.

Stakeholder Identification and Consultation

It is now accepted that consultation with stakeholders plays an important role in the conservation and asset management process. In the past, however, stakeholder concerns were often ignored, especially when they were seen to express antitourism sentiments. The need to include consultation has been slower to develop in the management of tangible assets than with intangible assets. Unfortunately, an attitude still exists in many parts of the developing world that the legitimate needs of local residents can be ignored in pursuit of hard currency provided by foreign tourists. However, most experts now recommend consultation be started as early in the planning process as possible (Pearson and Sullivan 1995).

There are two main challenges when considering stakeholders. The first is deciding who has a legitimate interest in the management of the asset; the second is to ensure that the consultation process is both fair and open. Depending on the size, significance, and

TABLE 11.4. Stakeholders

Theme	Common Considerations	CHM Considerations	Tourism Considerations
Stakeholder identification and consultation	Identifying all relevant stakeholders as early as possible in the process Inviting their participation throughout the process Being aware that there are dominant stakeholders with controlling interests in the asset Understanding their different involvement expectations and capabilities Noting any history of conflict or collaboration	Listening to stakeholders' concerns and incorporating feedback into day-to-day management once the asset has been fully developed as an attraction Understanding the perspective and agenda of the tourism sector and associated stakeholders	Listening to stakeholders' concerns and incorporating feedback into product development, marketing, and business strategies Understanding the perspective and agenda of the CHM and conservation sector and associated stakeholders
Types of stakeholders		Educational institutions, conservation and heritage NGOs, government agencies, museums, indigenous groups/ethnic minorities, religious groups, others	Local, national, state government tourism organizations, tour operators, local guides
Key stakeholder issues	Power and power relationships between stakeholders Agreement by controlling stakeholder(s) to allow the asset to be presented to visitors Awareness of impacts of tourism Ownership and copyright issues are addressed Commitment to an ongoing conservation	Controlling stakeholders and owners agree to visitation and conservation measures Designing interpretation that is culturally appropriate and suits visitors' needs CH manager understands and takes into account the role of volunteers and sponsors Robusticity and carrying capacity of the asset	Controlling stakeholders and owners support visitation and development Design and marketing of a viable product that is culturally appropriate and sustainable Ongoing costs of stakeholder consultation Potential of a long lead time to approvals given by other stakeholders to tourism ventures

political sensitivity of the tourism proposal, literally hundreds of potential stakeholders may claim an interest in it. Some will have an immediate and direct interest, such as tradition bearers, traditional owners, indigenous groups, ethnic minorities, or historical users, as well as tour operators and tour guides. Others will have an indirect though still legitimate interest. Research facilities, heritage NGOs, international heritage agencies, other agencies associated with heritage management, historical organizations, and conservation groups, along with local, regional, and national tourism NGOs, the local travel trade, and public-sector tourism bodies may all have some valid though not direct interest in the asset. However, if the proposed use is controversial, many other stakeholders who do not have a legitimate interest in the asset may also seek to assert their rights to become involved in its management. Sometimes it is those with the least direct interest in the asset who are the most vocal. One of the management challenges is to separate legitimate from illegitimate stakeholders.

The second key issue is to ensure that any consultation exercise is both fair and open. Again, in the past—and this practice still continues in some places today—consultation was undertaken as a rather cynical exercise aimed at being seen apparently to involve the public rather than genuinely seeking input into the planning and management process. Ideally, consultation should seek to involve all legitimate stakeholders in the entire planning process. Further, consultation seeks to have stakeholders with different viewpoints listen to and understand other stakeholders' concerns, with a view to seeking a mutually agreeable resolution of any real or imagined problems.

Stakeholder Issues

Stakeholders generally have a long history with one another. It is important to understand such issues as the power alliances that have formed between and among groups, which stakeholders have assumed the mantle of leadership, the history among stakeholders, whether there have been major conflicts, or if they have worked toward mutual solutions when commencing the consultative process. In addition, tourism often represents a powerful new stakeholder that can alter the power balance among existing stakeholders. Care must be used when including tourism interests to ensure that its true power position is recognized by all.

PEOPLE, SKILLS, AND FINANCIAL RESOURCES

Finally, no assessment is complete without assessing the skill, resources, and capabilities of the people involved and the resources available to them. Some of the considerations are identified in Table 11.5. The ability to deliver on visions and to manage cultural assets as tourism attractions in a sustainable manner is directly related to the skills of the people directly involved in any project. The human element can be a fatal flaw that turns good ideas into failed projects with significant management problems. Issues relating to the ability of the people involved to deliver on a project's goals and an assessment of their motives for becoming involved needs to be considered. If the skills are not present, does the person have the ability to acquire them himself or herself or the resources to buy them?

Buying skills raises a second fundamental question: does the proponent have sufficient financial resources to deliver on the idea? In general, it is difficult to acquire monies for conservation work. But it is generally easier to source funding for one-off development projects or site stabilization than it is for ongoing maintenance. Tourism assets, however, require ongoing maintenance. Where will the resources come from? Further, questions must be asked about the financial viability of proposals. Business plans must be developed and scrutinized closely to assess their reliability.

TABLE 11.5. People, Skills, and Financial Resources

Theme	CHM Considerations	Tourism Considerations
People	Skills of individuals involved Skill gaps Ability to fill skill gaps Motives for being involved	Skills of individuals involved Skill gaps Ability to fill skill gaps Motives for being involved
Resources	Amount of money/resources available Amount of money/resources needed Desired use for money and resources (maintenance, development, etc.) Possible sources of money/resources Tourism as a means to an end or as an end in itself	Amount of money/resources available Amount of money/resources needed Possible sources of money/resources Tourism as a means to an end or as an end in itself

Finally, two more crucial questions must be answered. Why is tourism being proposed? Is tourism an end in itself, or is it a means to another end? Tourism reasons must be the only reasons a cultural heritage asset is developed for tourism. By this, the authors mean that only assets with strong appeal to tourists, that are robust enough to cater for visitors, and that can be positioned uniquely and attractively in the marketplace should be developed as tourism attractions. Caution must be used if tourism is used as a justification for the pursuit of other objectives, such as a desire to conserve assets further, protect them from demolition, or as a means to getting assets listed on a heritage registry.

CONCLUSIONS

Now that this information has been gathered, it must be assessed in a meaningful manner. Although all this information is important, clearly some details (such as legislative context, values at stake, and financial resources) are more important than others. Likewise, more critical issues emerge from an asset-specific perspective as the evaluation process moves from the general to the specific. Chapter 12 discusses one means available using this information to direct the management process.

Chapter 12

Asset Auditing and Planning

> If site administrators, conservators, community leaders and tourism officials see themselves as part of a larger, over-all planning process, risks and waste can be avoided. (ICOMOS 1993: 28)

INTRODUCTION

The previous chapter identified a vast array of factors that must be considered when evaluating the tourism potential of cultural or heritage assets. The question now becomes: what to do with this information? This chapter presents a model that can be used to evaluate the information gathered on an asset-by-asset basis for a region or a group of assets. It will provide macroindicators about how assets could be managed and insights into how the relationship between tourism and cultural heritage management can be optimized (du Cros 2000; du Cros 2001). The model is tested using Hong Kong as a case study.

The reader is also introduced briefly to the formal planning process. The discussion on planning is not intended as a definitive site management or tourism operations planning document. Rather it is presented so the reader can appreciate the steps involved and considerations made in the planning process. Other sources exist that present the planning process in detail. If interested, the reader is encouraged to seek these sources: Ambrose and Paine 1993; Hall and McArthur 1998; Leask and Yeoman 1999; Lord and Lord 1999; ICOMOS 1993, 1999.

AN AUDIT MODEL

The information gathered must be processed systematically to ensure that valid conclusions about the tourism potential of assets can be drawn and, from here, appropriate management actions developed. The audit procedure outlined below enables such an evaluation to oc-cur. It will help asset managers and regional tourism planners to iden-tify which assets are best suited for cultural tourism development, the assets where tourism is not recommended, and assets where tourism may be an option but will need to be managed carefully.

As suggested in the previous chapter, the determination of tourism potential involves more than just an assessment of market appeal. It also involves assessing the asset's ability to cope with tourists, its robusticity. Although market appeal is clearly an important consider-ation from a tourism perspective, considering it in isolation is a sure recipe for future problems. To make tourism work and to achieve true sustainability, market appeal must also be correlated to the ability of the asset to cope with increased visitation or to be modified for use in a manner that does not compromise its values.

The relationship between these two dimensions can be shown in the Market Appeal-Robusticity Matrix in Figure 12.1. Audit proce-dures discussed in the following section enable the attraction's mar-ket appeal and robusticity to be assessed as being either low, moder-ate, or high. Different actions are proposed depending on where the asset is located in the matrix.

FIGURE 12.1. Market Appeal-Robusticity Matrix of Tourism Potential

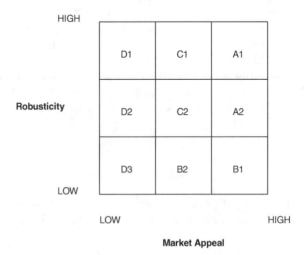

"A" grade assets are heritage places with moderate to high market appeal and high (A1) to moderate (A2) robusticity. They are ideally suited for significant tourism activity for they possess features that appeal to tourists and also can withstand significant use levels (see Photo 12.1). Only minimal to moderate conservation measures are required to protect the cultural values from the impact of heavy visitation.

"B" grade assets have high (B1) to moderate (B2) market appeal but are low in robusticity. Low robusticity may mean that the physical fabric of the asset is fragile or that its cultural values are extremely sensitive to significant impacts by visitors. Tourists may show strong interest in visiting these places but, because of their fragility, they have limited ability to cope with intense use. Some tourism use will likely occur regardless of management activity. As such, the management challenge becomes one of ensuring that visitation does not damage the cultural values of the asset. In some cases, visitation may need to be restricted or discouraged due to the fragility of the asset's amenity, fabric, and setting, possible public liability problems, dangers associated with modifying the asset for tourism use, or local sensitivity to tourism use. In other cases, it may be possible to put conservation and visitor management measures in place, which will allow greater tourism use to occur. Extreme options may also be considered for assets with exceptionally strong tourism appeal that are also exceptionally fragile. Tourism may be actively discouraged if it is felt the asset or its key nontourism stakeholders could not cope with visitation. Alternatively, purpose-built facilities located some distance from the asset may be considered, as has been done by the reconstruction of rock paintings at a visitors' center near the original Pleistocene place at Lascaux in France.

"C" grade assets have moderate tourism appeal and have high (C1) to moderate (C2) robusticity (see Photo 12.2). Two management options present themselves from a tourism perspective. Because these assets are robust, they many be able to withstand greater visitation levels than their current market appeal would suggest. A management approach to develop the asset's potential fully or to enhance the experience to widen its market appeal may be adopted. Alternatively, management plans may strive to maintain the status quo, with the recognition that tourism numbers will be limited.

PHOTO 12.1. Quebec City, Canada

Destinations such as the World Heritage–listed Quebec City are ideally suited to capitalize on cultural tourism. Quebec City enjoys the right combination of strong market appeal and high robusticity. Its sustainable competitive advantage rests, in part, on the fact that it is the only walled city in North America. In addition, it has a critical mass of heritage attractions concentrated tightly within the walls of the old city, providing visitors with much to see and do. The city is historically significant, with the Plains of Abraham being the most historic battlefield in Canada. In addition, the city offers visitors from English North America an exotic French experience. More important, though, the Old City is robust enough to withstand the pressures of large numbers of visitors without damaging the tangible or intangible fabric of the area.

PHOTO 12.2. Crown Point, New York State

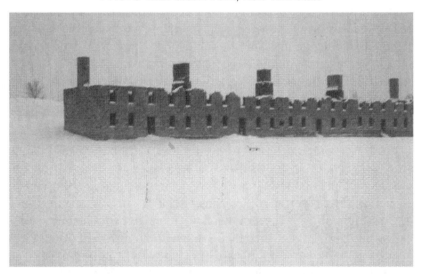

Some important heritage assets, such as the remains of the eighteenth-century Crown Point fort in upstate New York are robust but have limited tourism appeal. This site contains the remains of tow forts, an earlier small French fort and a much larger English fort. The English fort was the largest commissioned by the British in North America. However, since it never saw any action in the various French/English wars, the War of Independence, or the War of 1812, it has little historical significance. The nearby Fort Ticonderoga, originally built as Fort Carillon by the French, which saw much more action, is a more popular attraction.

"D" grade assets have low market appeal and are unlikely to attract significant visitation, unless the asset is commodified to such an extent that its intrinsic values would be almost totally sacrificed. These types of assets should be managed for reasons other than tourism. The biggest challenge may be to convince asset managers of their limited appeal.

AN AUDIT PROCEDURE

Chapter 11 identified a range of factors that must be considered when assessing how to integrate tourism with cultural heritage management. Although all factors must be taken into consideration, the list is too long to be easily translated into a practical audit tool that can be used to assess individual assets and locate them in the Market Appeal-Robusticity Matrix. The simplified audit procedure discussed below focuses on the most significant elements that must be evaluated. The elements are listed in Table 12.1. Some variables shown, such as icon status, uniqueness, historical value, and state of repair, are stand-alone items. Other variables, such as ambience and setting, access, an assessment of tourism flows, aesthetic values, and impact considerations, represent composites of elements identified in Chapter 11.

Each asset is graded according to these variables, with separate scores derived for the tourism and cultural heritage management subsets. Depending on the degree of rigor desired, scores can be assigned on a binary basis (yes/no) or by using a scaled point system (1 low rating to 5 high rating). An asset that has a management plan, for example, would get a higher grade than one without any kind of management regime. Likewise, an asset that is truly unique and has an interesting story that is relevant to the visitor would receive a higher score than one that is common with a story that is of interest only to local residents. In addition, some variables that are more critical to the evaluation process may receive a higher weight. Examples include icon status, fragility, and others. Once grades have been assigned to all indicators in each subset, the asset can be plotted on the matrix and its status determined.

Most of the variables are qualitative in nature. By its very nature, therefore, the assessment must be subjective. This poses both opportunities and challenges to prospective auditors. Subjective assessments are open to personal biases. As well, the efficacy of the audit depends on the ability of the auditor to evaluate the tourism elements from the perspective of a tourist, a nonlocal visitor who may not know much about the asset or its local history. Likewise, the CHM variables must be assessed from a cultural heritage management perspective. In short, caution is advised when conducting the audit. Indeed, the authors recommend that an external examiner conduct the audit to eliminate the risk of internal bias. As well, it is recommended that a region- or destinationwide audit be conducted to ensure consistency in application of the methodology and the production of a regional overview.

TABLE 12.1. Cultural Heritage Tourism Subindicators

Tourism

Market Appeal

- Ambience and setting
- Well-known outside local area
- National icon or symbol
- Can tell a "good story"—evocative place
- Has some aspect to distinguish it from nearby attractions
- Appeals to special needs or uses (e.g., pilgrimages, festivals, sports)
- Complements other tourism products in area/region/destination
- Tourism activity in the region
- Destination associated with culture or heritage
- Political support

Product Design Needs

- Access to asset's features
- Good transport/access to asset from population centers
- Proximity to other heritage attractions
- Amenity (toilets, parking, pathways, refreshments, availability of information)

Cultural Heritage Management

Cultural Significance

- Aesthetic value (including architectural value)
- Historical value
- Educational value
- Social value
- Scientific value
- Rare or common (locally, regionally, nationally)
- Representativeness (locally, regionally, nationally)

Robusticity

- Fragility of the asset
- State of repair
- Management plan or policy in place
- Regular monitoring and maintenance
- Potential for ongoing involvement and consultation of key stakeholders
- Potential for negative impacts of high visitation on
  —fabric of the asset(s) and
  —lifestyle and cultural traditions of local community(ies)
- Potential for modifications (as part of product development) to have negative impacts on
  —fabric of the asset(s) and
  —lifestyle and cultural traditions of local community(ies)

TESTING THE PROCEDURE—HONG KONG

This audit model was tested in Hong Kong during the summer of 2000. The test included an audit of twelve heritage places from archaeological sites to structures, dating from prehistoric times through the mid-twentieth century. This sample also comprised those places that were likely to have had some tourism use and/or a management policy as well as those that had never had any tourism use nor have had any active conservation management. The heritage places differed in scale from a building complex and site cluster to rock carvings on a single rock face.

Background information was gathered on each location prior to the commencement of the study. This information included an assessment of its ownership structure, management history, known cultural significance, available resources for interpreting the information, its level of access to the public, the existence of tourism products or nearby attractions, and an identification and evaluation of stakeholders who were likely to be involved in tourism, heritage conservation, and planning. A pro forma checklist was developed to collect background information systematically. Information about cultural heritage values was gathered from government-supported heritage agencies, public records offices, libraries, and informants. Background information on the tourism sector subindicators was mostly collected from tourism association publications, tourism product information, guidebooks, and tourism sector reports. Site inspections filled information gaps and proved essential to the completion of the assessment process.

After the assessment was completed, the scores for each of the assets were tabulated and plotted on the Market Appeal-Robusticity Matrix. The results are shown in Figure 12.2. Only one asset is shown as having high market appeal. It is located proximate to the downtown area, is unique, is recognized as important, and has an interesting story to tell. The rest of the assets were clustered around the "moderate" range for market appeal for a variety of reasons. Some of the assets had been commodified in a manner that is appropriate for attracting tourists, elevating the market appeal. For others with potentially strong market appeal, relative isolation or lack of product development opportunities hindered their ability to earn a higher ranking.

The heritage assets with the highest robusticity or cultural value ratings were two museum sites and the former Marine Police Headquarters. Each of these buildings had been restored or was in the process of being restored, which provided a form of site hardening. Assets that received a lower rating were those that had little evidence of a systematic management policy, were in a poor state of repair, or where local residents would be inconvenienced by heavy visitation. No assets examined were assessed as having low robusticity, although a few had some serious conservation planning issues still to be resolved.

FIGURE 12.2. Market Appeal-Robusticity Matrix for Hong's Kong's Heritage Attractions

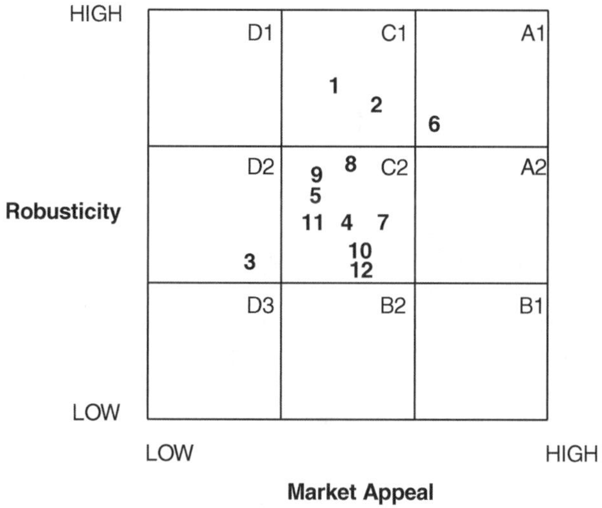

Key:
1. Sheung Yiu Folk Museum
2. Tai Po Market Railway Station Museum
3. Victoria Barracks
4. Rock Carving at Wong Chuk Hang
5. Tung Chung Fort
6. Former Marine Police Headquarters
7. Hong Kong Observatory
8. Cheung Shan Kwu Tsz (Monastery)
9. Site cluster at southern section of Lung Yuek Tau Heritage Trail
10. Wun Yiu (pottery kiln) Archaeological Site
11. Sai Kung Temple and nearby town precinct
12. Shek Kip Mei Housing Estate

Based on this assessment, recommendations were made about the efficacy of pursuing tourism and the manner in which tourism could be pursued at each of these assets. Suggestions ranged from a recommendation that tourism should not be pursued at certain assets, to giving tourism a lower priority in management plans, to the active de-marketing of fragile archaeological sites until they are stabilized, to suggestions that current management and development activities are appropriate, and, finally, to a recommendation that further commodification be considered to maximize tourism appeal.

Applying the Results: Issue Identification and Option Selection

The audit process facilitates the identification of key issues and the selection of possible management directions that will form the basis of the development of subsequent management plans. The following main options present themselves when this approach is applied:

1. Deciding not to identify tourism as an objective as the asset has insufficient market appeal
2. Selecting another asset for tourism use that is less costly to conserve or commodify
3. Continuing the development process with the original asset with a higher priority on conservation measures to better manage its cultural values in the face of projected visitation
4. Continuing the development process with the original asset with a higher priority on commodification and tourism product design needs to boost or enhance market appeal
5. Continuing the development process with the original asset with equal emphasis on conservation measures and commodification/product design needs

A further use of this model is that it offers guidance as to whether tourism or cultural heritage management should be the primary consideration in management decisions. Where the tourism potential is high and the asset is robust (A grade assets), perhaps tourism can take a leading role in the setting of management objectives. When the asset is fragile, however, cultural heritage management considerations must dominate, regardless of the tourism potential (B grade). Similarly, when tourism potential is low (D grade), there is little merit in identifying tourism as the lead management consideration, regardless of the level of robusticity. Where there is some tourism appeal and the asset is moderately to highly robust, opportunities exist for a more equal relationship between tourism and cultural heritage management objectives. Clarifying the objectives of assets will also help address stakeholder issues.

PLANNING

Ultimately, the application of the audit can be used to drive the development of management plans or management policies for individual assets, groups of assets, or national collections of assets. Some organizations prefer to identify policy guidelines, while others prefer to have more specific plans. Policies are useful at a macro level, but at a micro or asset-specific level, formal plans are recommended.

Many approaches can be taken to planning and many different terms used, but, ultimately, planning has one main goal: to move a place/asset/business/destination from its current position to a more favorable position. Likewise, many different planning models have been devised, some with a strong business focus, some with less of a business focus (see, for example, Pearce 1989; Aaker 1995; WTO 1994; Conlin 1996; Hayword and Walsh 1996; Joyce and Woods 1996; ICOMOS 1993; NTHP 1999). They all share a number of features in common. Simplified, the planning process involves the following steps:

- A realistic assessment of the current situation, including an internal and external analysis
- Consultation
- The establishment of a mission or vision
- The identification of options and the selection of the most feasible
- Establishment of quantifiable and assessable goals and objectives
- The creation of action plans to achieve the goals and objectives (budgets, programs, projects, actions)
- Establishing an evaluation and feedback mechanism to monitor achievement of the plan's objectives

As stated in the outset of this chapter, this book is not designed to be a planning manual for would-be cultural tourism managers. A number of good sources discuss the planning process in detail. This brief discussion of the component parts of management plans is being offered as an introduction to the type of issues that need to be considered.

Planning, by its nature, is an iterative process that often requires revisiting certain elements as the plan changes or initial conditions change. In a cultural tourism context, especially, effective planning is a consensus-building exercise that seeks to assuage as many stakeholder concerns as possible while also building partnerships between disparate groups. It is for this reason that cultural tourism planning is such a challenging task. However, by identifying CHM and tourism concerns at an early stage, a balance can be created that can be maintained throughout the development and management of the attraction. Silberberg (1995) describes the operationalization of this challenge as requiring close scrutiny of operating policies and practices to focus on aspects such as visitor management, partnerships, and packaging opportunities, while still continuing to meet heritage preservation and education mandates.

Embarking on the planning process can happen at any time during the life of an asset but is of most use and is most likely to be endorsed by all parties during the initial life-cycle stage of the asset, when it is in the process of being converted from an asset to an attraction. It is at this stage that some fundamental questions must be resolved, such as what options should be examined before converting the asset into a sustainable tourism attraction, who should lead the planning and management process, and how the key stakeholder group that actually controls the asset should work with the rest to reach an acceptable balance between tourism and conservation concerns.

Realistic Assessment

Planning will work only if it is grounded in reality. It is for this reason that much of Chapter 11 and the first half of this chapter are devoted to the development of an assessment and audit mechanism of both the tourism and cultural heritage values. As has been mentioned elsewhere in this book, asset managers and involved stakeholders are sometimes too close to the asset to evaluate its tourism potential in a realistic and unbiased manner. As a result, many people become enthusiastic about tourism where no such potential exists. By the same token, some people will resist the tourismification of the asset out of an unrealistic fear that its values will be compromised.

Consultation

Consultation must commence from the outset and be a regular part of the ongoing management of the asset, especially when indigenous stakeholders, traditional users, and tradition bearers may be asked to sacrifice something to achieve the asset's tourism potential. Consultation must be conducted in an open and transparent manner that allows the process to be fully participatory. The identification of leading stakeholders, key spokespeople, and main controller of the asset (where these differ) early in the process will make the entire planning process operate more smoothly.

It is important, as well, that the process be managed effectively to ensure that it does not break down into a series of autonomous parallel processes. A management framework must be designed and agreed upon among the stakeholders that allows for continual and regular communication to continue between task holders such that the process can be modified if necessary. Detailed advice on establishing such a framework according to the needs of asset and the stakeholders is given by several authorities but will not be expanded upon here (see Hall and McArthur 1998; NTHP 1999; AHC and TCA 1999).

Establishment of a Mission or Vision

Elucidating a clear mission or vision for the asset is much more easily said than done; until it is achieved, however, the rest of the planning process cannot proceed. Different stakeholders will view the asset differently and will value it for different reasons. Some may have unrealistic aspirations for the asset. Likewise, some stakeholders may view other interested parties with suspicion. Consultation and consensus building at this stage will alleviate potential problems that may emerge at a later state.

The mission or vision must be compatible with the asset itself. As discussed in the next chapter, it is as important to decide what the asset is *not,* what it will *not* offer and what type of tourist it will *not* be shaped for, as it is to decide what its core product, market, and message are. Some heritage places are attractive to tourists, while others have little or no tourism appeal. It is an underlying principle of cultural tourism that not all tourism attractions are equal and not all cultural assets are cultural attractions. Further, a cultural or heritage asset does not automatically become a tourism attraction without some form of commodification. These issues must be recognized from the outset.

Identification of Options and Selection of the Preferred Option

Knowing what an asset has to offer, how stakeholders are prepared to allow an asset to be used, and what everyone, collectively, wishes to do with the asset should enable asset mangers to develop a list of possible options to follow. These options must be scrutinized closely before deciding which one is best suited for the asset's shared vision.

The audit process will identify the desired, broad management direction to follow and which element should be the lead objective. But once the result of the initial assessment of potential is completed, a number of options will present themselves for consideration. They must be discussed and narrowed to the most workable one. This decision must be influenced, to a large degree, by an assessment of the skills, assets (human and financial), and other resources available, as well as by the wishes of stakeholders.

Establishment of Quantifiable Goals and Objectives

The development process must distill the above information in the proposed management framework into an action plan. When dealing with an entire region's set of cultural and heritage assets, a master plan may be required. It will usually follow internationally developed guidelines (Nordic World Heritage Office and UNESCO 1999). Specific action plans for individual assets will follow. Goals include both financial (where relevant) and nonfinancial (experiential, interpretive, conservation) objectives. In addition, measures must be designed to ensure that any adverse impacts are mitigated.

One feature of goals is that they must be *SMART: specific, measurable, attainable, realistic,* and *timely.* Goals are the benchmarks by which the success or failure of a cultural tourism product will be assessed. Unless they are specific and their attainment measurable, it will be impossible to determine how well the asset is performing. In addition, it is recommended that interim or milestone goals be identified so that organizations can assess how well they are performing during the life of the plan and how likely they are to achieve their targets. The failure to meet milestone goals may necessitate a revision of the plan. Likewise, exceeding milestones may not necessarily be good news, especially if they relate to visitor numbers at sensitive attractions. Again, if milestones are exceeded, the plan will need to be modified.

Creation of Action Plans

Once goals are established, action plans need to be developed to ensure that they can be achieved. Such plans may include conservation and monitoring of assets during development, actions for presenting an asset, marketing responsibly, accommodating key or special users other than tourism, avoiding or mitigating negative impacts, and continued consultation and involvement of key stakeholders. More detail on the types of actions listed above can be found in Hall and McArthur (1998), ICOMOS (1993), Uzzell and Ballantyne (1998), Leask and Yeoman (1999), and Lord and Lord (1999), to name a few. Clearly, all of these plans work toward the accomplishment of the same sets of goals, so care must be taken to ensure that they are integrated and compatible. Chapter 13 discusses how marketing can be used as a management tool to achieve a host of different objectives.

Evaluation and Feedback Mechanisms

Evaluation and feedback mechanisms form the last step of the current planning process and the first of the next planning round. These devices enable the asset managers to track success toward the achievement of stated goals. All aspects of the attraction's performance can be measured; which aspects are selected will depend on the core needs of the asset and the resources available. As a minimum, the effectiveness experiential aspects of the attraction should be assessed through visitor satisfaction surveys or other mechanisms. As well, the effect of tourism use on the state of the tangible or intangible assets should be monitored.

Finally, it should be noted that once an asset is developed to its full potential for cultural tourism, the work does not stop there. Conservation and economic demands associated with the day-to-day management and long-term survival of an asset as an attraction will require acknowledgment during the planning process and careful monitoring afterward (Clarke 1997). Most responsible professionals recognize this fact, but it should be emphasized clearly in the action plan or master plan that management and conservation of an attraction is an ongoing process.

Chapter 13

Marketing

INTRODUCTION

Marketing and cultural heritage management; are they compatible? Many people in the CHM sector cringe when advised to adopt a marketing perspective in the overall management of their assets. They equate marketing with sales maximization, even if that means misrepresenting the core values of the asset to broaden the consumer base. Likewise, many people also confuse marketing with advertising and promotion, again presenting whatever image maximizes sales, often to the detriment of the asset. In reality, however, sales and promotion represent the end product of the marketing process; they are a means to an end, a means to achieve broader management objectives, rather than an end in themselves. If conducted in an unplanned or uncoordinated way, sales or promotional activities can lead to the types of problems cited in this book.

Indeed, many of the adverse impacts noted in cultural tourism are a direct result of the failure to adopt a marketing management perspective rather than because of it. Because of a failure to identify clearly the core product, the target market, financial, and nonfinancial objectives, and a plan of action to achieve them, mixed messages can be sent to the public. As a result, the "wrong" type of person, expecting the "wrong" type of experience is likely to be attracted to the asset, which in turn forces asset managers to present their products in an inappropriate manner to satisfy consumer demand.

MARKETING AS A MANAGEMENT TOOL

Marketing is, or should be, an integral part of the overall management process used to develop facilities and services as tourism products, identify potential travelers and their needs and wants, price their products, communicate their appeal to target markets, and deliver them to their customers' satisfaction, in compliance with organizational goals (American Marketing Association as modified by Richardson 1996). Marketing, rather than being about visitation and sales maximization, therefore, is about adopting a customer-focused management tool that can be used to help cultural or heritage attractions achieve their wider organizational goals by linking customer desires with appropriate goods and services (adapted from Kotler and Turner 1989). Especially within a cultural tourism context, these goals may be nonfinancial as much as financial. In addition, responsible marketing must take into account the needs of the host population (Seaton and Bennett 1996) whose needs and uses of many cultural or heritage assets may be quite different from those of tourists.

Although adopting a marketing approach means considering assets as products that visitors can consume, it also means acknowledging that only certain types of visitors are desirable (see Photo 13.1). Indeed, one of the legitimate uses of marketing cultural or heritage assets is to de-market the asset, reduce demand, transfer demand between seasons, or shift pressure away from fragile areas to more robust ones. Thus, marketing may be as much about convincing some people not to use the product as it is about convincing the target audience to enjoy their experiences.

It is for this reason that Reverend Canon Brett adopts a marketing approach with the Canterbury Cathedral in England. He indicates that careful and accurate description of the character of the site and of the desired message management wishes to promote will do much to attract the visitor who has the right kind of interest in the cathedral (Brett 1999). He states, "Good marketing can be a useful means of selection [of appropriate visitors] which can help with problems of sustainability at high-profile attractions" (Brett 1999: 84). It is also for this reason that the Department of Canadian Heritage in Parks Canada uses a marketing or de-marketing approach to try to influence demand for services and to direct the message conveyed by the travel trade to the consumer (Whytock 1999).

Why a Marketing Approach Has Not Been Adopted

As discussed elsewhere in this book, the failure to consider marketing in all phases of strategic planning results in a loss of control over the product, often with catastrophic consequences. One of the

PHOTO 13.1. Guiyang Province, China

Adopting a marketing approach enables managers to exert control over their assets by positioning a desired type of experience for a desired type of visitor. As such, some of the adverse impacts of tourism caused by a less desirable type of tourist can be avoided, including this example from Guiyang in Western China, where visitors have damaged the site by "testing" the strength of paper windows.

reasons that "marketing" (used in its context of sales and advertising) has gotten so much deserved bad press over the years is that it has been undertaken without due consideration of specific objectives to be achieved or what message is to be conveyed. In all too many cases, sales targets are identified, advertising budgets set, and promotional material produced without asking the essential questions, "Why?" and "What do we really want to achieve from these efforts?" Part of the problem is that many of the people given marketing responsibility have little real knowledge of marketing. A second problem is that, surprisingly, few cultural tourism attractions have formalized marketing plans with clearly stated goals and objectives. As a result, they are placed in a reactive position, having to respond to consumer and travel trade demand, rather than leading it.

A third factor is that destinations become obsessed with increasing visitor numbers rather than providing quality experiences. Most destination marketers will talk about quality experiences, but when push comes to shove and when their performance is assessed, the first thing considered is visitor numbers, followed by economic impact. Quality of experience falls somewhat lower on the list. Thus, at a macro level, much marketing activity is directed at maximizing sales, which places pressure on cultural assets that are often showcased in promotional literature. The result is that many activities that fall under the broad moniker of marketing achieve little or actually work against the best interests of the asset. The failure to control the message sent and ensure that it is linked explicitly to the goals of the organization, subsequently creates opportunities for others to take control of the message conveyed.

UNIQUE FEATURES OF MARKETING IN CULTURAL TOURISM

Cultural tourism has a number of unique features that pose challenges to marketers as well as highlight the importance of considering marketing in the planning process. Nonfinancial objectives often have an equal or stronger role in the overall set of objectives than financial goals. Conservation, education, awareness building, creating pride in one's past, or even religious contemplation may be more important objectives than visitor numbers or financial gain. In fact, increased visitor numbers may actually work against the achievement of nonfinancial goals. Further, when considering the entire spectrum of cultural tourism attractions, only a small number are operated as viable business concerns. Most either generate no direct revenue from tourism or charge a nominal entry fee as a means of trying to recover some costs to augment private- and public-sector operating grants.

A second unique feature of cultural tourism is that tourists and local residents share the asset, creating the need to be cognizant of both external (tourist) and internal (local residents) markets. Part of the balancing act in developing cultural tourism products from extant cultural heritage assets is to gain community support for the tourism-ification of the asset, while at the same time ensuring that tourism use does not compromise the needs of local user. Again, a marketing approach will recognize that the actions of the secondary user, be it tourist or local resident, do not impinge on the needs of the primary user.

The third unique element is that many cultural or heritage asset managers fail to appreciate that their facilities are, indeed, tourist attractions and, therefore, must be managed, at least in part for tourism use. This circumstance is especially true if the asset is open to the public at no charge (such as historic houses, churches, or temples), or is operated as a nonprofit community service (community museums, historic buildings). Management must be convinced of their role in the tourism hierarchy before marketing issues can be considered.

THINKING STRATEGICALLY

Marketing should be considered an integral element in the overall planning and management process adopted for any cultural tourism attraction. In doing so, however, one must think strategically about the product, the market, and how to position the cultural tourism asset effectively in the marketplace. No cultural tourism product, nor any product for that matter, can be everything to everyone.

One of the biggest mistakes that inexperienced marketers (or people given the marketing role) make is to assume that their product or experience has universal appeal. Often this mistake is made naively by well-intentioned people who become absorbed by the asset and believe that everyone else, given the right chance, will find it as fascinating as they do. Because of this misguided belief, they embark on a series of unfocused promotional activities that send out unclear messages aimed at no one in particular. The result is the inefficient use of scarce resources, lowered visitation levels, lowered satisfaction levels, and the suboptimal performance of the asset on almost all levels.

Instead, attraction managers should learn lessons from successful organizations, both from within and outside of the cultural heritage management field, by identifying certain desired markets whose needs and wants are compatible with their product. Professional marketers know that certain segments of any market are more likely to want a product than other segments. Internationally recognized theme parks know that certain segments of the population are their core audience (usually families with younger children), while they know that demographic sectors will not be as interested. Luxury automobile manufacturers are uninterested in the majority of the population for they cannot afford their products. Instead, they position themselves as being above the norm and appeal to the wealthier buyer. In all cases, successful organizations shape their products and position them effectively to meet the needs and wants of their target users. Cultural tourism sector strategies try to do the same thing?

Thinking strategically is not that difficult, but it does involve clarity of vision, singularity of purpose, and discipline. The first element of any strategic marketing activity is to identify which product markets a business or organization will compete in and, by extension, to determine those it will not compete in (McKercher 1998c). Aaker (1995) asserts that the first element of strategic marketing is to answer the following six questions:

1. What products do I choose to offer?
2. What products do I choose not to offer?
3. What markets do I choose to target?
4. What markets do I choose not to target?
5. What competitors do I choose to compete with?
6. What competitors do I choose to avoid?

Products

Deciding what product an asset does not offer is as important as deciding what it does offer, for the products will determine who will visit and how these visitors will use an asset. Remember, from Chapter 9, a product, in a marketing sense, is the core benefit provided or the core problem solved. If the core benefit is to provide a deep spiritual experience, then the manner in which the product is shaped will be different than if the core benefit desired is a more secular one. Likewise, if the core desire is to educate or raise awareness among visitors, then, the product will need to be shaped differently than if the core benefit sought is to be an entertainment-oriented experience. Providing too broad an array of products or experiences for too diverse a group of people will end up satisfying no one. Reis and Trout (1993) suggest, instead, to focus on one or two core benefits and then communicate these benefits to the target audience. In this way, the product can become the automatic choice for the consumer.

Markets

Defining the product should also help define the likely user and, equally as important, who the likely user will not be. The first decision that many cultural or heritage managers need to make is whether or not to target tourists. Often this decision is taken out of their hands by destination marketing and travel trade organizations that decide to encourage people to visit some sites. However, attraction managers can exert a significant amount of influence over whether they wish tourists to visit through a variety of management actions that can enhance or inhibit access (operating hours, entrance fees, limits on visitation, encouraging/prohibiting bus tours, being included or excluded from tour packages, etc.).

Assuming the decision is made to accept tourists, the next decision is to define what type of tourist is wanted and what type is not wanted. Some types of tourists may be more compatible with the asset than others. Considerations, such as how long tourists will stay on site, what their backgrounds are, and prior knowledge of the asset, will influence how the product is shaped. If the target market is the casual or incidental tourist, then the attraction will need to be presented in an easily consumable manner. If the goal is to target the sightseeing cultural tourist, then a deeper experience can be provided that is still relatively accessible to the nonexpert. If, however, the target audience is the purposeful cultural tourist, the product will, again, have to be shaped in a different manner to suit this audience.

Competitors

It is hard for some people to understand that cultural tourism assets must compete with other tourism assets for a share of visitors. If the decision is made to pursue tourism, the decision has also been made to compete for tourists. Any cultural tourism attraction must compete for visitors with other cultural tourism attractions and also with other attractions aimed at the broader tourism market. Only a small percentage of cultural tourists are truly committed, purposeful cultural tourists. Most others will participate in a variety of activities during their visit, which undoubtedly will include cultural as well as noncultural activities. However, thinking that a cultural asset must compete with all other tourist attractions is a mistake. For starters, only about one-third of all tourists participate in cultural tourism activities at some time during their visit. And among this one-third, this book identifies five different segments (serendipitous, incidental, casual, sightseeing, and purposeful; see Chapter 9) that exhibit quite different behavior patterns.

To compete effectively (positioning the asset as a preferred place to visit), asset managers must know which other attractions are offering similar experiences that target the market. In the Hong Kong case study, for example, purposeful cultural tourists were the greatest consumers of museum experiences. By contrast, incidental cultural tourists were most interested in entertainment-oriented attractions, such as theme parks and IMAX cinema presentations. This knowledge would suggest that museums should compete with other museums for the purposeful cultural tourist dollar, and not worry about cultural theme parks, as they do not appeal to their main audience. Likewise, cultural theme parks need to compete effectively against other entertainment-oriented attractions, both within and outside of the cultural tourism realm, but need not feel they must compete against art galleries.

SUSTAINABLE COMPETITIVE ADVANTAGES

The ultimate goal of strategic marketing is to identify and exploit those attributes of an organization that give it a sustainable competitive advantage in the marketplace. A sustainable competitive advantage (SCA) is defined as a real competitive advantage that is sustainable over time in the face of competitor reaction (Aaker 1995). These are the unique features of an organization or attraction—the things it does well, or things its competitors do not do well. SCAs have a number of attributes:

- They are substantial enough to make a difference; a marginal advantage is meaningless.
- They are sustainable in the face of competitor reaction; in other words, they are immune to competitor actions.
- They must be real or perceived to be real by the consumer and must also be seen to be valuable to the consumer.

- They form a central platform in the overall positioning of the product.
- They must be rare among current competitors. (Aaker 1995; Bharadwaj, Varadarajan, and Fahy 1993)

There is evidence of strategic thinking, positioning, and developing SCAs everywhere in the cultural tourism sector. Why is it that most large cities have separate art museums, natural history museums, and historical museums? Why do some have separate art museums that specialize in different styles of art? Why do these museums not offer the same products? The answer, from a business perspective, is that each has effectively identified its SCA and has designed its product mix accordingly to capitalize on its own assets or on the asset gap offered by other museums. In doing so, each museum has clearly defined what products it offers and what it does not offer, which helps define who its customers are and are not. In the end, this approach enables each to segment the market, minimizing direct competition.

If the large players adopt such a strategic focus, does it not make sense that smaller players should also consider the same approach? Every cultural tourism attraction, be it a representation of tangible or intangible heritage, a primary attraction at a destination or a tertiary attraction, a museum, art gallery, historic building, fort, prison complex, industrial heritage complex, cultural show, or purpose-built theme park, needs to do something to differentiate itself from the myriad other cultural and heritage tourism products available to the tourist. Failure to do so will relegate it to the list of failed or poor-performing attractions. This differentiation must occur from the perspective of the tourist. What the tourist sees to be unique or different about a place matters more than what the asset managers feel is unique or different.

ROLE OF RESEARCH

Successful marketing is predicated on a sound understanding of the product on offer, the target market, and the underlying industry conditions. Product knowledge comes from being able to disassociate oneself from the product and look at it from the perspective of the consumer. It also comes from being able to enunciate the core product and assess how well the tangible product matches it. Often asset managers are too close to the product or experience to be able to examine it in an unbiased manner. The customers or specialist researchers are better able to accomplish these tasks.

Thus, research plays a vital role in the successful management, marketing, and delivery of quality experiences. Increasingly, the role of research is being recognized in the cultural tourism sector. Historically, what research was conducted tended to identify only the generic demographic profile of visitors and establish a crude level of satisfaction. Today, a more sophisticated approach to market research is being advocated (Wertheim 1994; Kerstetter, Confer, and Bricker 1998; Prentice, Witt, and Hamer 1998) that also seeks to identify motivational and psychographic reasons for visiting, desired experiences, and critical incidents that reflect the overall quality of experience. Wertheim (1994), for example, suggests that visitor surveys should consider, among other elements, visitor profile; details of the visit, such as time spent on site, areas visited, and expenditure; decision making in choosing the site, including effectiveness of advertising, recall of ads, main reason to visit; and attitudes and opinions about the site, such as rating of quality of information, ease of moving around, the entertainment/educational value, highlights of the visit, overall satisfaction, and suggestions for changes or improvements. To this, we would add finding out if the desired message was communicated effectively during the visit.

Effective research must be outcome oriented and conducted with specific objectives in mind. Again, a tactical or strategic approach to research is advocated. We have seen too many cases where small to medium-sized cultural and heritage attractions gather much information through various sources but never actually get around to analyzing it. The excuse offered is that staff members are simply too busy operating the attraction to take the time to analyze the data. Alternatively, we have also seen many places gather excessive amounts of data or conduct research exercises with no clear goal or outcome in mind.

One of the most abused research techniques is the SWOT (strength, weakness, opportunity, and threat) analysis. When done correctly, a SWOT analysis is an effective, easy-to-conduct research tool that can offer valuable insights to help an organization identify and capitalize on its SCAs. The SWOT analysis is, essentially, a comparative tool that enables an organization to assess its operations or one element of its operations against either industry norms or a known competitor, with specific outcomes in mind. In practice, however, far too many SWOT analyses are done without a context or clear goals. Instead of being goal oriented, the SWOT tends to identify a laundry list of items that serve no real purpose.

The failure to identify specific goals or a clear frame of reference in which the analysis is conducted will produce meaningless results. A 300-year-old building is just that: an old building. It is impossible to state whether its age is a strength, weakness, opportunity, or threat unless it is compared to something. If it is the oldest building in town and has an interesting history, then its age may be a strength. But a 300-year-old building in the midst of an ancient archaeological site may be a modern eyesore that detracts from the even older experience and, thus, may be considered a weakness. So although research is important, the purpose or desired outcomes from the research are more important than the act of gathering information. It is for this reason that the audit approach, mentioned in Chapter 12, is suggested as a preferred method.

PUTTING IT TOGETHER—THE MARKETING PLAN

Marketing activities are drawn together in a marketing plan that integrates the organization's overall goals and objectives and long-term marketing activities with the year's marketing efforts. Like all plans, marketing plans should be dynamic documents that outline a desired path but also provide the flexibility to alter the plan should market conditions change. Marketing plans generally consist of five or six elements (Richardson 1996; Seaton and Bennett 1996): (1) a situation analysis, (2) a review of the organization's mission, (3) objectives and strategies for both financial and nonfinancial goals, (4) an action plan, (5) a budget, and (6) a means to evaluate its effectiveness.

Like all plans, annual and interim targets that can be assessed quantitatively to assess progress toward overall goals need to be identified. One of the challenges with a marketing plan, or with any plan for that matter, is to be able to assess its effectiveness. Without specific, quantifiable targets, this task is almost impossible. How can one assess a goal of "encouraging our visitors to learn something about our asset" unless that goal can be assessed somehow?

THE FOUR Ps—THE MARKETING MIX

The marketing mix reflects how the plan is put into action. Defined as "the mixture of controllable marketing variables that the firm uses to pursue the sought level of sales in the target market" (Kotler 1984, as cited in Middleton 1994, p. 63) or other management objectives, these elements reflect the practical decisions that must be made when matching organizational objectives with consumers' needs and wants to the products or services provided. Each of the elements of the marketing mix, more commonly known as the four Ps of marketing (product, price, place, and promotion), should be crafted in such a way that these broader management objectives can be achieved.

Product

Adopting a marketing approach when considering product development empowers the asset managers, whereas the failure to do so results in a loss of control over the experience. Empowerment comes from being able to control the core product, and thus the experience, to reach the target audience. By contrast, the failure to adopt a marketing approach when developing products or to let external agencies, such as the travel trade, assume the product development role could very likely result in inappropriate products being created that will appeal to a less desirable type of user.

Price

Price is the only element of the marketing mix that produces revenue. As such, it serves a tactical as well as an economic role for an organization (Holloway and Robinson 1995). The price charged sends many signals about the likely value of the product being offered and, as such, must be commensurate with the quality of experience. People are more than willing to pay $10,000 or more for specialist cultural tours to exotic places because the perceived value will be equal to or greater than the cost. On the other hand, many people will balk at paying entry fees of $1 or $2 to visit a historic home out of concern that they will not receive value for money.

Price also plays a role of democratizer or discriminator of experiences. A low price may facilitate access for all. On the other hand, a high price may actively discourage some people from participating and, if the price is high enough, may exclude them on economic grounds. As such, it can be used to satisfy a management objective of reducing access. As a general rule of thumb, the more rare or unique the asset is, the greater its scarcity value, which means a high price can be justified.

Place

The place or distribution channels used to get the product into the marketplace, again, will influence the amount of visitation, the type of visitor, the quality of experience expected, the amount of information that can be disseminated, and control over that information. Essentially two types of distribution channels are available: *direct distribution,* where asset managers distribute the product directly to the consumer, and *indirect distribution,* where the product is distributed through a variety of intermediaries, most notably the travel trade. The role that these gatekeepers play in both information dissemination and expectation creation has already been discussed in Chapter 10 and, therefore, does not need to be raised again. Direct distribution channels provide the benefit of being able to control the message but at a cost of limited reach. On the other hand, the use of indirect distribution systems and, in particular, the inclusion of the attraction package tour itineraries will broaden the marketplace considerably but at the risk of losing control over the message and expected experience.

Promotion—Communicating the Message

Promotion, or getting the desired message across, is clearly a key element of the marketing mix for cultural tourism attractions. The basic aim of promotion is to prompt people into positive action after they have received information about the products or services offered (Richardson 1996). How well the message is conveyed and what messages are sent not only heighten or dampen interest in visiting cultural tourism attractions but also shape the type of experience visitors expect on arrival. It is for this reason that the message conveyed must be clear and unequivocal and must, at all times, convey a message that is compatible with the desired type of experience.

Communication or miscommunication is one of the legitimate complaints raised about tourism promotion in fragile environments. Advocates of codes of ethical conduct in terms of marketing (Wheeler 1995) lament the fact that untruthful, misleading, or incomplete messages are conveyed all too often to potential visitors. Others (D'Sa 1999; Sizer 1999) decry the lack of tourists with appropriate social consciousness consuming cultural tourism products and blame marketing. Communication of this type results in unrealistic expectations being created, irresponsible behavior being promoted or condoned, and, arguably the worst of all, the promotion of a mismatch between destinations and tourist types resulting in damage to assets or lower visitor satisfaction.

Effective communication will enable attractions to effectively segment the market and send messages that will appeal to the desired type of visitor. Further, it will also help perspective visitors self-select whether the product being offered is suitable for their needs. By contrast, ineffective or misleading communication will serve only to confuse the market, possibly driving away the desired visitor or attracting a less-desirable visitor.

CONCLUSIONS

Marketing is more than simply sales. It is a management approach that forms part of the overall management plan. Most important, it is also a tactical tool that can be used to accomplish a wide range of management objectives, including both financial and nonfinancial goals. To be effective, though, it must be focused tightly, strategic in its orientation, and based on a sound understanding of the marketplace.

Chapter 14

Presentation and Management
of Heritage Assets

INTRODUCTION

Use of or visitation to assets is an integral component of cultural heritage management. Forming an innate part of most management plans, the promotion of use fosters an understanding of its values and its context in the sociocultural heritage of a community and engenders greater community support for the further conservation of valuable tangible and intangible assets. Among other goals, presentation, therefore, aims to encourage visitors to value heritage assets now, to support keeping them for the future (Goulding 1999; Lowenthal 1998). To do this properly, the right assets need to be selected and highlighted, while measures for their commodification have to cover the needs of as broad an audience as possible.

How the asset is presented will influence how well it can be managed. If managers can control the message or presentation, they can also control the tourist and, in doing so, control the use of the asset. Indeed, CHM's main need in presenting assets to the public is to convey the message that they are valuable to society and therefore their ongoing conservation is important (Goulding 1999; Bell 1997; UNESCO World Heritage Centre 2000). Tourism can play a role. It is seen as ensuring the "survival of places and the continued support of society for them. . . . Intelligent and positive responses by the manager can mean more conservation funds, more employment, better place conservation and a more sympathetic community" (Pearson and Sullivan 1995: 279).

Problems can occur when tourism and cultural heritage management priorities are set separately. They can also develop when an asset's ability to withstand visitation impacts and its appeal are poorly understood. For instance, a heritage place under pressure from heavy visitation with little attention to its conservation management will suffer physical damage that will in turn affect its cultural values and eventually compromise the visitor experience. Poor planning, however, can also compromise intangible cultural values. Aspects of an asset's history, for instance, that should have been emphasized to encourage a proper understanding of its cultural significance can be subverted by the need to present the asset only as a form of entertainment (Urry 1990; Daniel 1996). Often the problem lies in the way such values are treated by the standardization of visitor experiences (Dodson and Clarke 1999; Henderson 1999). Setting commodification priorities properly, therefore, becomes a vital element in the overall management strategy.

Commodification usually involves some form of interpretation or, as the tourism sector prefers, the development of products. In the end, both tourism and cultural heritage management are talking about the same thing—presentation of assets—but they look at this issue from different perspectives. Interpretation tends to be a more all-encompassing idea. Ham (1992, as cited in Weiler and Ham 2001) believes that five main principles drive interpretation:

1. It is not teaching or instruction in an academic sense, although it does involve the transfer of information.
2. It must be enjoyable for visitors, for if it is made to be fun and enjoyable, noncaptive visitors are likely to pay attention longer.
3. It must be relevant for visitors, and visitors must be able to relate it to their own frame of reference.
4. It must be well organized so that visitors can follow it easily.
5. It should be focused around a few discrete themes, rather than simply presenting information in a disconnected manner.

Tourism, on the other hand, tends to focus on use values. For many in the tourism industry, the middle three elements (entertaining, relevant for the visitor, and easy to follow) take precedence over the other elements. The management challenge for cultural tourism attractions is to try to achieve more than just the provision of entertainment. If the tourist can learn something, even subliminally, then the visit has been worthwhile. Again, Weiler and Ham (2001) comment that visitors will forget much of the factual information presented but may still develop an appreciation of the overriding notion of the importance of the place. Perhaps this is an acceptable objective for casual and incidental cultural tourists, while presenting an opportunity for a deeper experience may be a worthwhile goal for sightseeing and purposeful visitors.

A further challenge to management is that cultural heritage assets must serve many "publics" with diverse needs, of whom tourism is just one. To encourage these publics or audiences to "need" heritage as an important aspect of their lives, the presentation of heritage assets must include a wide array of activities. Such activities might include educational programs for schools—special activities such as field schools and experiments with different modes of interpretation to engage the interest of these diverse audiences and assist absorption of the core message. The assets will also be subject to research activity that will further the study of particular aspects of the past and can be used as part of the asset's presentation. Different users, however, may have quite different management and presentation needs. Many historical assets, for example, may benefit schoolchildren on excursions as much as tourists. But children under twelve usually require such radically different programs that presenting the same material for adults will not lead to a positive experience for adults (Tilden 1977: 9). Cultural heritage management, therefore, must be aware of the needs and requirements of user groups such as these in the earliest stages of planning the conservation and management of an asset.

Two Cases: Integrating Tourism and Local Use

One example of tourism as the minority user of an asset is the Hindu temple complex of Pashupatinath, near Kathmandu in Nepal (see Photo 14.1). This complex is also World Heritage listed and is well known on the subcontinent first and foremost as a site of major significance to the Hindu religion. As such, it attracts a large number of pilgrims who outnumber other tourists at most times. An unspoken policy exists at the site complex: tourism operators and local guides should use a different entrance than the one used by pilgrims, and they should move visitors along a different route to view the main shrines. Some areas are restricted to tourist access. This is to allow pilgrims, many of whom come to the site to cremate their dead, to carry on with their rituals unhindered. It also prevents the tourists

PHOTO 14.1. Pashupatinath Hindu Temple, Near Kathmandu in Nepal

The Pashupatinath Temple Complex, near Kathmandu in Nepal, is a place of sacred significance for Hindus all over the subcontinent. It is holiest of the god Shiva's shrines in Nepal while being one of three important sites in the region and attracting large numbers of pilgrims. This World Heritage Site is under stress from external forces, such as pollution from industries upriver, as well as from poorly coordinated visitor management. The pollution of the sacred Bagmati River has become so extreme that in the dry season it barely flows past the temple complex.

Worshippers and pilgrims commonly outnumber tourists and are seen by the site's managers as the main user group for the whole complex. Currently the southern side of the Bagmati River is the main place that tourists are taken; non-Hindus can view Pashupatinath and Guyeshwari temples only from a distance. Tour groups are usually accompanied by a guide who brings them in by the southwestern entrance, avoiding the main gate and the majority of the temple complex on the northern side of the river where cremations and rituals occur. Tourists are also brought along the southern edge of the river past numerous souvenir shops up a small hill to where they can look across and down into the courtyard of the Pashupatinath Temple and watch the cremations along the riverbank from a distance. The Lonely Planet guide notes that some tourists have been known to treat those conducting cremations insensitively by crossing the river and getting up close to film the activity (Lonely Planet 2000: 231).

The problem is that not much has been done onsite to provide much information about visitor behavior at the complex or to improve information and interpretation about the site to tourists. The complex seems to rely entirely on the proficiency of guides that escort such groups and the ability of independent travelers to behave in accordance with the information provided in guidebooks. A very basic tourist information booth sits among the souvenir shops, but it provides little useful information (du Cros and Johnston 2001).

from unknowingly defiling areas where, for instance, leather from cattle should not be worn or only people of the Hindu faith should enter. However, problems can arise when independent travelers are poorly informed and wander into areas where they should not due to poor site presentation. The temple complex relies heavily on local guides to provide information on visitor etiquette and to keep visitors away from areas of special spiritual significance. Because of the lack of detailed information in guidebooks, on-site signage, and other site information (such as brochures stressing visitor etiquette that could be made available at the entrance) independent tourists risk the ire of other users, such as pilgrims and local priests.

In another example, the craftswomen of Fombori, a small village in West Africa, observed that nearby sister villages were making money from the sales of handicrafts and some ceremonial objects to tourists. Although keen to increase sales and production of secular objects themselves, they were wary that too much exposure to tourism would lead to heavy economic dependence on it, that it may also lead to sacred objects being offered for sale. Their initial solution was to establish a small museum and gift shop where handicrafts could be sold and ceremonial objects would only be exhibited. It was built with aid from the U.S. Agency for International Development (USAID) and several other international aid organizations. It opened in 1996 with much public acclaim.

However, it soon became obvious that they had misjudged the tourist demand for such an attraction, and revenue for ongoing activities fell far short of the costs of providing them. Visitation was sporadic; the building was closed more often than it was open. Many villagers also were reluctant to place their ceremonial objects in the museum. It was soon shut down altogether, whereupon it became infested with termites.

The villagers met and discussed the situation; they decided to make the museum a focal point for the community rather than a tourist attraction. They planned to set it up as a "culture bank," where villagers could deposit their ceremonial artifacts for display and curation while they acted as collateral for loans. The building itself was improved and made termite proof with further government aid; eventually, a museum specialist was provided by the West African Museums Programme and other aid programs. The culture bank expects to be self-sufficient in five years.

The culture bank as museum also works as a true community and cultural center with an activity program that includes artisan workshops, concerts, theater presentations, and traditional festivals, as well as classes in literacy and health. The Fombori Culture Bank has become the means to provide a small community with a lasting economic resource that does not compromise its values by allowing tourism requirements to drive the agenda. Fombori has not fallen into the trap of being so economically dependent on tourism that it needs either the revenue from legal or illicit sales of objects or perpetual government aid or funding. It has cultivated respect for tradition locally, worked to reinvigorate it, and made cultural preservation economically sustainable (Crosby and Ebbe 2000).

The tourist sector in this example appears initially to have requirements that are inimical to those of the local heritage managers and the host community. Tourists or tourism operators do not seem to be interested in this little village unless good deals can be struck and unusual or sacred items can be bought. The museum, in its mostly un-commodified state when it first opened, was not of great interest to tourists. Ironically, once the facility started to focus on local requirements and became a better facility as museum and for preserving and enacting local traditions, its tourism appeal increased as well. So, some requirements may overlap for tourism and heritage management, as uncommodified and poorly planned facilities are unlikely to be of use to either.

REINVESTMENT OF REVENUE IN CONSERVATION AS ONE BENEFIT OF TOURISM

Most conservation charters and codes make no direct mention of the importance of having a mechanism for the reinvestment of revenue gleaned from tourism into the conservation process. Only the 1999 ICOMOS Cultural Tourism Charter has stated that, from the cultural heritage management perspective, such a mechanism is beyond being a key benefit of tourism; it is also an obligation that the tourism sector should fulfill. Accordingly, it states that "a significant proportion of the revenue specifically derived from tourism programs to heritage places should be allotted to protection, conservation and presentation of those places, including their natural and cultural contexts" (ICOMOS 1999 [Article 5.3]).

Tourism is a way of bringing externally generated funds to a country or region, and, once there, a number of ways are used to tap its bounty directly without causing resentment. One of these ways is to levy a fee, outside of that charged as part of any tourism package, to ensure revenue goes directly to asset management and conservation. In the case of Bhaktapur, a World Heritage town in the Kathmandu valley in Nepal, visitors are more willing to part with the entrance fee levied if they know it is going directly to heritage conservation (Bhaktapur Council 2000). In other places, revenue generation could be a levy that is part of a lodging tax or a gate fee on entering a heritage place, museum, or historic park. Some type of conservation or cultural trust, which would have accessible procedures and audited accounts, would manage the levied funds toward implementing conservation measures.

How Important Is Self-Sufficiency?

Many instances exist of management or conservation plans being shelved through subsequent lack of resources to implement their recommendations. How important is achieving self-sufficiency or some kind of economic sustainability, therefore, for an asset that could become a major tourism attraction? A debate that still continues in some developed countries concerns how much government core funding of publicly owned heritage assets is actually needed. The disagreement revolves around whether it is possible for publicly accessible assets to achieve some level of economic sustainability or self-sufficiency through their own revenue generation (du Cros 1996; Garrod and Fyall 1998; Peacock 1998; Elliott 1998).

The question for publicly accessible assets is: If visitors cannot be charged in some way directly for their use of the asset, how do such assets still become self-sufficient, with adequate funds for maintenance and interpretation? Some sites and landscapes may be too remote for management authorities to afford to collect gate fees. Many governments have also been pushing for corporate sponsorship and partial privatization, which so far has received little encouragement from heritage managers (Boniface and Fowler 1993; Austrian Heritage Commission 1997; Peacock 1998).

Cases: Hadrian's Wall and Kakadu National Park

In seeking self-sufficiency, the principles of CHM could be put to the test when other types of activity (for example, mining) are proposed to cover shortfalls in revenue for reinvestment. Whether archaeological sites that are already tourist attractions, including those contained in World Heritage listings, should be subject to the pressures associated with becoming self-sufficient is an issue, according to some analysts, associated with placing heritage in the context of the real world (Boniface and Fowler 1993: 89). Can the cultural values of such heritage assets continue to be maintained in a sustainable way?

Boniface and Fowler (1993) use the example of the World Heritage listing of Hadrian's Wall in Britain as demonstrating how economics can clash with sustainability policies (see Photo 14.2). In

PHOTO 14.2. Hadrian's Wall, England

Hadrian's Wall, the ancient Roman fortification located in the north of England. Despite its World Heritage significance, it has not been immune to the threat of development. Its importance to the British tourism industry and its high cultural value are two good reasons for its continued preservation.

1991, an application to drill an exploratory bore hole for hydrocarbons near the wall was made by a mining company and approved by the regional planning authority. A public inquiry was called when the secretary of state intervened in the planning process. The planning authority declared at this point that it stood by its original decision but would not allow a mining license to be issued if the exploration located any resources. Boniface and Fowler (1993) thought that any such development was incompatible with the site's use for tourism and with its rural setting; they also noted that the mining would be potentially damaging to subsurface archaeological material. They saw the incident as setting the scene for a culture clash between the proposed exploitation of a cultural as well as a natural resource, a novel and, in many respects, highly successful universal concept of World Heritage (Boniface and Fowler 1993: 89). If such a listing had been privatized, would the result have been the same? How much mining revenue by the mining company might have been put toward allowing a site to be self-sufficient if the government had taken such a policy to its extreme?

In Australia, where parts of the World Heritage-listed Kakadu National Park have been excised for uranium mining, it is likely there will be an opportunity to find out the answers to the previous questions once the Jabiluka Mine is operational. However, any reinvestment in heritage offered by the mining company is unlikely to do much in the eyes of the mine's main opponents, the Mirrar people. It is hoped that more culturally appropriate ways will be found to attract reinvestment in other cases, to generate revenue other than that from mining or exploitative tourism.

FEES AND LEVIES RAISED AT THE SOURCE

However, if raising revenue is to be done by fees, what sort of fees should be charged? Also, if the objective of heritage managers is to present the asset to as broad an audience as possible, would using a high gate fee to ease visitation pressure on a heritage place be seen as a legitimate visitor management measure? Should publicly owned museums, previously offering free entrance, start charging fees if their core government funding has been reduced? Should they try selling off the less important objects in their collections by what is termed "de-accessioning" them? These questions are being asked in situations where demands on the public purse are many, a taxation base is narrowing, and the legacy of known heritage in public management is sizeable (Garrod and Fyall 1998; Peacock 1998; Elliot 1998). Whatever is decided in each case should uphold the sustainable use of the asset, as these issues are too new to be covered fully by current codes of planning and practice. Careful negotiations with other stakeholders, particularly community groups, schools, the tourism sector, and philanthropic agencies are therefore needed to ensure a workable solution.

Conservation Measures to Assist in Visitor Management

Heritage managers and others are finding that it is crucial to include such conservation measures as early on as possible in the development of a conservation policy for tangible heritage, then to continue reviewing their effectiveness later on. Most heritage managers and museum specialists would agree that planning for the commodification of tangible heritage assets for visitors is becoming a major area of their responsibilities. Those in the public sector are responsible for the major part of such work in the form of erecting signage, establishing visitor centers, publishing and disseminating brochures, holding exhibitions, developing volunteer or education programs, and introducing many other activities. How well all this integrates with visitor management and conservation measures is the test of a presentation program, particularly in the face of what may be privately or independently offered in private tour packages or guidebooks.

Many heritage managers dealing with tangible heritage, such as vulnerable historic buildings and archaeological sites, tend to concentrate on the conservation message rather than a cultural one in this important phase. For instance, they want to control the transmission of ideas promoting their site mainly "to manage demand so that the attraction is not damaged by over-use" (Muresan 1998: 41). Making assets more exclusive (e.g., only so many visitors or tours per day by appointment only) or more expensive are two ways around this overuse. By engaging the visitor's cooperation and explaining the reason for such measures, both the visitor's level of satisfaction and the heritage manager's conservation message may be served (Jacobs and Gale 1994).

Frequently, heritage managers fail to see that the negative physical impacts on an asset are the result of a mismatch between tourism promotion and on-site visitor experience. For instance, the management of the Great Pyramids of Giza was criticized by Evans and Fielding (1998) as showing that little effort had been made to actualize the site's informative potential by the heritage managers. If more interpretative on-site information had been provided previsit and on-site regarding visitor etiquette and the cultural values of the place, it would improve and control visitor experiences and the site's conservation (Evans and Fielding 1998: 86-91).

How intangible heritage can add to its presentation and its management also needs to be integrated into planning. Understanding potential impacts of visitors on such assets is not easy. Impacts on host communities can be anticipated, such as when increased traffic, litter, or loss of good seating at festivals to tourists bring ringing complaints. Impacts of visitation on how tradition bearers and others use traditional knowledge, skills, and types of cultural expression can be more difficult to anticipate and plan to mitigate. As stated in Chapter 4, these aspects of intangible heritage are dynamic and so cannot be kept in a state of total stasis. However, these assets should not be exploited or completely overwhelmed by the needs of tourism. Heritage managers are just as concerned as tradition bearers that monitoring the rate of change must be a significant part of any conservation or cultural policy seeking to manage this aspect of heritage with strong community involvement (Truscott 2000).

Provision of Site Information

Previsit preparation is not only about marketing an experience, it is also about providing the visitor with some point of reference for understanding the experience. In Australia, some heritage managers have realized that the public may be ignorant about archaeology and willing to learn a bit to prepare for a visit—information that may not be repeated. They are keen to encourage people to discover more about history and archaeology for themselves. These efforts must be sensitive to avoid impact on archaeological remains at Aboriginal

sites and respect the concerns of Aboriginal people who are traditional owners.

Drawing attention to visitor etiquette should not restrict an experience; it should be used instead as a way to make it special. Hence, an
explanation of the cultural reasoning behind the protective measures
that are being recommended is important to enlist the visitors' understanding and support. The Internet is becoming an increasingly important resource for site managers in visitor management and site
promotion. It allows them the opportunity to educate visitors directly
and before they arrive, without the message being filtered through
some other authority. This also benefits visitors who wish to bypass
more superficial sources of information and find out directly about a
destination for themselves. They can draw on local knowledge of all
kinds whether they have concerns about confronting a different cultural context or are just worried about locating it and the types of facilities available. One example is a Native American-run Web site for
a Hopi Reservation in Four Corners, Arizona. It has information on
etiquette, what to bring, existing facilities, intellectual property rights,
and cultural sensitivities, which would assist in educating visitors to
respect both the tangible and intangible heritage they would experience at the reservation (Hopi 2000). Another example of the use of
this principle is the signage around some Aboriginal sites in Australia
and recreational sites in America that enjoin the visitors' cooperation
in not littering or accessing restricted areas (Ballantyne 1998; Jacobs
and Gale 1994; Pearson and Sullivan 1995).

Interpreting the Asset

But what is really involved in interpretation? What role do tangible
remains at a site or museum play in the communication and perception of the past by site visitors? One basic definition of the main features of perception that one would expect to associate with a visitor
experience at a site is given by the philosopher Merleau-Ponty in *The
Phenomenology of Perception* (1982). This definition comprises the
subject as perceiver, the action perceived, and the content of what is
perceived. A visitor's experience of a site is more than a mechanical
perception of tangible heritage. If little context or explanation is associated with a site, the visitor tends to try to comprehend through analogy with other facets of previous experience. If this experience is not

informed by basic background information, the visitor will be trying to understand the site in a vacuum. Worse still, the visitor will have to resort to stereotypes and misconceptions accumulated over the years. In other words, if the experience is not shaped for the tourist, the tourist will shape the experience to suit his or her own needs.

Conversely, sites can also be overinterpreted to the point where the medium becomes more important than the message. To demonstrate a case of overinterpretation, Uzzell (1989: 5) fabricated part of a conversation between two visitors comparing "heritage experiences":

> Charles: Did you go to "Baldrick's Saxon Village"? I thought the twenty rack stereo and laser light show in the hunting scene was good. Amanda and Henry liked it too.

> Tim: It wasn't as good as the guillotine scene at the "Best of Times, Worst of Times" exhibition.

Silverstone (1989) is also concerned about the lack of integrity and definition in some interpretation: "The (American) heritage industry is in the business of mass communication and that the boundary between reality and fantasy, between myth and mimesis . . . is becoming increasingly blurred, increasingly indistinct" (Silverstone 1989: 189). The presentation of key heritage attractions, in some countries, places more emphasis on over elaborate interpretation programs that communicate messages poorly about past lifestyles and their material remains (Uzzell 1989). It can be argued that commodification of heritage through interpretation and associated strategies can be still be effective even if it is as simple as a text-bearing sign or museum label in the right place.

The presentation strategy or strategies adopted for an attraction will continually grow and develop as its effectiveness is monitored and new information is included from research where appropriate. Community and visitor attitudes and cultural changes all have some impact on the way assets are presented to visitors, as it is not possible to interpret assets in complete isolation from these influences. A classic case of community attitudes changing and a presentation being noticeably outdated is the history museum in Cape Town, South Africa, visited by the authors in early 1999. Here, temporary labels had been placed in one gallery to indicate that information in the main display no longer coincides with current views of indigenous groups, but funding is not available to update the gallery exhibit.

Finally, it is worth noting that some heritage assets have a more complicated message to convey than others. Challenges of this kind can arise in many ways. One is that the asset is visually and histori-cally complex, as in the case of the Roman Baths in Bath, England. Potentially a confusing site, it has been has been clearly labeled, and remains and their histories have been carefully pointed out. Another challenge can arise if the visitor is expected to choose between more than one historical narrative and interpretation of historical events (e.g., Museum of Sydney). This postmodernist approach is not al-ways successful, although it is one that is still in its infancy and relies heavily on the sophistication or level of historical understanding of the visitor. Whether this approach can be used with less sophisticated visitors and children is yet to be proved. Finally, the greatest chal-lenge in presenting heritage assets is to transform successfully and appropriately an asset to an attraction, which has a confronting his-tory or associations for the visitor.

Case Study: Canterbury Cathedral and "Golden Memories" for Tourists

One example of "best practice" site presentation or commodifica-tion is that of Canterbury Cathedral in Kent, England. The clergy who are the heritage managers of the asset have gone beyond presenting only the basics about cultural values and its historical development. It is important, Reverend Canon Peter Brent advises, to take care of all the microexperiences that add up to a "golden memory" for the visi-tor (Brett 1999). Microexperiences can include aspects of the initial entry into a heritage attraction or "welcome" facilities provided, in-formation (e.g., previsit information and explanation of visitor eti-quette), interpretation, staff service, and relationship of the attraction to its local surroundings and community. He notes that the welcome should be carried out by people rather than signs because it is friend-lier, and staff or volunteer guides can also present information about the asset at the onset. Such staff should be properly trained and identi-fiable in some way as associated with the attraction by badge or uni-form. Facilities also need to be as comfortable and convenient as pos-sible without compromising the attraction's cultural values. Brent notes that in comparison with the Canterbury Cathedral, some other attractions try to limit refreshments to prevent litter, which does not always work. He advises that other strategies are worth investigating if little is done to encourage visitors to take away their rubbish with them. In addition, facilities should also include advance reservations and good parking arrangements.

Information is distinguishable from interpretation as it tells people about a place (where and what things are) while interpretation tells them about its meaning and value. Again, Web sites, promotions by travel agencies, and a dissemination of general information brochures locally and regionally are important. Accordingly, based on the Canterbury Cathedral experience, free leaflet information and adequate but not invasive signage (according to the complexity of the attraction and the nature of its visitor flow patterns) should be provided. He advises that interpretation, in a balanced manner, should anticipate to some extent what visitors would like to know and introduce concepts about the attraction that are important to site managers. The narrative should also balance local aspects of the attraction's historical and cultural development with its regional or thematic context. Such interpretation should also be sensitive to nonphysical aspects of the attraction's value such as the "spirit of the place," particularly in the case of sacred or socially significant heritage assets. This ambience, Brett (1999) states, should not be overwhelmed by the latest in interpretative audiovisual aids, although these are useful in the more educational sectors of an attraction, such as its visitor center.

Of particular concern is the quality of interpretation offered by the human-guided tour. Those who conduct the tours should be well trained or informed, if this is under the control of the heritage manager of the asset. The staff of the attraction should be well trained and continue to upgrade that training on a regular basis. For instance, guides should add information to the tour itinerary as new discoveries are made.

Other Issues for Consideration

The relationship of the heritage asset to the local community should be one that includes the community as a stakeholder in how the attraction is managed. This will assist in the local promotion of the attraction and in preventing negative impacts on the community (such as littering and parking nuisances). Attractions closely associated with indigenous custodians of intangible heritage should have the tradition bearers from such groups closely involved in their management, and information should be available about visitor etiquette in light of cultural sensitivities. Such involvement also adds to a sense of authenticity about the "spirit of the place" and requires the visitor to be mindful of their presence in a memorable way (Moscardo 1996).

Souveniring can be a huge problem for heritage managers of particular types of assets. It should be managed to become a positive, not a negative, aspect of the memories people take away with them. Memorabilia that is freely available or easily purchased should be encouraged and promoted—making these items more attractive for visitors rather than removing fragments of tangible heritage from the attraction. However, a positive intangible reminder or "golden memory" is the best legacy of a visit and one that both CHM and tourism should strive for with a visitor to achieve sustainable cultural tourism.

Epilogue

What does the future hold for cultural tourism? Depending on your perspective, you might be extremely optimistic or extremely pessimistic about the future. On one hand, cultural tourism is arguably the fastest-growing aspect of tourism. Demand is high for cultural experiences and will only continue to grow as tourists become more sophisticated and as more people can afford to travel globally. On the other hand, our collective cultural heritage, the raw material of cultural tourism, is under threat from many sources. War, natural disasters, increasing population, developmental pressures, lack of management resources, lack of clear policy guidelines in some jurisdictions, and use pressures all combine to create a sector under stress.

Tourism is a true double-edged sword: it can be seen both as a threat and as a potential savior. Countless inquisitive tourists are overwhelming cultural attractions in virtually every corner of the world. In all likelihood, tourism activities will exert even more pressure in the future as more people seek to learn more about their own or others' heritage.

But let us not forget that tourism can be a powerful ally of cultural heritage management and a powerful tool to achieve true sustainable use of cultural heritage assets. The exposure gained by presenting cultural heritage assets for tourism consumption can foster greater awareness of the value of the asset and of the need to conserve its unique attributes. Moreover, tourism can provide the financial wherewithal to conserve assets, either directly through gate receipts or indirectly through tax revenue generated from tourism activities. As we have argued throughout this book, recognizing the tourism potential of cultural heritage assets and shaping the experiences to appeal to certain types of preferred users enables asset managers to retain or regain control over their assets. In doing so, tourism can be used as a tool to achieve broader management objectives.

Unfortunately, tourism's potential all too often is not being met, in spite of the rhetoric heard from many quarters. Tourism is viewed as a competitor and not as a collaborator. We have identified a number of reasons for this throughout this book, but, in short, tourism and cultural heritage management still largely function in parallel. Although they may share the resource, they value it for different reasons and seek to use it for different purposes. As a result, tourism and cultural heritage management have each assumed a different role in the product-development/product-marketing process. Cultural heritage managers and asset owners provide the raw materials. The tourism industry then transforms the raw asset into a tourism product and assumes the role of shaping the message communicated to the public to attract them to consume it. Sustainable cultural tourism cannot occur until and unless the product development/promotion roles are integrated with conservation goals.

The partnerships that have been discussed in this book relate primarily to the achievement of this task. How can key stakeholders work together to blend the identification, development, and promotion of cultural tourism into a seamless process? This book was structured to answer this question. Collaboration can only occur when one party understands what factors drive the other party. The legitimate needs and interests of tourism and cultural heritage management must also be understood, as must the role each party plays be appreciated in cultural tourism. In addition, some understanding of the consumer must be developed. Building on this foundation, the authors would encourage those reading this book to take care identifying and exploiting the tourism potential of cultural assets, so as to work within the use limits imposed by the physical or social characteristics of the assets in question.

In the end, though, the successful formation of a partnership between tourism and cultural heritage management is reliant on the will of all parties involved to work together to achieve common, mutually beneficial goals. The authors hope that this book can break down many of the barriers that have inhibited partnership information in the past. It is also hoped that by fostering a better understanding of the legitimate interests of cultural heritage management within the tourism industry and of the legitimate interests of tourism within the cultural heritage management sector, more professionals from both sectors will begin to appreciate the benefits of collaboration. Cultural tourism can survive only if its asset base is managed in a sustainable manner and sustainability can be achieved only if tourism and cultural heritage management work in partnership.

References

Aaker, David (1995). *Strategic market management,* Fourth edition. John Wiley and Sons, Brisbane.

Acott, T. G., La Trobe, H. L., and Howard S. H. (1998). An evolution of deep ecotourism and shallow ecotourism. *Journal of Sustainable Tourism* 6(3): 238-252.

Adande, A. (1995). Plea for a traditional arts and crafts museum. In Ardouin, C. and Arinze, E. (Eds.), *Museums and the community in West Africa* (pp. 68-82). West African Museums Programme and Villiers Publications, London.

AHC (Australian Heritage Commission) (1998). *Looking after heritage places: A guide for local communities.* Australian Heritage Commission, Canberra.

AHC and TCA (1999). *Draft heritage tourism guidelines.* Australian Heritage Commission and Tourism Council of Australia, Canberra.

Allcock, John B. (1995). International tourism and the appropriation of history in the Balkans. In Lanfant, Marie-Francoise, Allcock, John B., and Bruner, Edward M. (Eds.), *International tourism: Identity and change* (pp. 100-112). Sage Publications, London.

Ambrose, Timothy and Paine, Crispin (1993). *Museum basics.* ICOM and Routledge, London.

Anonymous (1998). Study released examining the correlation between cultural tourism and shopping. *Hotel Online Special Report.* Available at <http://www.hotel-online.com/Neo/News/PressReleases1998_4th/Dec98_Taubman.html>, 7 pp.

Anonymous (1999a). *Cultural/heritage tourism—Searching for the real experience.* California Division of Tourism, Sacramento. Available at <http://gocalif.ca.gov/research/historic.html>.

Anonymous (1999b). Like culture, will shop, survey finds. *Lodging Hospitality* 55(9): 17.

Anonymous (1999c). Quebec City: World Heritage Treasure Incentive (Canada's Destination Supplement), pp. 35-38.

Anonymous (1999d). Study says Pennsylvania's rich heritage attracts 12% of total leisure expenditures. *Hotel Online Special Report* 3. Available at <http://www.hotel-online.com/Neo/News/PressReleases1999_3rd/Aug99_PAtourism.html>, 3 pp.

Anonymous (n.d.). Cultural tourism: Where do we go from here? *Delaware Valley Grantmakers,* Philadelphia. Available at <http://www.libertynet.org/dvg/gpca.html> (retrieved June 6, 2000).

Antolovic, Jadran (1999). Immovable cultural monuments and tourism. In *Cultural Tourism Session Notes XII Assembly* (pp. 103-118). ICOMOS, Mexico.

Ap, John (1999). Arts/cultural tourism. Position paper prepared for the Arts/Cultural Tourism Working Group. Hong Kong Tourist Association and Hong Kong Arts Development Council, Hong Kong Polytechnic University, 16 pp.

Ardouin, Claude and Arinze, Emmanuel (1995). *Museums and the community in West Africa.* West African Museums Programme and Villiers Publications, London.

Ashworth, Gregory (1995). Managing the cultural tourist. In Ashworth, G. J. and Dietworst, A. (Eds.), *Tourism and spatial transformation: Implications for policy and planning,* (pp. 265-284). CABI Publications, Wallingford.

Ashworth, Gregory (1999). Tourism in the communication of senses: 'Place' displacement in New Mexico. *Tourism Culture and Communications* 1(2): 115-128.

Ashworth, Gregory and Tunbridge, J.E. (2000). *The tourist-historic city: Retrospect and prospect of managing the heritage city.* Pergamon, New York.

Australia ICOMOS (1998). *Cultural heritage places policy.* Australia ICOMOS, Canberra.

Australia ICOMOS (2000). Australia ICOMOS Web site. <http:/www.icomos.org/australia/>.

Australian Heritage Commission (1997). Australia's national heritage: Options for identifying heritage places of national significance. Discussion paper. Australian Heritage Commission, Canberra.

Australian Heritage Commission and Tourism Council Australia (1999). Draft heritage tourism guidelines. Discussion paper. Australian Heritage Commission and Tourism Council, Canberra.

Bachleitner, Reinhard and Zins, Andreas H. (1999). Cultural tourism in rural communities: The resident's perspective. *Journal of Business Research* 44(3): 199-209.

Bahaire, Tim and Elliott-White, Martin (1999). Community participation in tourism planning and development in the historic city of York, England. *Current Issues in Tourism* 2(2/3): 243-276.

Ballantyne, Roy (1998). Interpreting "visions": Addressing environmental education goals through interpretation. In Uzzell, David and Ballantyne, Roy (Eds.), *Contemporary issues in heritage and environmental interpretation* (pp. 77-97). The Stationary Office, London.

Bazin, Clause-Marie (1995). Industrial heritage in the tourism process in France. In Lanfant, Marie-Francoise, Allcock, John B., and Bruner, Edward M. (Eds.), *International tourism: Identity and change* (pp. 113-126). Sage Publications, London.

Belk, Russell W. and Costa, Janeen Arnold (1995). International tourism: An assessment and overview. *Journal of Macromarketing* 15(2): 33-49.

Bell, D. (1997). *The historic Scotland guide to international conservation charters.* The Stationary Office, Edinburgh.

Belland, Greg and Boss, Erin (1994). Cultural and historical sites: Assessing the tourism potential. *ICOMOS Canada* 3(3), available at <http://www.icomos.org/canada/bulletin/vol3_no3_belland_e.html>.

Bennett, Tony (1993). History on the rocks. In Frow, John and Morris, Meagan (Eds.), *Australian Cultural Studies: A Reader* (pp. 222-240). Allen and Unwin, Sydney.

Bernstein, Judith and Awe, Susan C. (1999). *Wired travelers: Tourism and tourism Web sites.* MCB Press, 16 pp. Available at <http://www.emerald-library.com/brev/24027df1.htm>.

Berry, S. (1994). Conservation, capacity, and cashflows—Tourism and historic building management. In Seaton, A. V. (Ed.), *Tourism: State of the Art* (pp. 712-718). John Wiley and Sons, Chichester.

Bhaktapur Council (2000). Harmonious hobnobs between heritage and tourism: The success story of Bhaktapur. Report to UNESCO by Bhaktapur Council. Available online at UNESCO Web site: <http://www.unescobkk.org/culture/bhaktapur/Casestudy.pdf>.

Bharadwaj, S. G., Varadarajan, P. R., and Fahy, J. (1993). Sustainable competitive advantage in service industries: A conceptual model and research propositions. *Journal of Marketing* 57(4): 83-89.

Bickford, Anne (1983). The patina of nostalgia. *Australian Archaeology,* 13: 1-7.

Bird, Drayton (2000). *Marketing insights and outrages: A collection of pithy pieces from* Marketing m*agazine.* Kogan Page, London.

Birkhead, Jim, De Lacy, Terry, and Smith, Laurajane (1992). *Aboriginal involvement in parks and protected areas.* Australian Institute of Aboriginal and Torres Strait Islander Studies, Canberra.

Blackwell, C. (1997). Tourism and cultural tourism: Some basic facts. *Preservation Issues* 7(3), available at <http://www.umsl.edu/services/library/blackstudies/culttour.htm> (retrieved June 6, 2000).

Bond, Marybeth (1997). *Women travelers: A new growth market.* PATA, Singapore, 5 pp.

Boniface, Priscilla (1998). Tourism culture. *Annals of Tourism Research* 25(3): 746-749.

Boniface, P. and Fowler, P. (1993). *Heritage and tourism in "the Global Village."* Routledge, London.

Bonn, M. A. and Brand, R. R. (1995). Identifying market potential: The application of brand development indexing to pleasure travel. *Journal of Travel Research* 34(2): 31-35.

Boorstin, D. (1964). *The image: A guide to pseudo events in America.* Harper and Row, New York.

Bowes, Bob (1994). Cultural tourism: Are we on the brink? *ICOMOS Canada* 3(3), available at <http://www.icomos.org/canada/bulletin/vol3_no3_bowes_e.html> (retrieved June 6, 2000).

Boylan, Patrick J. (1992). Museums 2000 and the future of museums. In Boylan, P. J. (Ed.), *Museums 2000: Politics, people, professionals and profit* (pp. 1-21). Museums Association. In conjunction with Routledge, London.

Brett, Reverend Peter C. (1999). Principles of visitor management and care for historical sites, with special reference to Canterbury Cathedral. In *Cultural Tourism Session Notes XII Assembly* (pp. 83-92). ICOMOS, Mexico.

Brooks, Graham (1993). Visitation to major heritage sites—Some essential planning considerations. *Proceedings of the ICOMOS 10th General Assembly on Cultural Tourism, Sri Lanka*, pp. 14-19.

Brooks, Graham (2000). ICOMOS Tourism Charter. Paper given at UNESCO Bhaktapur Workshop, April. Available online at <http://www.unescobkk.org/culture/bhaktapur/index.htm>.

Brown, Linden (1997). *Competitive marketing strategy.* Nelson, Melbourne.

Budowski, Gerardo (1976). Tourism and conservation: Conflict, coexistence or symbiosis? *Parks* 11(4): 3-6.

Budowski, Gerardo (1977). Tourism and conservation: Conflict, coexistence or symbiosis? *Environmental Conservation* 3: 27-31.

Bull, Adrian (1991). *The economics of travel and tourism.* Pitman, Melbourne.

Burgess, L., Limb, M., and Harrison, C. M. (1988). Exploring environmental values through the medium of small groups. *Environmental and Planning Analysis* 20: 457-476.

Byrne, Dennis (1991). Western hegemony in archaeological heritage management. *History and Anthropology* 5: 269-276.

Campbell, B. (1994). Aboriginal cultural tourism: The market. *ICOMOS Canada Bulletin* 3(3), available at <http://www.icomos.org/canada/bulletin/ vol3_no3_campbell_e.html> (retrieved June 6, 2000).

Cantacuzino, Sherban (1995). Towards the sustainable city. In *ICOMOS ethics, principles and methodology* (pp. 7-14). ICOMOS, Paris.

Cass, Ginny and Jahrig, Shannon (1998a). Heritage tourism: Montana's hottest travel trend. *Montana Business Quarterly* 36(2): 8-18.

Cass, Ginny and Jahrig, Shannon (1998b). The united people's powwow and cultural rendezvous: A cultural event. *Montana Business Quarterly* 36(2): 17.

Chacko, Harsha E. (1997). Positioning a tourism destination to gain a competitive edge. From *Asia Pacific Tourism Association Journal,* as cited in *Hotel Online Ideas and Trends.* Available at <http://www.hotel-online.com/Neo/Trends/ Asia PacificJournal/PositionDestination.html>.

Chavas, J. P., Stoll, J., and Sellar, C. (1989). On the commodity value of travel time in recreational activities. *Applied Economics* 21: 711-722.

Cheung, Sydney C. H. (1999). The meanings of a heritage trail in Hong Kong. *Annals of Tourism Research* 26(3): 570-588.

Clarke, J. (1997). A framework for approaches to sustainable tourism. *Journal of Sustainable Tourism* 5(3): 222-233.

Clements, Christine J., Schultz, John H., and Lime, David W. (1993). Recreation, tourism and local residents. *Journal of Parks and Recreation Administration* 1(4): 78-91.

Coathup, David C. (1999). Dominant actors in international tourism. *International Journal of Contemporary Hospitality Management* 11(2/3): 69-72.

Cohen, Eric (1972). Toward a sociology of international tourism. *Social Research* 39: 164-182.

Cohen, Eric (1979). A phenomenology of tourist experiences. *Sociology* 13: 170-201.

Conlin, Michael V. (1996). Revitalising Bermuda: Tourism policy and planning in a mature destination. In Harrison, L. and Husbands, W. (Eds.), *Practicing responsible tourism* (pp. 80-102). John Wiley and Sons, Brisbane.

Copley, Paul and Robson, Ian (1996). Tourism, arts marketing and the modernist paradox. In Robinson, Mike, Evans, Nigel, and Callaghan, Paul (Eds.), *Tourism and culture: Image, identity and marketing* (pp. 15-34). The Centre for Travel and Tourism/British Education Publishers, Sunderland, UK.

Costa, Jorge and Feronne, Livio (1998). *Sociocultural perspectives on tourism planning and development.* Virtual Conference Centre, MCB Press, 14 pp. Available at <http://www.mcb.co.uk/services/conferenc/jan98/eit/paper4-3.htm>.

Craik, Jennifer (1997). The culture of tourism sites. In Rojek, Chris and Urry, John (Eds.), *Touring cultures: Transformations of travel and theory* (pp. 113-136). Routledge, London.

Craik, Jennifer (1999). Interpretive mismatch in cultural tourism. *Tourism Culture and Communications* 1(2): 115-128.

Craine, K. (1999). *Incorporating cultural tourism into National Tourism Week activities.* Tourism Industry Association of America, Washington. Available at <http://www.tia.org/caledar/ntwcultural.stm>, 2 pp.

Crosby, Todd Vincent and Ebbe, Katrinka (2000). The Culture Bank: A community-based museum provides micro-credit. *The Urban Age Magazine,* Cultural Heritage Issue, World Bank Web site, September 6, 2000. Available at <http://www.world bank.org/html/fpd/urban/urb_age/culture/mail.html>.

Cuattingguis, Nana (1993). Cultural tourism in Sweden. In *International Scientific Symposium on Cultural Tourism, ICOMOS 10th General Assembly, Sri Lanka* (pp. 43-50). ICOMOS International Committee, Paris.

Cumming, Valerie, Merriman, Nick, and Ross, Catherine (1996). *Museum of London.* Scala Books and the Museum of London, London.

Dambiec, Dieter (2000). Indigenous peoples' folklore and copyright law. University of Queensland Web site, November 2, 2000 <http:/www.ozemail.com.au/-dambiec/indigenous-llm-essay.html>.

Dana, Leo P. (1999). The social cost of tourism. *Cornell Hotel and Restaurant Administration Quarterly* 40(4): 60-63.

Daniel, Y. P. (1996). Tourism dance performances: Authenticity and creativity. *Annals of Tourism Research* 23(4): 780-797.

Davidson, Jim and Spearritt, Peter (2000). *Holiday business: Tourism in Australia since 1870.* Melbourne University Press, Melbourne.

de Kadt, E. (1979). *Tourism: Passport to development.* Oxford University Press, New York.

Derrett, R. (1996). The tourism culture of cultural tourism: Planning through community consultation. In Robinson, M., Evans, N., and Callaghan, P. (Eds.), *Tourism and cultural change* (pp. 61-74). Centre for Travel and Tourism, Business Education Publishers, Sunderland, UK.

Dev, C. S., Morgan, M. S., and Shoemaker, S. (1995). A positioning analysis of hotel brands—Based on travel-manager perceptions. *Cornell Hotel and Restaurant Administration Quarterly* 36(6): 48-55.

Diamond, A. H. (1993). Chaos science. *Marketing Research: A Magazine of Management and Applications* 5(4): 8-14.

Diarrassouba, T. M. (1995). Proposed centre of popular arts and traditions embracing the local museum at Boundiali. In Ardouin, C. and Arinze, E. (Eds.), *Museums and the community in West Africa* (pp. 95-99). West African Museums Programme and Villiers Publications, London.

Dickinson, Rachel (1996). Heritage tourism is hot. *American Demographics* 18(9): 13-14.

Dienne, D. (1994). Routes as part of our cultural heritage. In ICOMOS and Ministry of Culture, Spain (Eds.), *Routes as part of our cultural heritage* (pp. 45-48). Meeting of Experts, ICOMOS and Ministry of Culture, Madrid.

DKS (1999). *Pennsylvania heritage tourism study,* D. K. Shifflet and Associates, prepared for Pennsylvania Department of Conservation and Natural Resources, 63 pp., plus appendixes.

Dodd, T. H. (1995). Opportunities and pitfalls of tourism in a developing wine industry. *International Journal of Wine Marketing* 7(1): 5-16.

Dodson, Rob and Clarke, Alan (1999). Multiculturalism: A dynamic approach to tourism policy and management. In Heung, Vincent and Ap, John (Eds.), *Tourism 2000: Asia Pacific's role in the new millenium* (pp. 230-237). Conference Proceedings of the Asia Pacific Association, Hong Kong.

Doggett, L. (1993). Multi-cultural tourism development offers a new dimension in travel. *Business America* 114(8): 8-10.

Domicelj, Joan (1995). A question of authenticity: Cultural diversity. In Larsen, Knut (Ed.), *Proceedings of the Nara Conference on Authenticity in relation to the World Heritage Convention* (pp. 301-304). UNESCO World Heritage Centre (France), Agency for Cultural Affairs (Japan), ICCROM (Italy), and ICOMOS (France).

Drezner, T. and Drezner, Z. (1996). Competitive facilities: Market share and location with random utility. *Journal of Regional Science* 36(1): 1-15.

D'Sa, Eddie (1999). Wanted: Tourists with a social conscience. *International Journal of Contemporary Hospitality Management* 11(2/3): 64-68.

du Cros, Hilary (1996). Committing archaeology in Australia. Doctoral thesis. Monash University, Melbourne.

du Cros, Hilary (1999). Planning and developing sustainable cultural heritage tourism: Flying the Australian way. Conference paper no. 16 presented to International Conference on Heritage and Tourism in Hong Kong, December.

du Cros, Hilary (2000). Planning for sustainable cultural heritage tourism in Hong Kong. Unpublished report to the Lord Wilson Heritage Trust, Hong Kong.

du Cros, Hilary (2001). A new model to assist in planning for sustainable cultural heritage tourism. *International Journal of Tourism Research,* 3(2): 165-170.

du Cros, Hilary and Johnston, Chris (2001). Tourism tracks and sacred places. Conference paper given at the ICOMOS Making Tracks: Heritage Routes Conference, Alice Springs, May.

Duan, Song-Ting and Duan, Ling (2000). Dayan Ancient City, Lijiang. Unpublished report to UNESCO.

Eden, G. (1990). Gordon River reprieve. *Australian Ranger Bulletin* 5(4): 11-12.

Elliot, Gerald (1998). Museums and galleries: Storehouses of value? In Peacock, A. (Ed.), *Does the past have a future? The political economy of heritage* (pp. 117-134). The Institute of Economic Affairs, London.

English Heritage Web site (2000). Conservation areas, January 15, available at <http:/www.english-heritage.org.uk/knowledge/conservation/management.asp>.

EPCG (1995). *Packaging and selling to the United States.* Economic Planning Group of Canada for Tourism Canada, Ottawa.

Evans, Katie and Fielding, Lindsay (1998). Giza (Egypt). In Shackley, Myra (Ed.), *Visitor management: Case studies from World Heritage sites* (pp. 82-99). Butterworth-Heinemann, London.

Evans, M. R., Fox, J. B., and Johnson, R. B. (1995). Identifying competitive strategies for successful tourism development. *Journal of Hospitality and Leisure Marketing* 3(1): 37-45.

Faulkner, Bill and Russell, Rosslyn (1997). Chaos and complexity in tourism: In search of a new perspective. *Pacific Tourism Review* 1(2): 93-102.

Fodness, Dale and Murray, Brian (1997). Tourist information search. *Annals of Tourism Research* 24(3): 503-523.

Formica, Sandro and Uysal, Muzaffer (1998). Market segmentation of an international cultural-historic event in Italy. *Journal of Travel Research* 36(Spring): 16-24.

Foster, Douglas (1985). *Travel and tourism management.* MacMillan, London.

Fowler, P. (1996). Heritage tourism, tourism heritage—Towards a respectful relationship. In Robinson, M., Evans, N., and Callaghan, P. (Eds.), *Tourism and cultural change* (pp. 75-78). Centre for Travel and Tourism, Business Education Publishers, Sunderland, UK.

Fyall, Alan and Garrod, Brian (1996). Sustainable heritage tourism: Achievable goal or elusive ideal? In Robinson, M., Evans, N., Callaghan, P. (Eds.), *Managing cultural resources for tourism* (pp. 50-76). Business Education Publishers, Sunderland, UK.

Galla, Amareswar (1995). Authenticity: Rethinking heritage diversity in a pluralistic framework. In Larsen, Knut (Ed.), *Proceedings of the Nara Conference on authenticity in relation to the World Heritage Convention* (pp. 315-322). UNESCO World Heritage Centre (France), Agency for Cultural Affairs (Japan), ICCROM (Italy), and ICOMOS (France).

Gallagher, Mary Lou (1995). Taking a stand on hallowed ground. *Planning* 61(1): 10-15.

Garrod, Brian and Fyall, Alan (1998). Beyond the rhetoric of sustainable tourism. *Tourism Management* 19(3): 199-212.

Garrod, Brian and Fyall, Alan (2000). Managing heritage tourism. *Annals of Tourism Research* 27(3): 682-708.

Getz, Don (1993). Impacts of tourism on residents' leisure: Concepts, and a longitudinal case study of Spey Valley, Scotland. *Journal of Tourism Studies* 4(2): 33-44.

Getz, Don (1994). Residents' attitudes towards tourism: A longitudinal case study of Spey Valley, Scotland. *Tourism Management* 15(4): 247-258.

Ghose, Sarah (1992). The people's participation in science museums. In Boylan, Patrick (Ed.), *Museums 2000* (pp. 84-89). Museums Association and Routledge, London.

Gilbert, David C. (1992). Touristic development of a viticultural region in Spain. *International Journal of Wine Marketing* 4(2): 25-32.

Giles, Dari (1995). Heritage tours for conventioners. *Black Enterprise* 25(8): 96-98.

Goodrich, Jonathan N. (1997). Cultural tourism in Europe. *Journal of Travel Research* 35(3): 91.

Gorman, A. (1988). Tourism: Trojan horse or white knight? The role of social impact analysis. In Faulkner, B. and Fagence, M. (Eds.), *Frontiers of Australian tourism: The search for new perspectives in policy development and research* (pp. 199-210). Bureau of Tourism Research, Canberra.

Goudie, Simon, Khan, Farieda, and Killen, Darryll (1996). Tourism beyond apartheid. In Well, Patricia (Ed.), *Keys to the marketplace: Problems and issues in cultural and heritage tourism* (pp. 65-86). Hisarlick Press, Middlesex, UK.

Goulding, Christina (1999). Interpretation and presentation. In Leask, Anna and Yeoman, Ian (Eds.), *Heritage visitor attractions: An operations management perspective* (pp. 54-68). Cassells, London.

Gratton, C. and Richards, G. (1996). The economic context of cultural tourism. In Richards, G. (Ed.), *Cultural tourism in Europe* (pp. 71-86). CAB International, Oxon, UK.

Greer, T. and Wall, G. (1979). Recreational hinterlands: A theoretical and empirical analysis. In Wall, G. (Ed.), *Recreational land use in southern Ontario* (pp. 227-246). Dept. of Geography Publication Series #14, Waterloo University, Waterloo, Canada.

Hall, C. Michael (1999). Rethinking collaboration and partnership: A public policy perspective. *Journal of Sustainable Tourism* 7(3/4): 274-289.

Hall, C. Michael and McArthur, Simon (1998). *Integrated heritage management,* The Stationery Office, London.

Hannabuss, Stuart (1999). Postmodernism and the heritage experience. *Library Management* 20(5): 295-302.

Hawkins, Donald E. (1994). Ecotourism: Opportunities for developing countries. In Theobald, William F. (Ed.), *Global tourism: The next decade* (pp. 261-273). Butterworth Heinemann, Melbourne.

Hayword, K. Michael and Walsh, Laurel J. (1996). Strategic tourism planning in Fiji: An oxymoron, or providing for coherence in decision making? In Harrison, L. and Husbands, W. (Eds.), *Practicing responsible tourism* (pp. 103-122). John Wiley and Sons, Brisbane.

Henderson, Joan (1999). The challenges of heritage conservation in the new millenium: Singapore's Chinatown. In Heung, Vincent and Ap, John (Eds.), *Tourism 2000: Asia Pacific's role in the new millenium* (pp. 94-103). Conference Proceedings of the Asia Pacific Association, Hong Kong.

Hiam, Alexander (1990). *The vest pocket CEO: Decision making tools for executives.* Prentice-Hall, Englewood Cliffs, NJ.

Hollingshead, Keith (1996). Culture and capillary power: Texas and the quiet annihilation of the past. In Robinson, Mike, Evans, Nigel, and Callaghan, Paul (Eds.), *Tourism and culture: Image, identity and marketing* (pp. 49-98). The Centre for Travel and Tourism/British Education Publishers, Sunderland, UK.

Hollingshead, Keith (1999). Tourism as public culture: Horne's ideological commentary on the legerdomain of tourism. *International Journal of Tourism Research* 1(4): 267-292.

Holloway, J. C. and Robinson, C. (1995). *Marketing for tourism,* Third edition. Longman, Harlow.

Hong Kong Leisure and Cultural Services Department (2000). *Hong King Heritage Museum: Branch Museums.* Pamphlet published by the Hong Kong Leisure and Cultural Services Department.

Hopi Cultural Preservation Office (2000). Hopi visitor information Web site, February 11, 2000. Available at <http:/www.nau.edu/~hcpo-p/visit/>.

Hovinen, Gary R. (1995). Heritage issues in urban tourism: An assessment of new trends in Lancaster County. *Tourism Management* 16(5): 381-388.

Hughes, Howard L. (1996). Redefining cultural tourism. *Annals of Tourism Research* 23(3): 707-709.

Hughes, Howard L. (1998). Theatre in London and the interrelationship with tourism. *Tourism Management* 19(5): 445-452.

Human, Brian (1999). Kodachrome icons: Photography, place and the theft of identity. *International Journal of Contemporary Hospitality Management* 11(2/3): 80-84.

ICOMOS (1976). ICOMOS Cultural Tourism Charter (first version). ICOMOS, Paris.

ICOMOS (1978). *The Venice Charter.* ICOMOS, Paris.

ICOMOS (1993). Cultural tourism. Tourism at World Heritage cultural sites: The site manager's handbook. Unpublished report to the International Scientific

Committee 10th General Assembly. International Specialized Committee on Cultural Tourism, Columbo.

ICOMOS (1994). The Venice Charter. *ICOMOS Scientific Journal Series* No. 4. ICOMOS, Paris.

ICOMOS (1999). Cultural Tourism Charter. ICOMOS, Paris. Web site February 2, 2000, available at <http://www.icomos.org>.

ICOMOS (2000). Cultural Tourism International ICOMOS, available at <http://www.international.icomos.org/icomos/e_touris.htm> (retrieved June 6, 2000).

ICOMOS Australia (1994). The Australia ICOMOS charter for the conservation of places of cultural significance (the Burra Charter). In Marquis-Kyle, P. and Walker, M. (Eds.), *The illustrated Burra Charter* (pp. 69-71). Australia ICOMOS, Canberra.

IDCCA (1997). Illinois Heritage Tourism Program. Illinois Department of Commerce and Community Affairs, Bureau of Tourism, Chicago.

Ito, Nobuo (1995). "Authenticity" inherent in cultural heritage in Asia and Japan. In Larsen, Knut (Ed.), *Proceedings of the Nara Conference on authenticity in relation to the World Heritage Convention* (pp. 35-46). UNESCO World Heritage Centre (France), Agency for Cultural Affairs (Japan), ICCROM (Italy), and ICOMOS (France).

Jackson, E. and Wong, R. (1982). Perceived conflict between urban cross country skiers and snowmobilers in Alberta. *Journal of Leisure Research:* 42-62.

Jackson, Mervyn S., White, Gerard N., and Schmierer, Claire L. (2000). Predicating tourism destination choices: Psychographic parameters versus psychological motivations. *CAUTHE 2000 Conference Proceedings,* pp. 57-63. La Trobe University/Bureau of Tourism Research, Canberra.

Jackson, Mervyn S. (2000). Predicting Australian mass tourism flow using Hofstede's cultural model. *CAUTHE 2000 Conference Proceedings,* pp. 47-56. La Trobe University/Bureau of Tourism Research, Canberra.

Jacob, G. R. and Schreyer, R. T. (1980). Conflict in outdoor recreation: A theoretical perspective. *Journal of Travel Research* 12(4): 368-380.

Jacobs, Jane and Gale, F. (1994). *Tourism and the protection of Aboriginal cultural sites.* Australian Heritage Commission, Special Publication Series No. 10, Canberra.

Jafari, Jafar (1996). Tourism and culture: An inquiry into paradoxes. *Proceedings of the Round Table Debate on Culture, Tourism, Development: Crucial issues for the 21st Century* (pp. 43-47). UNESCO, Paris.

Jamieson, Walter (1994). The challenge of cultural tourism. *ICOMOS Canada* 3(3), available at <http://www.icomos.org/canada/bulletin/vol3_no3_jamieson_e.html> (retrieved June 6, 2000).

Jamieson, Walter (1995). The use of indicators in monitoring: The economic impact of cultural tourism initiatives. *ICOMOS Canada* 4(3), available at <http://www.icomos.org/canada/bulletin/vol4_no3_jamieson_e.html> (retrieved June 6, 2000).

Jansen-Verbeke, Miriam (1998). Tourismification and historical cities. *Annals of Tourism Research* 25(3): 739-741.

Jarrett, I. (1996). Hard-earned recognition. *Asian Business* 32(5): 26-27.

Johansson, Per and Montagari, Reza (1996). The value of travel time: An empirical study using repeated samples of non-business trips. *Tourism Economics* 2(4): 353-368.

Johnston, Chris (1994). What is social value? Discussion paper. Australian Heritage Commission, Canberra.

Jokilehto, Jukka (1995). Authenticity: A general framework for the concept. In Larsen, Knut (Ed.), *Proceedings of the Nara Conference on authenticity in relation to the World Heritage Convention* (pp. 17-36). UNESCO World Heritage Centre (France), Agency for Cultural Affairs (Japan), ICCROM (Italy), and ICOMOS (France).

Jones, Clive B. (1998). *The new tourism and leisure environment,* Economic Research Associates, 16 pp. Available at <http://wwww.hotel-online.com/ Neo/ Trends/ERA/ERANewEnvironment.html>.

Jones, Clive B. and Robinett, John (1998). *The future of theme parks in international tourism,* Economic Research Associates, 11 pp. Available at <http://wwww.hotel-online.com/Neo/Trends/ERA/ERARoletheneparks.html>.

Jordan, Troy (1999). Back to the future. *Asian Business* 35(6): 23.

JOST (1999). *Journal of Sustainable Tourism,* Special Issue on Collaboration and Partnerships, 7(3/4).

Joyce, Paul and Woods, Adrian (1996). *Essential strategic management.* Butterworth Heinemann, Oxford.

Kaplan, F. (1994). *Museums and the making of "ourselves": The role of objects in national identity.* Leicester University Press, London.

Kavanagh, Gaynor (1994). *Museum provision and professionalism,* Routledge, London.

Kemmerling Clack, Jan (1999). Cultural tourism: An overview of impact, visitors and case studies. In Moisey, R. N., Nickerson, N. P., and Klenosky, D. B. (Eds.), *Navigating global waters—30th annual conference proceedings, travel and tourism research association* (pp. 154-159). Boise, Idaho.

Kerr, Alastair (1994). Strange bedfellows: An uneasy alliance between cultural conservation and tourism. *ICOMOS Canada* 3(3). Available at <http://www.icomos.org/canada/bulletin/vol3_no3_kerr_e.html> (retrieved June 6, 2000).

Kerstetter, D., Confer, J., and Bricker, K. (1998). Industrial heritage attractions: Types and tourists. *Journal of Travel and Tourism Marketing* 7(2): 91-104.

King, Brian, Pizam, Abe, and Milman, Ady (1993). Social impacts of tourism: Host perceptions. *Annals of Tourism Research* 20: 650-665.

Koffi, A. (1995). Sociohistorical factors for improved integration of local museums: Zaranou and Bonoua. In Ardouin, C. and Arinze, E. (Eds.), *Museums and the community in West Africa* (pp. 87-94). West African Museums Programme and Villiers Publications, London.

Korean National Commission (2000). A case study of Hahoe Village in Andong, Korea. Unpublished report to UNESCO.

Kotler, Phillip and Turner, Ronald E. (1989). *Marketing management.* Prentice-Hall, Scarborough.

Larsen, Knut (Ed.) (1995a). *Proceedings of the Nara Conference on authenticity in relation to the World Heritage Convention.* UNESCO World Heritage Centre (France), Agency for Cultural Affairs (Japan), ICCROM (Italy), and ICOMOS (France).

Larsen, Knut (1995b). "The test of authenticity" and national heritage legislation. In Larsen, Knut (Ed.), *Proceedings of the Nara Conference on authenticity in relation to the World Heritage Convention* (pp. 363-364). UNESCO World Heritage Centre (France), Agency for Cultural Affairs (Japan), ICCROM (Italy), and ICOMOS (France).

Leask, Anna and Fyall, Allan (2000). World Heritage sites: Current issues and future implications. In Robinson, Mike, Evans, Nigel, Long, Phillip, Sharpley, Richard, and Swarbrooke, John (Eds.), *Reflections of international tourism. Tourism and heritage relationships: Global, national and local perspectives* (pp. 287-300). Centre for Travel and Tourism and Business Education Publishers, Ltd., Sunderland.

Leask, Anna and Yeoman, Ian (1999). *Heritage visitor attractions: An operations management perspective.* Cassel, London.

Leiper, Neil (1990). Tourist attraction systems. *Annals of Tourism Research* 17: 367-384.

Leon, Warren and Rosenzweig, Roy (1989). *History museums in the United States: A critical assessment.* Board of Trustees of the University of Illinois, Illinois.

Lewis, Robert (1984). Theoretical and practical considerations in research design. *Cornell Hotel Restaurant Administration Quarterly* 24(4): 25-35.

Liu, Juanita, Sheldon, Pauline J., and Var, Turgut (1987). Resident perceptions of the environmental impacts of tourism. *Annals of Tourism Research* 14: 17-37.

Lonely Planet (2000). *Nepal.* Lonely Planet Publications, Melbourne.

Lord, Gail Dexter and Lord, Barry (1999). *The manual of museum planning,* Second edition. The Stationary Office, London.

Lowenthal, David (1985). *The past is a foreign country.* Cambridge University Press, Cambridge.

Lowenthal, David (1995). The changing criteria of authenticity. In Larsen, Knut (Ed.), *Proceedings of the Nara Conference on authenticity in relation to the World Heritage Convention* (pp. 121-136). UNESCO World Heritage Centre (France), Agency for Cultural Affairs (Japan), ICCROM (Italy), and ICOMOS (France).

Lowenthal, David (1998). Selfishness in heritage. In Uzzell, David and Ballantyne, Roy (Eds.), *Contemporary issues in heritage and environmental interpretation* (pp. 26-36). The Stationary Office, London.

MacCannell, Dean (1973). Staged authenticity: Arrangements of social space in a tourist setting. *American Journal of Sociology* 79: 585-603.

Macintosh, Barry (1999). The National Parks Service and Cultural Resources. *Cultural Resource Management* 22(4): 40-44.

Madrigal, Robert (1993). A tale of tourism in two cities. *Annals of Tourism Research* 20: 336-353.

Manning, R. E. (1985). Crowding norms in backcountry settings: A review and synthesis. *Journal of Leisure Research* 17(2): 75-89.

Marquis-Kyle, Peter and Walker, Meredith (1992). *The illustrated Burra Charter.* Australia ICOMOS and the Australian Heritage Commission, Canberra.

Mason, Gary (1996). Manufactured myths: Packaging the exotic for visitor consumption. In Robinson, Mike, Evans, Nigel, and Callaghan, Paul (Eds.), *Tourism and culture: Image, identity and marketing* (pp. 121-137). The Centre for Travel and Tourism/British Education Publishers, Sunderland, UK.

McBryde, Isobel (1992). The past as symbol of identity. *Antiquity,* 66: 261-266.

McDonald, George F. and Alsford, Stephen (1989). *Museum for the Global Village: The Canadian Museum of Civilization.* Canadian Museum of Civilization, Hull.

McIntosh, Alison J. and Prentice, Richard R. C. (1999). Affirming authenticity: Consuming cultural heritage. *Annals of Tourism Research* 26(3): 589-612.

McIntosh, Robert W. and Goeldner, Charles R. (1990). *Tourism principles, practices, philosophies,* Sixth edition. John Wiley and Son, New York.

McKean, J., Johnson, D., and Walsh, R. (1995). Valuing time in travel cost demand analysis: An empirical investigation. *Land Economics* 71(1): 96-105.

McKercher, Bob (1992). Tourism as a conflicting land use: Northern Ontario's outfitting industry. *Annals of Tourism Research* 19(3): 467-481.

McKercher, Bob (1993). Some fundamental truths about tourism: Understanding tourism's social and environmental impacts. *Journal of Sustainable Tourism* 1(1): 6-16.

McKercher, Bob (1996). Understanding attitudes to tourism in protected areas. In Richins, H., Richardson, J. and Crabtree, A. (Eds.), *Taking the next steps* (pp. 229-234). The Ecotourism Association of Australia, Brisbane.

McKercher, Bob (1998a). The effect of distance decay on visitor mix at Victorian coastal destinations. *Pacific Tourism Review* 2(3/4): 215-223.

McKercher Bob (1998b). The effect of market access on destination choice. *Journal of Travel Research* 37(August): 39-47.

McKercher, Bob (1998c). *The business of nature-based tourism.* Hospitality Press, Melbourne.

McKercher, Bob (1999). A chaos approach to tourism. *Tourism Management* 20(4): 425-434.

McKercher, Bob and Chow, Billie S. M. (2001). Cultural distance and cultural tourism participation. *Pacific Tourism Review* 5(1/2): 21-30.

McKercher, Bob and Davidson, Penny (1995). Women and commercial adventure tourism: Does the industry understand its dominant market? In Faulkner, B.,

Fagence, M., Davidson, M., and Craig-Smith, S. (Eds.), *Tourism research and education in Australia* (pp. 129-140). Bureau of Tourism Research, Canberra.

McKercher, Bob and du Cros, Hilary (1998). I climbed to the top of Ayers Rock and still didn't see Uluru! In Faulkner, D., Tideswell, C., Weaver, D. (Eds.), *Progress in Tourism and Hospitality Research 1998* (pp. 376-386). CAUTHE/BTR Canberra.

McKercher, Bob and du Cros, Hilary (1999). The fundamental truths of cultural tourism. In Heung, V. C. S., Ap, J., and Wong, K. K. F. (Eds.), *Tourism 2000, Asia Pacific's Role in the New Millennium* (pp. 272-279). APTA, Hong Kong.

McKercher, Bob and Robbins, Bill (1998). Business development issues affecting nature-based tourism operators in Australia. *Journal of Sustainable Tourism* 6(2): 173-188.

Mercer, D. (1996). Native peoples and tourism: Conflict and compromise. In Theobald, W. F. (Ed.) *Global tourism: The next decade* (pp. 124-146). Butterworth Heinemann, Melbourne.

Merleau-Ponty, M. (1982) (C. Smith, trans.). *The phenomenology of perception.* Routledge and Kegan Paul, London.

Middleton, Victor (1994). *Marketing travel and tourism,* Second edition. Butterworth Heinemann, Oxford.

Mill, Robert C. and Morrison, Alastair (1985). *The tourism system.* Prentice-Hall International, London.

Miller, Julie (1997a). Cultural tourism worthy of note. *Hotel and Motel Management* 212(15): 7.

Miller, Julie (1997b). Travel trends point to market stronghold. *Hotel and Motel Management* 212(8): 1, 28.

Milman, Ady and Pizam, Abe (1988). Social impacts of tourism in Central Florida. *Annals of Tourism Research* 15: 19-24.

Mitchell, Vincent M. and Greatorex, Michael (1990). Consumer purchasing in foreign countries: A perceived risk perspective. *International Journal of Advertising* 9: 295-307.

Morrison, Alison (1998). Small firm co-operative marketing in a peripheral tourism region. *International Journal of Contemporary Hospitality Management* 10(5): 191-197.

Moscardo, Gianna (1996). Mindful visitors: Heritage and tourism. *Annals of Tourism Research* 23(2): 376-397.

Muresan, Alexandra (1998). The fortified church of Biertan (Transylvania). In Shackley, Myra (Ed.), *Visitor management: Case studies from World Heritage sites* (pp. 26-45). Butterworth-Heinemann, London.

Nishimura, Yukio (1994). Changing concept of authenticity in the context of Japanese conservation history. In Larsen, Knut (Ed.), *Proceedings of the Nara Conference on authenticity in relation to the World Heritage Convention* (pp. 175-184). UNESCO World Heritage Centre (France), Agency for Cultural Affairs (Japan), ICCROM (Italy), and ICOMOS (France).

NTHP (1999). *Getting started: How to succeed in heritage tourism.* National Trust for Historic Preservation, Washington, 45 pp.

O'Grady, R. (1981). *Third World Stopover,* World Council of Churches, Geneva.

Orbasli, Aylin (2000). Tourists in historic towns. E&FN Spon, London.

Otake, Tomoko (1997). Heritage area seeks respect from tourists. *Japan Times Weekly* 37(1): 12.

Paige, John and McVeigh, Mary (1999). Planning for jazz. *Cultural Resource Management,* 8: 20-22.

Palmer, Catherine (1999). Tourism and symbols of identity cities. *Tourism Management* 20: 313-321.

Parks Australia (1999). Uluru-Kata Tjuta National Park, draft plan of management. Parks Australia and Uluru-Kata Tjuta Board of Management, Canberra.

Parks Canada (1994). *Guiding principles and operating policies, Parks Canada.* Canadian Heritage, Ottowa.

Parlett, G., Fletcher, J., and Cooper, C. (1995). The impact of tourism on the old town of Edinburgh. *Tourism Management* 16(5): 355-360.

Peacock, Alan (1998). The economist and heritage policy: A review of the issues. In Peacock, A. (Ed.), *Does the past have a future? The political economy of Heritage* (pp. 1-26). The Institute of Economic Affairs, London.

Pearce, Douglas (1989). *Tourism development,* Second edition. Longman, London.

Pearce, Phillip L. (1995). From culture shock and culture arrogance to cultural exchange: Ideas towards sustainable sociocultural tourism. *Journal of Sustainable Tourism* 3(3): 143-154.

Pearce, P. L. (1996). Tourism-resident impacts: Examples, explanations and emerging solutions. In Theobald, W. F. (Ed.), *Global tourism: The next decade* (pp. 103-124). Butterworth Heinemann, Melbourne.

Pearson, Michael and Sullivan, Sharon (1995). *Looking after heritage places: The basics of heritage planning for managers, landowners and administrators.* Melbourne University Press, Melbourne.

Peleggi, Maurizio (1996). National heritage and global tourism in Thailand. *Annals of Tourism Research* 23(2): 432-448.

Petzet, Michael (1995). "In the full richness of their authenticity"—The test of authenticity and the new cult of monuments. In Larsen, Knut (Ed.), *Proceedings of the Nara Conference on authenticity in relation to the World Heritage Convention* (pp. 85-100). UNESCO World Heritage Centre (France), Agency for Cultural Affairs (Japan), ICCROM (Italy), and ICOMOS (France).

Picard, Michel (1995). Cultural heritage and tourism capital: Cultural tourism in Bali. In Lanfant, Marie-Francoise, Allcock, John B., and Bruner, Edward M. (Eds.), *International tourism: Identity and change* (pp. 44-66). Sage Publications, London.

Pigram, John J. (1984). Tourism in the coastal zone: The question of public access. In O'Rourke (Ed.), *Contemporary issues in Australian tourism* (pp. 1-14). IAG, Sydney.

Pinkley, R. L. (1990). Dimensions of conflict frame: Disputant interpretations of conflict. *Journal of Applied Psychology* 75(2): 117-126.

Plog, Stanley (1974). Why destination areas rise and fall in popularity. *The Cornell HRA Quarterly* 1(4): 55-58.

Prentice, Richard (1993). *Tourism and heritage attractions.* Routledge, London.

Prentice, Richard C., Witt, Steven F., and Hamer, Clare (1998). Tourism as experience: The case of heritage parks. *Annals of Tourism Research* 25(1): 1-24.

Prideaux, Bruce, and Kininmont, Lee-Jaye (1999). Tourism and heritage are not strangers: A study of opportunities for rural heritage museums to maximise tourism visitation. *Journal of Travel Research* 37(February): 299-303.

Quirk, P. J. (1989). The cooperative resolution of policy conflict. *American Political Science Review* 83(3): 905-921.

Readings on Cultural Respect (2000). Web site available at <http://www.hanksville. org/sand/intellect/NAbibBell.html> (retrieved February 14, 2000).

Richards, Greg (1996a). Introduction: Cultural tourism in Europe. In Richards, G. (Ed.), *Cultural tourism in Europe* (pp. 3-18). CAB International, Oxon, UK.

Richards, Greg (1996b). Production and consumption of European cultural tourism. *Annals of Tourism Research* 23(2): 261-283.

Richards, Greg (1996c). The scope and significance of cultural tourism. In Richards, G. (Ed.), *Cultural tourism in Europe* (pp. 19-46). CAB International, Oxon, UK.

Richardson, John I. (1996). *Marketing Australian travel and tourism: Principles and practice.* Hospitality Press, Melbourne.

Richelieu, David Anthony (1999). San Antonio, Texas, to develop new historic-, cultural-tour programs. *San Antonio Express News,* October 18. Available online at <http://www.hotel.-online.com/Neo/News/1999_Oct_15/k.SNT.940274118.html>.

Ries, A. and Trout, J. (1986). *Positioning.* McGraw-Hill, New York.

Ries, A. and Trout, J. (1993). *The 22 immutable laws of marketing.* Harper Collins, London.

Ritzer, George and Liska, Allan (1997). "McDisneyization" and "post-tourism": Complementary perspectives on contemporary tourism. In Rojek, Chris and Urry, John (Eds.), *Touring cultures: Transformations of travel and theory* (pp. 96-111). Routledge, London.

Robb, John G. (1998). Tourism and legends: Archaeology and heritage. *Annals of Tourism Research* 25(3): 579-596.

Robinson, Mike (1999). Collaboration and cultural consent: Refocusing sustainable tourism. *Journal of Sustainable Tourism* 7(3/4): 379-397.

Rojek, Chris (1997). Indexing, dragging, and the social construction of tourist sites. In Rojek, Chris and Urry, John (Eds.), *Touring cultures: Transformations of travel and theory* (pp. 52-74). Routledge, London.

Rosenbaum, Alvin (1995a). Cultural resources and sustainable tourism: The end of tourism as we know it. Lecture for the International Institute of Tourism Studies, George Washington University, 8 pp. Available at <http://www.al.net/ endtourism. html> (retrieved June 6, 2000).

Rosenbaum, Alvin (1995b). A regional development strategy: National heritage tour routes. Paper prepared for Pennsylvania's Heritage Partnerships Conference, 5 pp. Available at <http://www.al.net/Strategy.html> (retrieved June 6, 2000).

Rössler, Mechtild (1994). Cultural landscapes, itineraries and canals for the World Heritage list. In ICOMOS and Ministry of Culture, Spain (Eds.), *Routes as part of our cultural heritage* (pp. 59-70). Meeting of Experts, ICOMOS and Ministry of Culture, Madrid.

Rowe, M. (1996). Beyond heads in beds. *Lodging Hospitality* 52(1): 42-44.

Rudd, Michelle A. and Davis, James A. (1998). Industrial heritage tourism as Bingham Canyon Copper Mine. *Journal of Travel Research* 36(3): 85-89.

Russell, Roslyn, and Faulkner, Bill (1999). Movers and shakers: Chaos makers in tourism development. *Tourism Management* 20(4): 411-423.

Ryan, Chris (2000). Tourist experiences, phenomenographic analysis, post-positivism and neural network software. *International Journal of Tourism Research* 2(2): 119-132.

Ryan, Chris and Dewar, Keith (1995). Evaluating the communication process between interpreter and visitor. *Tourism Management* 16(4): 295-303.

Schweitzer, Carol (1999). The hot ticket to cool meetings. *Association Management* 51(8): 121-130.

Seaton, Tony V. and Bennett, Marion M. (1996). *The marketing of tourism products: Concepts, issues and cases.* International Thompson Business Press, Boston.

Selwitz, R. (1998). Multi-branding opportunities need special strategies. *Hotel and Motel Management* 213(9): 34-36.

Shackley, Myra (1998). Preface. In Shackley, M. (Ed.), *Visitor management: Case studies from World Heritage sites* (p. xiii). Butterworth Heinemann, Oxford.

Sharples, Liz, Yeoman, Ian, and Leask, Anna (1999). Operations management. In Leask, Anna and Yeoman, Ian (Eds.), *Heritage visitor attractions: An operations management perspective* (pp. 22-38). Cassell, London.

Sharpley, Richard (2000). The consumption of tourism revisited. In Robinson, Mike, Long, Philip, Evans, Nigel, Sharpley, Richard, and Swarbrooke, John (Eds.), *Motivations, behaviours and tourist types* (pp. 381-392). Centre for Travel and Tourism/Business Education Publishers.

Silberberg, Ted (1995). Cultural tourism and business opportunities for museums and heritage sites. *Tourism Management* 16(5): 361-365.

Silva, Roland (1994). The significance of the Venice International Charter for the conservation and restoration of monuments and sites, with special reference to eastern countries (pp. 40-44). Reprinted in ICOMOS, The Venice Charter, 1964-1994. ICOMOS, Paris.

Silverstone, Roger (1989). Heritage as media: Some implications for research. In Uzzell, D. (Ed.), *Heritage interpretation,* Volume 2 (pp. 138-148). Belhaven Press, London.

Singh, T. V., Thuens, H. L., and Go, F. (Eds.) (1989). *Towards appropriate tourism: The case of developing countries.* European University Studies, Peter Lang, Frankfurt.

Sizer, Stephen R. (1999). The ethical challenges of managing pilgrimages to the Holy Land. *International Journal of Contemporary Hospitality Management* 11(2/3): 85-90.

Sjögren, Tomas and Brännäs, Kurt (1996). Recreational travel time conditional on supply, work travel time, and income. *Tourism Economics* 2(3): 268-275.

Sletvold, Ola (1996). Viking heritage: Contexts and commodification. In Robinson, Mike, Evans, Nigel , and Callaghan, Paul (Eds.), *Tourism and culture: Image, identity and marketing* (pp. 217-230). The Centre for Travel and Tourism/British Education Publishers, Sunderland, UK.

Snepenger, David, Meged, Kelli, Snelling, Mary, and Worrall, Kelly (1990). Information search strategies by destination naïve tourists. *Journal of Travel Research* 29(1): 13-16.

Sofield, T. and Li, S. (1998). Tourism development and cultural policies in China. *Annals of Tourism Research* 25(2): 362-392.

Spearritt, Peter (1991). Money, taste and industrial heritage. In Rickard, J. and Spearritt, P. (Eds.), *Packaging the past? Public histories* (pp. 33-45). Melbourne University Press and Australian Historical Studies, Melbourne.

Squire, Shelagh J. (1996). Literary tourism and sustainable tourism: Promoting 'Anne of Green Gables' in Prince Edward Island. *Journal of Sustainable Tourism* 4(3): 119-134.

Stalker, P. (1984). Visions of poverty, visions of wealth *The New Internationalist,* 142(December): 7-9.

Stebbins, Robert A. (1996). Cultural tourism as serious leisure. *Annals of Tourism Research* 23(4): 948-950.

Stewart, Susan I. and Vogt, Christine A. (1999). A case-based approach to understanding vacation planning. *Leisure Sciences* 21: 79-95.

Stocks, Jayne (1996). Heritage and tourism in the Irish Republic—Towards a giant theme park. In Robinson, Mike, Evans, Nigel, and Callaghan, Paul (Eds.), *Tourism and culture: Image, identity and marketing* (pp. 251-260). The Centre for Travel and Tourism/British Education Publishers, Sunderland, UK.

Stovel, Herb (1998). *Risk preparedness: A management manual for world cultural heritage.* ICCROM, Rome.

Sugaya, H. Bill (1999). Cultural tourism—International policies and perspective. Presentation made to the International Conference on Heritage and Tourism, Hong Kong.

Sugaya, H. Bill and Brooks, Graham (1999). Heritage development and tourism. In *Cultural Tourism Session Notes XII Assembly* (pp. 1-14). ICOMOS, Mexico.

Swarbrooke, J. (1995). *The development and management of visitor attractions.* Butterworth Heinemann, Oxford.

TC (1991). *Investigative study on the cultural tourism sector.* Tourism Canada, Ottawa.

TCA (1998). *Our heritage—It's our business—TCA action plan.* Tourism Council of Australia, Sydney.

Temple, Helen (1988). Historical archaeology and its role in the community. Master's thesis, University of Sydney.

Tighe, Anthony J. (1986). The arts/tourism partnership. *Journal of Travel Research* 24(3): 2-5.

Tilden, Freeman (1977). *Interpreting our heritage,* Third edition, University of North Carolina Press, North Carolina.

Timothy, Dallen J. (1997). Tourism and the personal heritage experience. *Annals of Tourism Research* 24(3): 751-754.

Titchen, Sarah (1996). *World Heritage Newsletter* No. 10, Cultural Landscapes: Uluru-Katatjuta. Available at <http://www.unesco.org/whc/news/10newsen.htm#story4>.

Truong, T. and Hensher, D. (1985). Measurement of travel time values and opportunity cost model from a discrete-choice model. *The Economic Journal* 95(June): 438-451.

Truscott, Marilyn (1994). *Heritage places, past, present and future.* Department of Communications and the Arts, Canberra.

Truscott, Marilyn (2000). Intangible heritage values in Australia. *ICOMOS News* 10(1): 4-11.

Tufts, Steven and Milne, Simon (1999) Museums: A supply side perspective. *Annals of Tourism Research* 26(3): 613-631.

Tunbridge, J. E. and Ashworth, Gregory (1996). Dissonant heritage: The management of the past as a resource in conflict. John Wiley and Sons, Chichester.

TVS (1995). *Cultural tourism: Statistical bulletin July 1995.* Tasmanian visitor survey, Hobart, Tasmania. Available at <http://www.tased.edu.au/aststas/pucsspct.htm> (retrieved July 19, 1999).

UNESCO (1996). More about the World Heritage Convention. Web site available at <http:/www.unesco.org/whc/ab_conve.htm#debut>.

UNESCO (1998). Draft decisions recommended by the program and external relations commission, 155th Session of the Executive Board. November 2, 1998, Resolution 3.5.5. World Heritage Committee, Kyoto, Japan.

UNESCO (1999). Interim report on the project concerning the proclamation by UNESCO of masterpieces of oral and intangible heritage of humanity. Report of the 157th Session of the Executive Board, UNESCO, Paris.

UNESCO (2000a). Managing Living Human Treasures, February 11, 2000. Available at <http://www.unesco.org/culture/heritage/intangible/treasures/html_eng/method.htm>.

UNESCO (2000b). Living Human Treasures, available at <http://www.unesco.org/culture/legalprotection/index.html>.

UNESCO and Nordic World Heritage Office (1999). Sustainable tourism and cultural heritage. A review of development assistance and its potential to promote sustainability. UNESCO and Nordic World Heritage Office, Norway.

UNESCO World Heritage Centre (2000). World Heritage Convention, available at <http://www.unesco.org/whc/>.

UNESCO World Heritage Centre (2001). News, available at <http://www.unesco.org/whc/>.

Urry, John (1990). *The tourist gaze.* Sage, London.

U.S. Department of the Interior (1993). Code of Federal Regulations 36 CFR Part/title 65, National Historic Landmarks Program. U.S. Department of the Interior, Washington.

U.S. Department of the Interior (1995). How to apply the National Register criteria for evaluation. National Register Bulletin 15, U.S. Department of the Interior, National Park Service. Cultural Resources, Washington.

USICOMOS (1996). *The ICOMOS International Committee on Cultural Tourism.* US/ICOMOS Newsletter Number 6, Special Edition.

Uzzell, David (1989). Introduction: The visitor experience. In Uzzell, D. (Ed.), *Heritage interpretation,* Volume 2 (pp. 1-15). Belhaven Press, London.

Uzzell, David and Ballantyne, Roy (Eds.) (1999). *Contemporary issues in heritage and environmental interpretation: Problems and prospects.* The Stationary Office, London.

Van der Borg, J., Costa, P., and Gotti, G. (1996). Tourism in European heritage cities. *Annals of Tourism Research* 23(2): 306-321.

Van der Borg, J. and Russo, A. P. (1998). Tourism management in European cities: Networking practices and sharing experiences. In Van Borg, J. and Russo, A. P. (Eds.), *Tourism management in heritage cities* (pp. 1-22). UNESCO, Venice.

VICNET (1996). Cultural Tourism Industry Group home page. Available at <http://home.vicnet.net.au/~ctig/> (retrieved November 15, 1999).

Vogt, Christine A. and Fesenmaier, Daniel R. (1998). Expanding the functional information search model. *Annals of Tourism Research* 25(3): 551-578.

Vukonic, Boris (1996). Marketing culture as a tourist commodity. In Robinson, Mike, Evans, Nigel, and Callaghan, Paul (Eds.), *Tourism and culture: Image, identity and marketing* (pp. 289-296). The Centre for Travel and Tourism/British Education Publishers, Sunderland, UK.

Wager, Jonathon (1995). Developing a strategy for the Angkor World Heritage site. *Tourism Management* 16(7): 515-523.

Wallace, M. (1994). The future of history museums. In Kavanagh, G. (Ed.) *Museum provision and professionalism* (pp. 71-81). Routledge, London.

Walle, Alf H. (1993). Tourism and traditional people: Forging equitable strategies. *Journal of Travel Research* 31(3): 14-19.

Waller, J. and Lea, S. E. G. (1999). Seeking the real Spain? Authenticity in motivation. *Annals of Tourism Research* 26(1): 110-129.

Walsh, R., Sanders, L., and McKean, J (1990). The consumptive value of travel time on recreational trips. *Journal of Travel Research* summer: 17-24.

Wang, N. (1999). Rethinking authenticity in tourism experience. *Annals of Tourism Research* 26(2): 349-370.

Warren, Karen (1989). A philosophical perspective on the ethics and resolution of cultural property issues. In Maunch Messenger, Phyllis (Ed.), *The ethics of collecting cultural property: Whose culture? Whose property?* (pp. 1-26). University of New Mexico Press, Albuquerque.

Weil, S. (1994). The proper business of a museum: Ideas or things? In Kavanagh, G. (Ed.), *Museum provision and professionalism* (pp. 82-89). Routledge, London.

Weiler, Betty and Ham, Sam (2001). Tour guides and interpretation in ecotourism. In D. Weaver (Ed.), *The Encyclopedia of Ecotourism* (pp. 549-564). CABI publications, London.

Weiler, Betty and Richins, Harold (1995). Extreme, extravagant and elite: A profile of ecotourists on earthwatch expeditions. *Tourism Recreation Research,* 20(1): 29-36.

Welgemoed, Marietha (1996). The tourist guide as culture broker: A South African scenario. In Robinson, Mike, Evans, Nigel, and Callaghan, Paul (Eds.), *Tourism and culture: Image, identity and marketing* (pp. 297-302). The Centre for Travel and Tourism/British Education Publishers, Sunderland, UK.

Wertheim, Marion E. (1994). Market research for heritage attractions. *Journal of Vacation Marketing* 1(1): 70-74.

Wheeler, Marion (1995). Tourism marketing ethics: An introduction. *International Marketing Review* 12(4): 38-49.

Whytock, John K. (1999). National historic sites and national parks in Canadian heritage tourism. Presentation made to the International Conference on Heritage and Tourism, Hong Kong.

Wood, Sean (1999). Fort Worth, Texas, uses cowboy culture to lure foreign tourists. *Fort Worth Star-Telegram,* October 13. Available online at <http://www.hotel.online.com/Neo/News/1999_Oct_13/k.FTT.939921277.html>.

World Bank (2000). Web site, April 5, 2000, available at <http://wbln0018.world bank.org/essd/kb.nsf/>.

World Monuments Fund (2000). Web site available at <http://www.columbia.edu/cu/mca/wmf/html/programs/aboutwmf.html>.

World Monuments Watch (2000). List of 100 most endangered sites. Available online at <http://worldmonuments.org/html/programs/watch.html>.

WTO (1985). *The states' role in protecting and promoting culture as a factor in tourism development and the proper use and exploitation of the national cultural heritage of sites and monuments for tourists.* World Tourism Organization, Madrid.

WTO (1994). *National and regional tourism planning.* World Tourism Organization, Routledge, New York.

WTO (1995). *Accra Declaration on the WTO-UNESCO Slave Route Programme.* World Tourism Organization, Madrid.

Zeppel, Heather (1992). *Cultural tourism in Australia: A growing travel trend.* Material Culture Unit/Department of Tourism, James Cook University, Townsville, Australia.

Zeppell, Heather and Hall, C. Michael (1991). Selling art and history: Cultural heritage and tourism. *Journal of Tourism Studies* 2(1): 29-45.

Index

Aaker, David, 206
accidental cultural tourists, 141
allocentric tourists, 118
Antolovic, Jadran, 135, 141
archaeological sites, 67
artisans, 89, 91
Ashworth, Gregory, 108
assessment
  asset-specific
    current and potential uses and
      users, 179-180
    intangible assets, 179
    tangible assets, 178-179
  financial resources, 183-184
  people, 183-184
  setting
    access, 177
    physical, 177
    sociohistorical, 176
  skills, 183-184
  stakeholder and consultation issues,
    180-182
  tourism potential of assets, 172
  in wider context
    cultural/heritage assets, 174, 175
    legislative/political, 173, 174
    tourism activity, 174, 175-176
ATLAS, 141
attractions. *See also* products
  development of
    building, 111-112
    bundling, 112
    circular tours, 113-114
    festivals, 114
    heritage networks, 113-114
    linear tours, 113-114
    precincts, 113
  features of
    focusing on quality and
      authenticity, 127

attractions, features of *(continued)*
    making asset come alive, 125
    making experience participatory,
      125
    making experience relevant to
      tourist, 125-127
    telling a story, 122, 124-125
  hierarchy of, 109-110
auditing
  Hong Kong test, 192-195
  market appeal-robusticity matrix,
    186-189
  model of, 185-189
  procedure, 189-195
augmented products, 104
authenticity
  commodification versus, 76-78
  core management issue for, 74
  cultural space and, 94-96
  in cultural tourism products, 40-42
  defined, 73
  Eastern viewpoint of, 75-76
  factors for consideration in, 76
  passion for, 73-74
  testing for, 74-75
Ayers Rock. *See* Uluru-Kata Tjuta
  National Park

Ballantyne, Roy, 199
Bennett, Marion M., 162-163
Boniface, Priscilla, 144, 222, 223
branding, of destinations, 155-162
Brett, Reverend Peter C., 202, 228-229
Brussels Charter on Cultural Tourism,
  66
Budowski, Gerardo, 15
buildings, 67
bundling, 112, 119

California Cultural Tourism Coalition,
113-114
*Canada National Historic Sites
Criteria,* 72
Canterbury Cathedral, 202, 228-229
case studies
Canterbury Cathedral, 228-229
Fombori Culture Bank, 219-220
Hadrian's Wall, 222-223
Hong Kong, 147-150
Kakadu National Park, 223
New Orleans Jazz National
Historical Park, 91-92
Pashupatinath Temple Complex,
217-219
Uluru-Kata Tjuta National Park,
93-94
casual cultural tourists, 39, 144-147
cataloging, of assets, 175
CHM. *See* cultural heritage
management (CHM)
circular tours, 113-114
coexistence, between tourism and
cultural heritage management,
15, 16, 19
Cohen, Eric, 117
commercial media, as gatekeepers, 165
commodification, 76-78, 115, 216
communication, in tourism promotion,
214
conflict, between tourism and cultural
heritage management, 15
consultation
in assessment, 180-182
in management process, 81-82
in planning, 197
consumption
debate over, 116
environmental bubble, 116-122
of experiences and products, 8, 115
strangeness versus familiarity,
116-122
Convention Concerning the Protection
of the World Cultural and
Natural Heritage, 55-56
core products, 103-104
Craik, Jennifer, 40, 121
cultural heritage assets
as cultural tourism products, 8, 32
destination-branding of, 155-162

cultural heritage assets *(continued)*
overuse of, 60
physical deterioration of, 61
tourism potential of, 32-33
use of, 7
cultural heritage management (CHM),
2-3, 7
conservation policy development,
224-225
core concepts of
accessibility of assets, 46-48
conservation of intrinsic values,
46
conservation of representative
sample, 44-46
differences in assets, 48-50
evolving framework, 50-54
as ongoing structured activities,
50-54
resources versus heritage, 44
stakeholders, 57-58
sustainability, 56-57
tangible and intangible heritage
assets, 48, 50
cultural significance, 191
defined, 43
evolution of, 13-15
fees and levies raised at source,
223-224
importance of self-sufficiency, 221
integrating tourism and local use,
217-220
interpretation of assets, 226-228
life cycle of
increased professionalism, 51,
52, 53
initial legislation, 51, 52
inventory, 51, 52
review, 51, 52, 53
stakeholder consultation, 51, 52,
53
presentation of assets, 215-220
principles of, 45
provision of site information,
225-226
reinvestment of revenue in
conservation, 220-223
relationship of asset to local
community, 229-230
robusticity, 191

cultural heritage management (CHM)
(continued)
tourism and, 58-60
blissful ignorance, 19-20
comparison, 14
conflict, 15, 16, 21
consequences of relationships
between, 21-23
consideration of tourist needs, 59
full cooperation, 17
mild annoyance, 20-21
parallel existence, 19-20
partnership, 9-10, 17, 23-24
peaceful coexistence, 15, 16, 19
revenue reinvestment, 62
symbiosis, 15
visitor management, 224-225
cultural landscapes, as tangible heritage
assets, 67-70
cultural property
loss of control over, 61
movable, 70-71
cultural space, 94-96, 176, 179
cultural tourism. *See also* tourism
activities, 5
authenticity versus
commodification, 76-78
authenticity versus reality, 40-42
challenging products versus
intimidating products, 39-40
competition for use of resources,
12-13
conflicts occurring in, 11-12
control of information in, 153-155
definitions of
experiential, 3, 4-5
motivational, 3, 4
operational, 3, 5-6
tourism derived, 3, 4
as distinct product category, 1
elements of
consumption of experiences and
products, 8
tourism, 6-7
tourists, 8
use of cultural heritage assets, 7
environmental bubbles and, 119
future of, 231-232
implications for, 150-151

cultural tourism *(continued)*
lack of cross communication in,
13-14
paradoxes of, 7
principles of, 27
Cultural Tourism Charter, 220
cultural tourists, 39
behavior of, 36-38, 61, 117
defined, 137
demographics of, 135-139
as element of cultural tourism, 8
typology, 139-147
case study, 147-150
casual type, 39, 144-147
centrality dimension, 140-142
depth of experience, 142-143
incidental type, 39, 144-147
purposeful type, 39, 144-147
serendipitous type, 39, 144-147
sightseeing type, 39, 144-147
culture, concept of, 97
custodians, 92-93

Dana, Leo P., 25
direct distribution, 213
distance decay, 33
distribution channels, 213
domestic travelers, 147
Duan, Ling, 62
Duan, Song-Ting, 62

ecotourism, 150
edutainment, 17, 165
Endangered World Heritage List, 56
*English Heritage Conservation Areas
Criteria,* 72
*English Heritage Criteria for Historic
Buildings Register,* 72
environmental bubble, 116-122
defined, 117
extreme formation of, 120-121
ethnic tourism, 131, 132
European Association for Tourism and
Leisure Education (ATLAS),
141
Evans, Katie, 225
experiential definitions, of cultural
tourism, 4-5

family, as gatekeepers, 165
festivals, 114, 119, 132-133
Fielding, Lindsay, 225
Fombori Culture Bank, 219-220
4 P's of marketing, 212-214
Fowler, P., 144, 222, 223
friends, as gatekeepers, 165

gatekeepers
    defined, 154
    dissemination of information by,
        154-162
    effects of, on message to tourists,
        169-170
    features of, 163, 170
    role of, 162-169
    types of
        asset, 164
        commercial media, 165
        friends and family, 165
        inbound tour operators, 167-168
        local tour operators, 166-167
        on-site guide/interpreter, 164-165
        opinion formers, 163
        opinion leaders, 163
        retail travel agents, 168-169
        tour escorts, 167
        tour wholesalers, 168
        tourism media, 166
general cultural tourists, 141
Goeldner, Charles R., 146-147
Goulding, Christina, 157
Greatorex, Michael, 118

Hadrian's Wall, 222-223
Hall, C. Michael, 199
Ham, Sam, 216-217
heritage, defined, 7
heritage cities, 67-70
heritage designation status, 50
heritage networks, 113-114
heritage planning, stages of, 66
heritage routes, 67-70
Hong Kong
    audit procedure test, 192-195
    cultural tourism case study, 147-150
Hughes, Howard L., 39, 120

IATF, 55
IBOs, 167-168
ICCROM, 55
ICOM, 53, 55
ICOMOS. *See* International Council
        on Monuments and Sites
        (ICOMOS)
inbound tour operators (IBOs), as
        gatekeepers, 167-168
incidental cultural tourists, 39, 144-147
indirect distribution, 213
infotainment, 165
intangible heritage, 48, 50
    artisans, 89, 91
    assessment, 83-84, 179
    authenticity and cultural space,
        94-96
    case studies, 91-92, 93-94
    changes imposed by tourism, 96-97
    culturally appropriate use of, 97-98
    custodians, 92-93
    defined, 83
    living human treasures, 89
    performers, 89, 91
    recognition of, 84-88
    religious figures, 92-93
    stakeholder consultation in
        management of, 98-99
    sustainability, 97-98
Inter-Agency Task Force (IATF), 55
International Centre for the Study of
        the Preservation and
        Restoration of Cultural
        Property (ICCROM), 55
International Council on Monuments
        and Sites (ICOMOS), 3, 7, 11,
        54, 220
International Council of Museums
        (ICOM), 53, 55
international travelers, 146
International Union for the
        Conservation of Nature
        (IUCN), 55
interpretation, principles of, 216
IUCN, 55

Journal of Sustainable Tourism, 15

Kakadu National Park, 223
Korean Cultural Properties Protection
    Act of 1962, 85

Leask, Anna, 199
linear tours, 113-114
living human treasures, 85, 89
local tour operators, as gatekeepers,
    166-167
Lord, Barry, 199
Lord, Gail Dexter, 199
Lowenthal, David, 13

MacCannell, Dean, 143
management option continuum, 79-80
market access, 33
market appeal-robusticity matrix,
    186-189
marketing
    approach to product development,
        107-109
    failure to consider, 202-204
    as management tool, 201-204
    mix
        place, 213
        price, 212-213
        product, 212
        promotion, 213-214
    plan, 211-212
    role of research in, 209-211
    strategic thinking in
        competitors, 207-208
        markets, 206, 207
        products, 206
    sustainable competitive advantages
        as goal of, 208-209
    unique features of, 204-205
mass tourism, 116
"Masterpieces of Oral and Intangible
    Heritage," 85
McArthur, Simon, 199
McIntosh, Alison J., 143
McIntosh, Robert W., 146-147
midcentric tourists, 118-119
Minority Business Development
    Agency, 131

Mitchell, Vincent M., 118
Morris, William, 74
motivational definitions, of cultural
    tourism, 4
multicultural tourism, 131
museums, 47
    challenges faced by, 53-54
    defined, 53
    as tangible heritage assets, 70-71
mythmaking, 128, 129

Nara Conference on Authenticity, 75
Nara Document on Authenticity, 75
National Trust for Historic Preservation
    (NTHP), 125
New Orleans Jazz National Historical
    Park, 91-92
NTHP. *See* National Trust for Historic
    Preservation (NTHP)

on-site guides/interpreters, as
    gatekeepers, 164-165
operational definitions, of cultural
    tourism, 5-6
opinion formers, 163
opinion leaders, 163
overinterpretation, 227

packaged guided tours, 120
Palmer, Catherine, 127
Pashupatinath Temple Complex,
    217-219
Pennsylvania Department of
    Conservation and Natural
    Resources, 141-142
perception, as element of interpretation,
    226-227
performers, 89, 91
The Phenomenology of Perception
    (Merleau-Ponty), 226
place, concept of, 178-179
planning
    consultation, 197
    creation of action plans, 199
    establishment of mission or vision,
        197-198

planning *(continued)*
  establishment of quantifiable goals
      and objectives, 198-199
  evaluation and feedback
      mechanisms, 199-200
  identification of options, 198
  nature of, 196
  realistic assessment, 196-197
  selection of preferred opinion, 198
  steps in, 195
Plog, Stanley, 118-119
precincts, 113, 119
Prentice, Richard C., 143
primary attractions, 109-110
products, 5, 8. *See also* attractions
  benefits of standardizing,
      modifying, and
      commodifying, 123-124
  conceptual levels of, 103-104
  creation of, 122-127
  features of, 122-127
    focusing on quality and
        authenticity, 122, 127
    making asset come alive, 122,
        125
    making experience participatory,
        122, 125
    making experience relevant to
        tourist, 122, 125-127
    telling a story, 122, 124-125
  marketing approach to, development
      of, 107-109
  to satisfy consumer needs, 104-107
  standardization of, 156-162
  transformation of assets into,
      101-102, 115, 122-127
    building stories around assets,
        128, 130-131
    emphasizing otherness, 128, 131
    making asset a fantasy, 128,
        133-134
    making asset a spectacle, 128,
        132-133
    making asset fun, light, and
        entertaining, 128, 134
    making asset triumphant, 128, 132
    mythologizing assets, 128, 129
    showing direct link from past to
        present, 128, 131-132

proximity, influence on visitation
    levels, 33, 35
psychocentric tourists, 118
purpose-built cultural theme parks,
    120-121
purposeful cultural tourists, 39,
    144-147

Recommendation on the Safeguarding
    of Traditional Culture and
    Folklore
  conservation, 86
  dissemination, 88
  identification and inventory, 86
  international cooperation, 88
  preservation, 86
  protection, 88
Reis, A., 206
religious figures, 92-93
research, role in marketing, 209-211
retail travel agents, as gatekeepers,
    168-169
revenue
  fees and levies raised at source,
      223-224
  reinvestment of, in conservation,
      220-223
risk theory, 118
Rojek, Chris, 128
Ruskin, John, 74
Ryan, Chris, 157

SCA, 208-209
Seaton, Tony V., 162-163
secondary attractions, 110
self-sufficiency, 221
serendipitous cultural tourists, 39,
    144-147
serious leisure, 142-143
sightseeing cultural tourists, 39,
    144-147
Silberberg, Ted, 196
Silverstone, Roger, 227
SMART (specific, measurable,
    attainable, realistic, timely)
    goals, 198-199
souveniring, 230

specific cultural tourists, 141
stakeholders, 12-13
  in assessment, 180-182
  consultation with, 58, 98-99
  external, 58
  multiple, 57-58
Stebbins, Robert A., 142-143, 146
strangeness reduction, 120-122
strangeness versus familiarity, 116-122
  effects on product delivery, 120-122
  perceived risk and, 118
  tourist behavior from perspective of, 117
Sugaya, H. Bill, 138-139
sustainability, 2-3, 11, 56-57, 77-78, 171-172
sustainable competitive advantage (SCA), 208-209
SWOT (strength, weakness, opportunity, and threat) analysis, 210-211
symbiosis, between tourism and cultural heritage management, 15

tangible heritage, 48, 50
  accessibility of, 79-81
  assessment, 178-179
  cultural significance of, 71-73
  culturally appropriate use of, 77-78
  defined, 65
  process-driven conservation of, 66
  scope of
    archaeological sites, 67
    buildings, 67
    cultural landscapes, 67-70
    heritage cities, 67-70
    heritage routes, 67-70
    movable cultural property, 70-71
    museums, 70-71
  sustainability, 77-78
tangible products, 104
tertiary attractions, 110
theatre tourism, 110
3Rs, of ownership claims, 53-54
Timothy, Dallen J., 143
tour escorts, as gatekeepers, 167
tour wholesalers, as gatekeepers, 168

tourism, 2. *See also* cultural tourism
  attractions as driving force of
    hierarchy of attractions, 31
    role of cultural heritage attractions, 32
    tourism potential of cultural assets, 32-33
  changes to intangible heritage imposed by, 96-97
  conservation requirements and, 62
  control of, 30
  cultural heritage management and
    blissful ignorance, 19-20
    comparison, 14
    conflict, 15, 16, 21
    consequences of relationships between, 21-23
    consideration of tourist needs, 59
    full cooperation, 17
    mild annoyance, 21
    parallel existence, 19-20
    partnership, 9-10, 17, 23-24
    peaceful coexistence, 15, 16, 19
    symbiosis, 15
    use of assets, 59-60
    working relationships, 19
  cultural tourism as form of, 6-7
  dependency, 60
  evolution of, 13-15
  factors influencing visitation levels
    access and proximity, 33, 35
    time availability, 35-36
  features of, 116
  limited beneficiaries of, 61
  market appeal, 191
  mass, 116
  nature of
    as commercial activity, 26-28
    as consumption of experiences, 28
    as demand-driven activity, 30-31
    as entertainment, 28-30
  negative impacts of, 60-61
  positive impacts of, 61-62
  product design needs, 191
  social impact of, 25-26
  tourist behavior and
    controlling actions of tourists, 36
    need for controlled experiences, 36-37

tourism, tourist behavior and *(continued)*
  need for user-friendly tourism
    products in mainstream
    markets, 38
  understanding, 25-26
  unplanned infrastructure
    development, 61
tourism media, as gatekeepers, 166
tourism-derived definitions, of cultural
    tourism, 4
tourismification, 12, 26, 28
tourists. *See* cultural tourists
Travel and Tourism Administration,
    131
Trout, J., 206

Uluru-Kata Tjuta National Park, 93-94
UNESCO (United Nations Educational,
    Scientific, and Cultural
    Organization)
  Endangered World Heritage List, 56
  "Masterpieces of Oral and
    Intangible Heritage," 85
  Recommendation on the
    Safeguarding of Traditional
    Culture and Folklore, 86
  World Heritage Areas, 69-70
  World Heritage Centre, 56
  World Heritage Convention, 43, 75
  World Heritage List, 56

United States Agency for International
    Development (USAID), 219
*United States National Historic
    Landmark Criteria,* 72
*United States National Register of
    Historic Sites Criteria,* 71
Urry, John, 116
USAID, 219
Uzzell, David, 199, 227

Venice Charter, 43, 54-55, 66, 74

Walt Disney Company, 21
Warren, Karen, 53
Weiler, Betty, 216-217
Wertheim, Marion E., 210
World Conservation Union. *See*
    International Union for the
    Conservation of Nature
    (IUCN)
World Heritage Areas, 69-70
World Heritage Centre, 56
World Heritage Convention, 43, 74
World Heritage List, 56
WTO (World Tourism Organization),
    4, 39, 135, 147

Yeoman, Ian, 199